PF
for y

John Honeybourne

Michael Hill

Jon Wyse

D0186145

Stanley Thornes Publishers Ltd

Text © John Honeybourne, Michael Hill, Jon Wyse, 1998

Original line illustrations © Stanley Thornes (Publishers) Ltd

The right of John Honeybourne, Michael Hill and Jon Wyse to be identified as authors of this work has been asserted by them in accordance with the Copyright, Designs and Patents Act, 1988.

All rights reserved. No part of this publication may be reproduced or transmitted in any form or by any means, electronic or mechanical, including photocopy, recording or any information storage and retrieval system, without permission in writing from the publisher or under licence from the Copyright Licensing Agency Ltd. Further details of such licences (for reprographic reproduction) may be obtained from the Copyright Licensing Agency Limited, of 90 Tottenham Court Road, London W1P 0LP

First published in 1998 by:
Stanley Thornes (Publishers) Ltd
Ellenborough House
Wellington Street
Cheltenham
GL50 1YW
UK

98 99 00 01 02 / 10 9 8 7 6 5 4 3 2 1

A catalogue record for this book is available from the British Library.
ISBN 0 7487 3277 2

Typeset by Paul Manning
Printed and bound in Italy by STIGE, Turin

Contents

How to use this book iv
Acknowledgements vi

Part One: Anatomy and Physiology
1   Structure and Function of the Body   1
2   The Skeletal System   7
3   The Muscular System   15
4   The Cardiovascular System   23
5   The Respiratory System   31
6   The Nervous System   39
7   The Endocrine and Digestive Systems   44
    Exam Questions: Anatomy and
        Physiology   48
    Revision Guide: Anatomy and
        Physiology   50

Part Two: Factors Affecting Performance
8   Defining Fitness   52
9   Physique   61
10 Diet and Exercise   68
11 Drugs in Sport   77
12 Learning Skills   83
13 Mental Preparation   95
    Exam Questions: Factors
        Affecting Performance   102
    Revision Guide: Factors Affecting
        Performance   104

Part Three: Health, Safety and Training
14 Health-Related Exercise   106
15 Training Methods   112
16 Effects of Training and Activity   117
17 Safe Practice in PE and Sport   123
18 Sports Injuries and First Aid   128
    Exam Questions: Health, Safety
        and Training   136
    Revision Guide: Health, Safety
        and Training   138

Part Four: Participation in Sport
19 Definitions and History of Sport   140
20 Reasons for Participation   147
21 Factors Affecting Participation   155
22 The Local Organisation of Sport   161
23 The National Organisation of Sport   167
24 The International Organisation of
        Sport   174
    Exam Questions: Participation
        in Sport   182
    Revision Guide: Participation
        in Sport   184

Part Five: Issues in PE and Sport
25 Politics and Sport   186
26 Coaching, Facilities and Finance   190
27 Sponsorship in Sport   194
28 Excellence in Sport   201
29 Amateurs and Professionals   207
30 The Role of the Media in Sport   212
31 Women in Sport   219
32 Behaviour in Sport   225
    Exam Questions: Issues in PE
        and Sport   230
    Revision Guide: Issues in PE
        and Sport   232

Appendix: Rules, Tactics and Techniques   234
Glossary   242
Index   249

How to use this book

The aim of this book is to provide a user-friendly text for use by PE students and their teachers. Although written mainly with GCSE students in mind, it will also prove invaluable to students of a wide range of courses, from A-level through to NVQ, GNVQ and other vocational qualifications.

The content is relevant to all GCSE syllabuses currently offered and emphasises the practical aspects. The book allows for differences in ability and has a number of features to aid understanding. It is divided into five parts:

- **Part 1: Anatomy and Physiology** deals with the structure and function of body organs affecting sports performance

- **Part 2: Factors Affecting Performance** covers the influence of diet, drugs, skill acquisition and mental preparation

- **Part 3: Health, Safety and Training** explores the link between health and fitness and gives some useful information on safety procedures and sports injuries

- **Part 4: Participation in Sport** looks at the socio-cultural aspects of Physical Education, including the history of sport and the organisation of sport at local, national and international level

- **Part 5: Issues in PE and Sport** covers sport and politics, coaching, sponsorship, the role of the media and women in sport

The **Appendix: Rules, Tactics and Techniques** includes essential information on applying skills in sport, the rules, and winning strategies. Also included are typical exam questions and hints on how to answer them. All the most popular school or college sports are covered: athletics, badminton, basketball, cricket, football, hockey, netball, rugby league, rugby union, swimming and tennis.

Finally, the **Glossary** provides a quick reference guide to all the key words and concepts used in the book.

Features

As you read the book, you will notice several features designed to aid learning:

- Each main Part of the book is divided into chapters which are relevant to most schemes of work

- Each chapter begins with a clear statement of aims

- **Definition boxes** in the margin explain key words and phrases used in the text

- The **Quick Quiz** feature tests understanding of the main content of each section – all the answers will be found in the text or diagrams

- **Quick Tasks** are based on topics covered in the text and are graded in difficulty

- The **Fast Forward** feature takes you to a later page where the topic is dealt with more fully

- The **Rewind** feature takes you back to an earlier page where the topic is dealt with more fully

- The **Match It!** feature requires you to match phrases or words from the text in a way that reinforces understanding

- **Sport in Action** exercises require you to apply the knowledge gained in each chapter to real-life sporting situations

- **Key words** are listed at the end of each chapter so that you can check that you understand each one

- The **Revise It!** feature appears at the end of each chapter and ensures that you know and understand the key elements that you need to pass an examination at this level

- Each main Part of the book includes typical **Examination Questions**, and a **Revision Guide** summarising all the key concepts and containing suggestions for **Further Reading**.

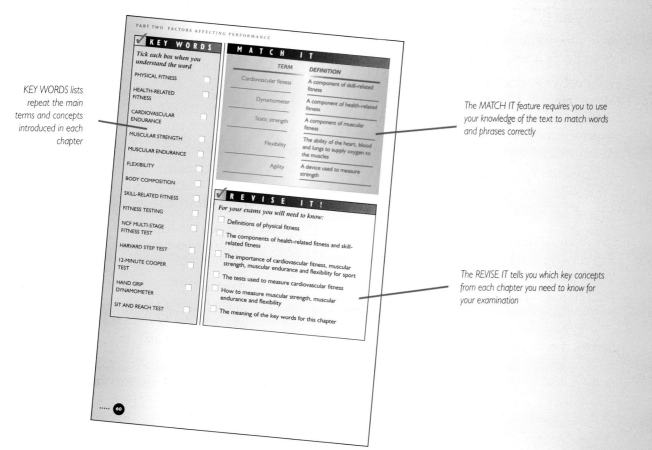

REWIND takes you back to an earlier page where the topic was introduced

DEFINITION BOXES explain key words and phrases used in the text

QUICK TASKS – short graded activities based on topics covered in the text. More challenging tasks appear on a darker coloured box

QUICK QUIZ tests your understanding of the material covered in each section

FAST FORWARD takes you to a later page in the book where the topic is explained more fully

2 Muscular endurance

The ability of a muscle to work for a sustained period of time is also important in most sports. Not having a good level of muscular endurance leads to muscle fatigue, causing our arms and legs to feel tired and heavy. This often means that our performance becomes worse, and some cases we may have to stop playing.

Muscular endurance is also important for maintaining our body **posture**. Even when we are sitting, we constantly use muscles to keep us upright, and it is these muscles that must maintain their **muscle tone**.

3 Flexibility

This third component of muscle fitness is linked to the muscular and skeletal systems. Muscles that are not stretched regularly become tight, causing pain when we stretch them. A loss of flexibility can also be caused by problems in the joints, such as worn-down cartilage or lack of synovial fluid.

Flexibility is important in most sports as it helps to reduce the risk of injury. Swimmers, javelin throwers and tennis players all need good shoulder flexibility, while gymnasts need a high level of all-round flexibility. Flexibility is often called **suppleness** or **mobility**.

General fitness and specific fitness

So far we have examined the components needed for **general fitness**. If certain fitness components are more important than others in a sport, then people playing that sport also need a level of **specific fitness**. For instance, a sprinter needs a high level of strength, speed and power, but cardiovascular fitness and agility are less important.

Similarly, the standard of competition will affect fitness levels: an Olympic athlete will have greater levels of fitness than a club athlete. Training to achieve specific fitness is described in Chapter 15.

FITNESS TESTING

Now that we know which components of fitness are important for our own particular sport, it is useful to find out how each of these components can be measured. By carrying out a number of fitness tests, we can get a picture of our current state of fitness. From this we can identify strengths and weaknesses and then work to improve the weaker areas.

Also, by repeating fitness tests after completing a training programme (at least a few months later) and comparing them with tests carried out earlier, it is possible to see how fitness levels have improved.

Performing press-ups requires a good level of muscular endurance

◄◄ REWIND
POSTURE   see page 8

FLEXIBILITY
The range of movement we have in a joint

QUICK TASK
1) Can you think of three examples of sports requiring static, explosive and dynamic strength?

2) Re-read the section on muscle fibre types on page 18, Chapter 3. Which of the muscle fibre types is mainly used when we apply maximum strength?

QUICK QUIZ
1) Define the term 'physical fitness'.
2) Name three health-related components of physical fitness.
3) What is meant by the term **aerobic**?
4) What type of strength do we use when we push in a rugby scrum?
5) Which sports require good shoulder flexibility?
6) In what way is fitness 'specific'?

FAST FORWARD ►►
TRAINING FOR FITNESS   see page 112

KEY WORDS lists repeat the main terms and concepts introduced in each chapter

✓ KEY WORDS
Tick each box when you understand the word

- PHYSICAL FITNESS ☐
- HEALTH-RELATED FITNESS ☐
- CARDIOVASCULAR ENDURANCE ☐
- MUSCULAR STRENGTH ☐
- MUSCULAR ENDURANCE ☐
- FLEXIBILITY ☐
- BODY COMPOSITION ☐
- SKILL-RELATED FITNESS ☐
- FITNESS TESTING ☐
- NCF MULTI-STAGE FITNESS TEST ☐
- HARVARD STEP TEST ☐
- 12-MINUTE COOPER TEST ☐
- HAND GRIP DYNAMOMETER ☐
- SIT AND REACH TEST ☐

MATCH IT

TERM	DEFINITION
Cardiovascular fitness	A component of skill-related fitness
Dynamometer	A component of health-related fitness
Static strength	A component of muscular fitness
Flexibility	The ability of the heart, blood and lungs to supply oxygen to the muscles
Agility	A device used to measure strength

The MATCH IT feature requires you to use your knowledge of the text to match words and phrases correctly

✓ REVISE IT!
For your exams you will need to know:

☐ Definitions of physical fitness

☐ The components of health-related fitness and skill-related fitness

☐ The importance of cardiovascular fitness, muscular strength, muscular endurance and flexibility for sport

☐ The tests used to measure cardiovascular fitness

☐ How to measure muscular strength, muscular endurance and flexibility

☐ The meaning of the key words for this chapter

The REVISE IT tells you which key concepts from each chapter you need to know for your examination

Acknowledgements

The authors and publishers would like to thank the following organisations for help in the preparation of this book and for giving permission for the reproduction of their logos:

British Olympic Association, page 171
Central Council of Physical Recreation, page 171
'Let's Kick Racism Out of Football' campaign, page 227
National Coaching Foundation, page 171
SportsAid Foundation, page 171
UK Sports Council, page 155
Womens Sports Foundation, page 157

We are also grateful to the following for permission to reproduce photographs:

BBC, page 223
Corbis, pages 78 and 169
Getty Images, pages 19, 36, 118 and 222
J. Allan Cash Ltd, pages 71 and 140
Mark Leech, pages 92, 110, 125, 131, 141, 153, 157, 17, 191, 195, 199, 201, 208, 209, 219, 225, 226, 227, 228
Martyn F. Chillmaid, page 69
Mary Evans Picture Library, page 145
Nike (UK) Ltd, page 199
PA News, page 221
Puma, pages 195 and 203
Sally and Richard Greenhill, pages 27 and 64
Sponsorship Bureau International Ltd, page 196
Supersport Photographs, pages 75, 91, 97, 123, 125, 143, 151, 152, 159, 172, 190, 191, 202, 204, 207, 210, 221
The Associated Press Ltd, page 179

Structure and Function of the Body

CHAPTER 1

The aim of this chapter is to help you:

○ Understand the technical language that will be used in this part of the book

○ Describe the nature of **cells, organs** and **systems**

○ Recognise the different systems in the **human body**

An understanding of the internal workings of the human body is of great importance to students, teachers and coaches of PE and sport. Knowing how the body operates is crucial when we participate in sport and evaluate sports performance.

BODY STRUCTURE AND FUNCTION

To understand how the body works when performing a sporting action, you need to be familiar with the following words:

● **Structure** – how something is put together in the body. We will be looking at the basic elements of the human body and considering how they fit together (this is what is meant by the word **anatomy**)

● **Function** – how the parts of the body work. We will be looking at the specific role (or job) of the basic elements of the human body (this is what is meant by the word **physiology**)

● **Location** – the position of the body part within the human body. For example, the **diaphragm** (a dome-shaped smooth muscle which helps us to breathe) is located just below the lungs at the base of the thoracic (chest) cavity

Anatomy and physiology are closely related, because the structure of an organ is linked to its **function**. For example, a description of the structure of an organ such as the stomach also involves describing its function – the digestion of food.

ANATOMY
The structure of the body

PHYSIOLOGY
The function of the different body parts

LOCATION
The position of parts within the human body

Cells, tissues and organs

The human body is made up millions of microscopic units called **cells**. These are the basic living unit of all animals (and plants). There are about ten million million cells in the human body. Each contains a **nucleus**, which controls the way the particular cell functions. This is normally located near the centre of the cell.

Cells that have a similar structure and function and work closely together form a **tissue**. Each type of tissue is highly specialised to perform specific functions. **Skeletal muscle** is an example of a type of tissue. Its function is to contract to produce movement.

NUCLEUS
Element normally located near the centre of a cell which controls the way it functions

TISSUE
Cells that have similar structure and function and work closely together

SKELETAL MUSCLE
Type of muscle tissue whose function is to produce movement of the body. It is attached to the bones

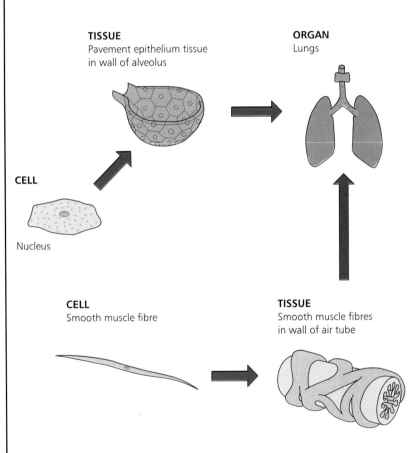

Relation of cells, tissues and organs

ORGAN
Two or more types of tissue that work to perform a common function

1) What is the function of skeletal muscle?

2) How many cells are there in the human body?

3) Which is the largest organ in the human body?

4) Where in a cell would you normally find the nucleus?

An **organ** consists of two or more types of tissue that work to perform a common function. The eyes, heart, and spinal cord are examples of organs. So is the skin: it is the largest organ in the human body, approximately the size of a single bed if laid out flat. Other major organs in the body include the brain, heart, lungs, stomach, liver, pancreas, kidneys, and bladder.

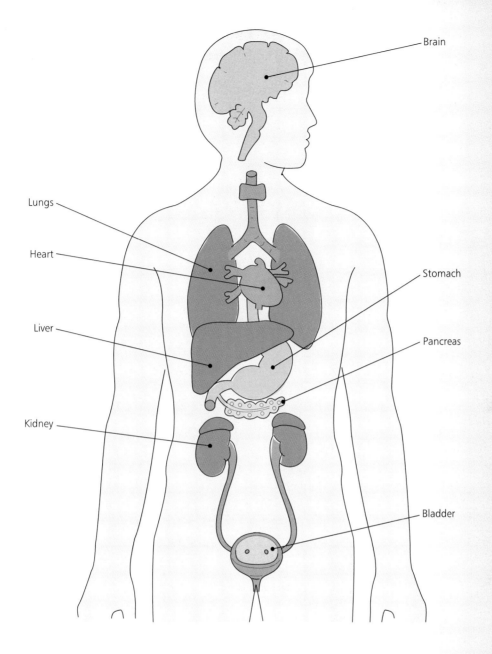

The organs of the human body

BODY SYSTEMS

As we have begun to see, the body is made up of lots of different organs. Whilst each organ has a specific function, some organs seem to work together.

For example, the **heart** pumps blood which is carried around the body through a network of arteries, capillaries and veins. Each of these organs makes up a part of the **cardiovascular system**. This system has the main function of carrying oxygen (in the blood) to the cells of the body, and carrying waste products (such as carbon dioxide) away from these cells.

> *CARDIOVASCULAR SYSTEM*
> *System governing the circulation of blood and the transport of oxygen and nutrients to the cells of the body, and of waste products away from these cells*

THE MAIN BODY SYSTEMS

Within the human body there are a number of different systems. We shall look at them briefly here before going on to examine them in more detail in Chapters 2–7.

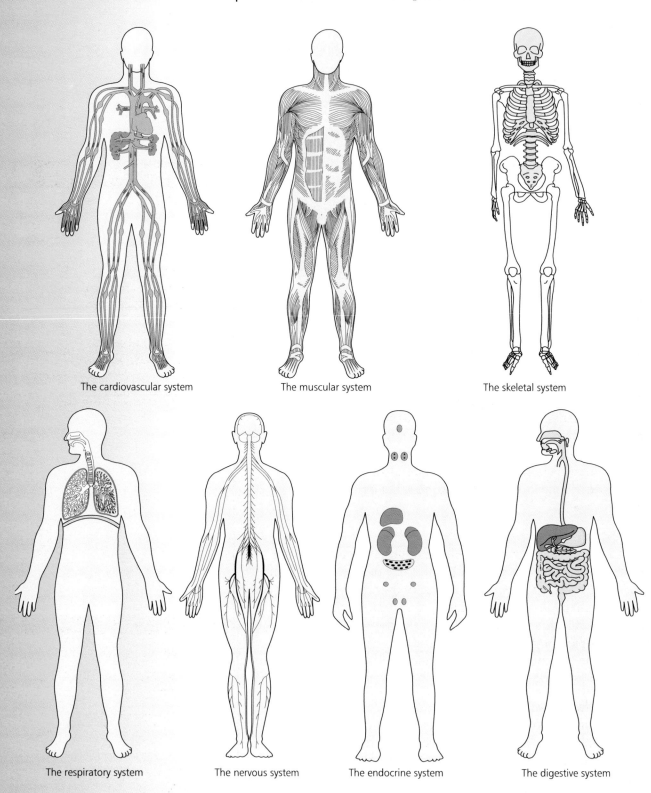

The cardiovascular system

The muscular system

The skeletal system

The respiratory system

The nervous system

The endocrine system

The digestive system

The main body systems

The skeletal system

The 206 bones of the skeleton make up the body's skeletal system. Also included are the **joints** (where two or more bones meet), and **connective tissues** called cartilage and ligaments. These are important as they allow us to move our bodies.

The muscular system

When we think of muscles, we are mainly concerned with **skeletal muscle**, which is connected to bones by tendons. But we also have two other types of muscle: cardiac and smooth. **Cardiac muscle** is found only in the heart, whilst some **smooth muscle** is located in the digestive system.

The cardiovascular system

This system is mainly concerned with the circulation of **blood** and with carrying **oxygen** and **nutrients** to the cells of the body and waste products away from these cells. The main organ in this system is the heart, and there is a network of blood vessels called **arteries**, **capillaries and veins** which help to circulate the blood to all parts of the body.

The respiratory system

The breathing process is very important, as it enables us to get oxygen into our body and **carbon dioxide** out. These two gases have to pass through a number of air passages and also our lungs as they move into and out of our bloodstream.

The nervous system

The reason we are able to play sport is because we can control our movements. The control centre for these **voluntary movements** is the brain. The function of the brain is to tell our muscles to shorten in order to move the bones of our skeleton. The brain also controls a large number of **involuntary movements**, including blinking, sneezing and even our heartbeat.

The endocrine system

This body system is made up of a number of organs that are located all around the human body. These organs include the adrenal glands, pancreas, and the sexual organs (testes in males, ovaries in females). These organs produce **hormones** (types of chemical substance) which help our body to function properly. For example, the adrenal glands produce a substance called adrenaline which helps us to increase our heartbeat quickly in response to threat or danger.

The digestive system

Though most of do not pay much attention to what we eat, the role of the digestive system is of great importance. It is in our stomach that our food begins to be broken down into useable nutrients. As it passes through the gut, these nutrients are taken out by the cells and used for growth, repair and as a source of energy.

CONNECTIVE TISSUE
Any material in the body which connects two or more organs. Cartilage, ligaments and tendons are dense (thick) connective tissues, whilst fat is a less dense connective tissue. Blood is a liquid connective tissue

FAST FORWARD

NUTRIENTS   see page 45

QUICK TASK

1) Describe how some of the main body systems are linked.

2) List the seven body systems described on the left. Write next to each one why each is important in helping us to play sport.

QUICK QUIZ

1) Where would you find a joint?

2) In which body system would you find arteries?

3) Name the three main types of muscle tissue found in the human body.

4) What is the substance produced by the adrenal glands? Why is this important for sports performers?

✓ KEY WORDS

Tick each box when you understand the word

STRUCTURE/ □
ANATOMY

FUNCTION/ □
PHYSIOLOGY

LOCATION □

NUCLEUS □

TISSUES □

SKELETAL MUSCLE □

ORGAN □

SKELETAL SYSTEM □

MUSCULAR SYSTEM □

CARDIOVASCULAR □
SYSTEM

RESPIRATORY SYSTEM □

NERVOUS SYSTEM □

ENDOCRINE □
SYSTEM

DIGESTIVE SYSTEM □

CONNECTIVE TISSUE □

M A T C H   I T

TERM	DEFINITION
Endocrine	System responsible for breathing
Brain	The way in which a group of cells is put together
Respiratory	The role of a specific organ
Function	System responsible for releasing hormones in our body
Structure	Group of cells that perform a common function
Tissue	Main organ of the nervous system

✓ R E V I S E   I T !

For your exams you will need to know:

□ How our bodies can be sub-divided into body systems, organs, tissues, and cells

□ The main function of the major body systems

□ How these body systems work together

□ How the body systems contribute to sporting actions

□ The meaning of the key words for this chapter

The Skeletal System

CHAPTER 02

The aim of this chapter is to help you:

- Identify the **major bones** in the human body
- Describe the **functions** of the bones in the skeletal system
- Understand the important role played by the **vertebral column**
- Explain the function of other tissues that are connected to bones
- Identify the different types of **joints** in the body
- Understand that **different movements** are possible at different joints

The skeletal system (our bones and joints) is an extremely important part of the body. Without it we would be a shapeless 'blob' of muscle, blood and other tissues. We would find it very difficult to move around, and playing sport would be impossible!

THE HUMAN SKELETON

There are 206 bones in the human body. These bones are made up of water (45%), calcium and phosphorous (35%), and other organic materials (20%). The calcium and phosphorous are **minerals** which give the bones their hardness. The organic materials consist mainly of a substance called **collagen**, which allows the bones to be squashed and twisted a little without breaking (although they will break if squashed and twisted too much).

Every bone in the human body has tiny blood vessels called **capillaries**. These help to keep our bones healthy, especially as we grow in size during our teenage years. Although bones are normally associated with dead things, the bones of the human skeleton are very much alive!

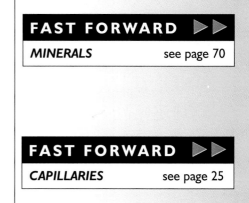

FAST FORWARD ▶▶
MINERALS   see page 70

FAST FORWARD ▶▶
CAPILLARIES   see page 25

Functions of the skeleton

The human skeleton has a number of different functions:

- To provide **shape** for our bodies
- To support the body in the correct position or **posture**
- To **support** the internal organs
- To **protect** the delicate vital organs of the body
- To provide sites for **muscle attachment**
- To work as a **lever system**
- To enable us to make large and fine **movements**
- To produce red and white **blood cells**

The human skeleton, with the axial skeleton in dark brown and the appendicular skeleton in light brown

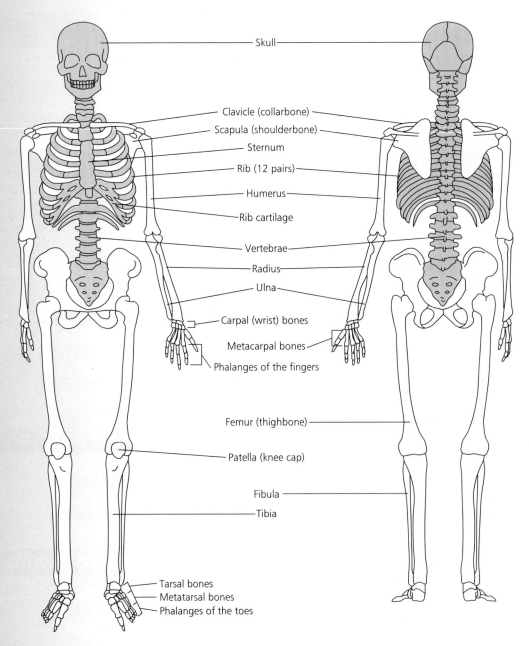

Skull

Clavicle (collarbone)
Scapula (shoulderbone)
Sternum
Rib (12 pairs)
Humerus
Rib cartilage
Vertebrae
Radius
Ulna
Carpal (wrist) bones
Metacarpal bones
Phalanges of the fingers

Femur (thighbone)

Patella (knee cap)

Fibula
Tibia

Tarsal bones
Metatarsal bones
Phalanges of the toes

The human skeleton can be split into two parts:

- The **axial skeleton** is the central part of the skeleton, and this is made up of the skull (or cranium), the spine (or vertebrae), the twelve pairs of ribs, and the breastbone (or sternum)

- The **appendicular skeleton** consists of the remaining bones. These are 'attached to' the axial skeleton as shown below:

QUICK TASK

Make a list of as many of the major bones in the body as you can think of. Write next to each if it is a long bone, a short bone, a flat bone, or an irregular bone. Notice how each type of bone is found in different areas of the body.

SHOULDER GIRDLE AND ARMS	HIP GIRDLE AND LEGS
Shoulder blades (scapula)	Hip bone (pelvis)
Collar bones (clavicle)	Thigh bone (femur)
Bones of the upper arm (humerus)	Knee caps (patella)
Forearm bones (ulna and radius)	Shin bones (tibia and fibula)
Bones of the hand (carpals and metacarpals) and fingers (phalanges)	Bones of the foot (tarsals and metatarsals) and toes (phalanges)

Types of bone

There are four main types of bone in our body:

- **Long bones** have a long thin section called a shaft, which has an enlarged head at each end (see diagram)

- **Short bones** are smaller and cube-shaped

- **Flat bones** are broad, plate-like bones that have a slightly curved surface

- **Irregular bones** are complex in form and can take a variety of different shapes. These normally have bits that stick out, known as projections

- A fifth type of bone is called a **sesamoid bone**, and is located entirely in a tendon. The two knee caps (known as patella) are examples of this type of bone.

Long bones help us to move our body when we are playing sport, and it is therefore important to know how they are structured. Generally, they are made up of two types of bone tissue:

- **Compact bone** is an extremely tough material that forms the outside layer of a bone, and is the tissue we find in the shaft of a long bone.

- **Spongy bone** is located inside the heads of long bones. It resembles a honeycombed criss-cross pattern like scaffolding, giving the bone strength without a large amount of weight.

Long bones are very strong, but they are not heavy. This is because they have a hollow in the middle of the shaft, known as the **marrow cavity**. This is where white blood cells are produced.

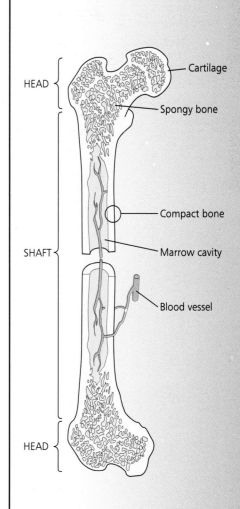

A typical long bone

STRUCTURE AND FUNCTION OF THE VERTEBRAE

The **spine** is made up of 33 irregular bones called **vertebrae**. These are split into five different sections. The bones in each section are slightly different in form and function.

The five sections of the human vertebrae

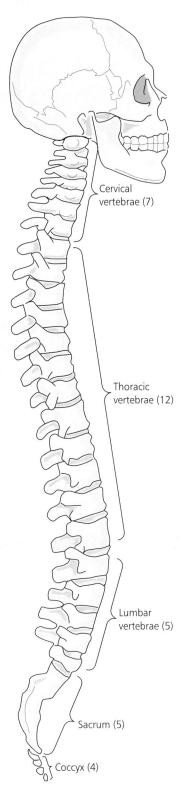

Cervical vertebrae (7)

Thoracic vertebrae (12)

Lumbar vertebrae (5)

Sacrum (5)

Coccyx (4)

Cervical vertebrae The top 7 vertebrae form the neck. The top 2 bones are the atlas and the axis. They enable us to nod and shake our head. The other vertebrae also help with movements of the head and the neck, such as twisting and bending.

Thoracic vertebrae These 12 vertebrae are level with the chest and connect with the ribs. They allow a slight amount of movement.

Lumbar vertebrae These 5 large vertebrae form the lower back. The large muscles of the back are attached to them, allowing a great amount of movement (bending forwards, backwards, from side to side and twisting). It is the region most likely to suffer from injuries, mainly due to poor posture.

Sacral vertebrae These 5 vertebrae are joined directly (or fused) together. The pelvis is attached to the sacrum, and it is here that the weight of the upper body is carried.

Coccyx The base of the spine, consisting of 4 vertebrae fused together. Muscles of the groin area are attached to these similar vertebrae.

Cartilage and ligaments

Cartilage

Cartilage is a connective tissue that is found in a variety of forms in the human body. When we are born, our entire skeleton is made up of cartilage. As we grow older this cartilage is gradually replaced by bone. This process is known as **ossification**. In long bones, the cartilage in the shaft is the first area to be converted into bone, followed by the cartilage in the heads. Bone growth occurs in the area where the shaft meet the heads.

Types of cartilage

There are three main types of cartilage in the human body:

- **Yellow elastic cartilage** is extremely flexible cartilage that provides shape for the ear lobe and the tip of the nose. The epiglottis is also made from this type of cartilage

- **White fibrocartilage** is a tougher, less elastic cartilage that acts as a shock absorber. It is found between the vertebrae of the spine, and also in the knee to prevent the bones from jarring

- **Blue articular (hyaline) cartilage** is found at joints (where two bones meet) and covering the ends of bones. Its slippery surface prevents the bones from wearing each other down, and it also produces synovial fluid

Ligaments

These are strong, non-elastic tissues that connect bone to bone, normally found at a joint. For example, at the knee there are a number of ligaments: two cross from the femur to the tibia inside the joint, and others connect the femur to the tibia and the fibula outside of the **joint capsule**.

They also have the function of preventing unwanted movements of the knee joint – we do not want our knee to bend from side to side! Compare the role of ligaments with tendons.

> **CARTILAGE**
> *Connective tissue found in a variety of forms in the human body*

QUICK QUIZ

1) How many bones are there in the appendicular skeleton?

2) Can you name the major bones in the leg?

3) List five functions of the human skeleton.

4) Where are white blood cells produced?

5) Why are there blood vessels running through bones?

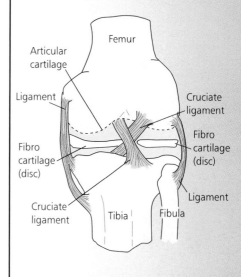

The knee joint showing ligaments

S P O R T I N A C T I O N

Can you complete the following table?

Cartilage	Colour	Structure	Function	Location
Elastic	?	?	Provides shape	?
Fibrocartilage	White	Tough fibrous material	?	Between vertebrae
Articular	Blue	?	Prevents bones from wearing down	?

Section through a movable, or synovial joint

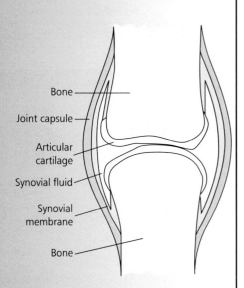

The structure of movable or **synovial** joints contains a number of similar features. These include **articular cartilage**, **synovial fluid** (contained within a **synovial cavity**), a **synovial membrane**, a **joint capsule** and surrounding **ligaments**. These synovial joints permit a greater degree of movement (although movement may be restricted by the shape of the connecting bones, ligaments and tendons). They are located throughout the body, e.g. at hips, knees, ankles, shoulders, elbows and wrists.

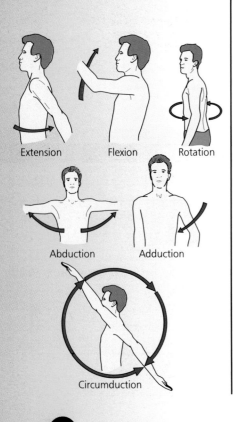

Extension   Flexion   Rotation

Abduction   Adduction

Circumduction

THE SKELETON IN ACTION

The reason we are able to move when we play sport is because our bones are not all joined together. Where two or more bones meet, a **joint** is formed. Each of our joints can be said to fall into one of three categories:

- **Immovable** These are located between flat bones connected by fibrous material. This means that no movement is possible. Examples include the joints between the bones of the skull and the bones of the hip

- **Slightly movable** These are bones connected by cartilage, which allows a small amount of movement. Examples include the joints between the bones of the vertebrae. (Can you remember which type of cartilage is found here?)

- **Movable** Also known as **synovial joints**, these contain a number of similar features, including articular cartilage, synovial fluid (contained within a synovial cavity), a synovial membrane, a joint capsule, and surrounding ligaments. Synovial joints permit a greater degree of movement, although this may be restricted by the shape of the connecting bones, ligaments and tendons. They are located throughout the body, e.g. at the hips, knees, ankles, shoulders, elbows and wrists

One important joint that we have not described is the **knee joint** *(see diagram on page 11)*. The knee joint looks like a condyloid joint, but the surrounding ligaments restrict the movement of the knee so that it functions like a hinge joint.

Movement terms

There are a number of specialised names for the movement of joints. The most common ones are shown and defined below:

- **Flexion** Decrease in the angle between two bones. When we bend our arm, the ulna moves closer to the humerus. This is flexion of the elbow

- **Extension** Increase in the angle between two bones. Straightening our arm is known as extension of the elbow

- **Abduction** Movement of a limb away from an imaginary vertical line down the middle of the body. Moving our arm away from our side is known as abduction of the shoulder

- **Adduction** Movement of a limb towards the imaginary mid-line of the body. Returning our arm back to our side is known as adduction of the shoulder

- **Rotation** Circular movement. When we turn our head from side to side, this is rotation of the atlas-axis joint

- **Circumduction** A combination of flexion, extension, abduction, adduction and rotation. This movement is possible at the shoulder when we move our arm in a circle

Six types of synovial joint

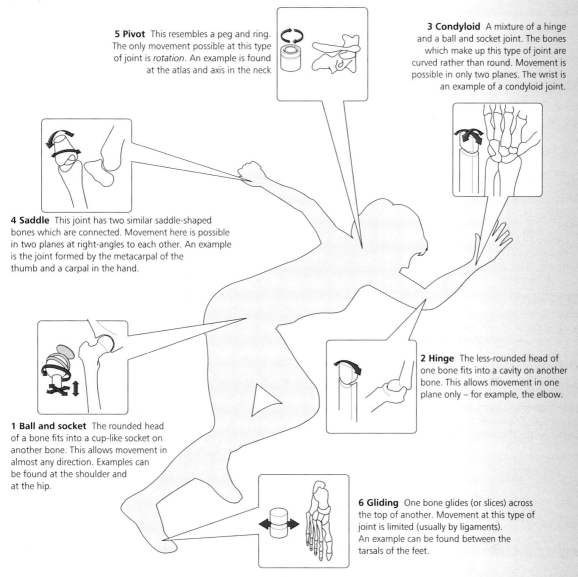

5 Pivot This resembles a peg and ring. The only movement possible at this type of joint is *rotation*. An example is found at the atlas and axis in the neck

3 Condyloid A mixture of a hinge and a ball and socket joint. The bones which make up this type of joint are curved rather than round. Movement is possible in only two planes. The wrist is an example of a condyloid joint.

4 Saddle This joint has two similar saddle-shaped bones which are connected. Movement here is possible in two planes at right-angles to each other. An example is the joint formed by the metacarpal of the thumb and a carpal in the hand.

1 Ball and socket The rounded head of a bone fits into a cup-like socket on another bone. This allows movement in almost any direction. Examples can be found at the shoulder and at the hip.

2 Hinge The less-rounded head of one bone fits into a cavity on another bone. This allows movement in one plane only – for example, the elbow.

6 Gliding One bone glides (or slices) across the top of another. Movement at this type of joint is limited (usually by ligaments). An example can be found between the tarsals of the feet.

S P O R T   I N   A C T I O N

Emma is a long-jumper. In the course of a circuit training session she performs a number of exercises. Can you describe the various joint movements taking place during each one?

EXERCISE	JOINT(S)	MOVEMENT(S)
Sit-ups	Hip	Flexion
Chin-ups	Elbow	
Star jumps	Shoulder	
	Hip	
Press-ups	Elbow	
	Shoulder	
Squat thrusts	Knee	
	Hip	

QUICK QUIZ

1) How many vertebrae are there in the spine?

2) Where would you find an immovable joint? Can you think of more than one example?

3) What do you find inside the synovial cavity?

4) How many directions can a ball and socket joint move in?

5) What type of joint is the knee?

6) Define the term 'flexion'.

✓ KEY WORDS

Tick each box when you understand the word

AXIAL AND APPENDICULAR SKELETON ☐

LONG, SHORT, FLAT, AND IRREGULAR BONES ☐

COMPACT AND SPONGY BONE ☐

CERVICAL, THORACIC, LUMBAR, SACRAL, AND COCCYX ☐

CARTILAGE ☐

LIGAMENTS ☐

IMMOVABLE, SLIGHTLY MOVABLE, AND MOVABLE/ SYNOVIAL JOINTS ☐

BALL AND SOCKET JOINT ☐

HINGE JOINT ☐

CONDYLOID JOINT ☐

SADDLE JOINT ☐

PIVOT JOINT ☐

GLIDING JOINT ☐

FLEXION/EXTENSION ☐

ABDUCTION/ ADDUCTION ☐

ROTATION ☐

CIRCUMDUCTION ☐

MATCH IT

TERM	DEFINITION
Circumduction	A connective tissue connecting two bones together
Ligament	A movement combining extension, flexion, adduction, abduction and rotation
Clavicle	A sesamoid bone located near the tibia
Patella	A structure found at a synovial joint
Articular cartilage	The collarbone

✓ REVISE IT!

For your exams you will need to know:

☐ The major bones of the human skeleton, including the five regions of the vertebral column

☐ Which bones are classified as long, short, flat or irregular

☐ The functions of the human skeleton

☐ That bones grow and develop from cartilage (the process of ossification)

☐ The functions of cartilage and ligament

☐ The structure and location of movable (synovial) joints, and the location of immovable and slightly movable joints

☐ How we describe the types of movement at specific joints

☐ The meaning of the key words for this chapter

The Muscular System

CHAPTER 03

The aim of this chapter is to help you:

- Describe the characteristics of **muscle**
- Understand how **skeletal muscle** is structured
- Identify the **major muscles** in the body
- Explain the role of **tendons**
- Describe how muscles develop **force**
- Understand how muscles enable **movement** to occur

As we have seen, the skeleton provides a framework for our body, and is held together by a number of connective tissues such as ligaments and cartilage. Muscle is also a connective tissue, supporting our joints as well as various organs within the body. Muscle enables us to maintain our body position and to move our body parts. It is therefore extremely important when we play sport.

TYPES OF MUSCLES

There are three main types of muscle found in the human body:

- **Smooth** This type of muscle is located in the lining of the stomach and gut, the walls of blood vessels and inside our eyes. It performs a number of different functions, each of which takes place without our conscious control (e.g. digesting our food, dilating our blood vessels and our pupils). Smooth muscle works automatically and is referred to as **involuntary muscle**.

- **Cardiac muscle** is found only in the heart. Its function is to force the blood around the body. This is a special kind of involuntary muscle: as well as working automatically, cardiac muscle does not get tired!

> INVOLUNTARY MUSCLE
> Muscle that works automatically

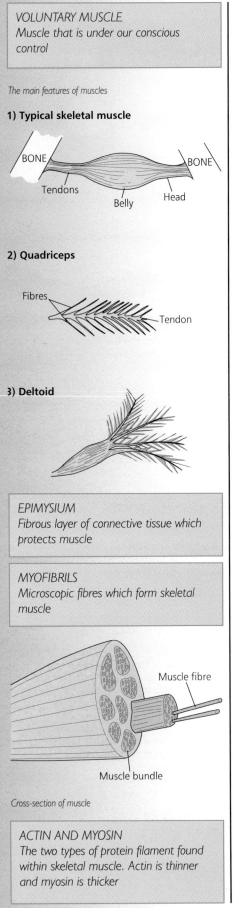

VOLUNTARY MUSCLE
Muscle that is under our conscious control

The main features of muscles

1) Typical skeletal muscle

BONE
BONE
Tendons
Belly
Head

2) Quadriceps

Fibres
Tendon

3) Deltoid

EPIMYSIUM
Fibrous layer of connective tissue which protects muscle

MYOFIBRILS
Microscopic fibres which form skeletal muscle

Muscle fibre

Muscle bundle

Cross-section of muscle

ACTIN AND MYOSIN
The two types of protein filament found within skeletal muscle. Actin is thinner and myosin is thicker

- **Skeletal muscle** is what we normally think of when we talk about muscles. Skeletal muscle forms approximately 40% of our body weight, and is responsible for bodily movement, posture, facial expressions and many other movements. Since these muscles are under our conscious control, we call them **voluntary muscles**

All three types of muscle tissues **contract** to allow movement to occur. Because they are elastic, they are able to shorten and be stretched. After movement, they return to their original length. For the rest of this chapter we shall concentrate on skeletal muscles.

SKELETAL MUSCLES

There are over 650 skeletal muscles in our body, around 150 of them in the head and neck. Most are named according to their **number of heads** (e.g. **biceps** and **triceps**), **shape** (e.g. **deltoid**), **location** (e.g. **rectus abdominus**), and **size** (e.g. **gluteus maximus**).

Fortunately we do not need to know the names of all of them, but there are several major muscles that we need to be able to identify. These are shown in the diagram opposite.

The structure of skeletal muscles

Skeletal muscles vary greatly in shape and size but generally consist of a belly, heads and **tendons**. This basic plan can alter, and the muscle can have multiple heads and tendons according to its function.

Each muscle consists of a bundle of fibres contained by a fibrous layer of connective tissue. This is known as the **epimysium**, and its function is to protect the muscle and to help it to slide smoothly past nearby muscles, bones and other organs as it changes in length.

Inside the epimysium, the muscle is further grouped into bundles. Each of these is divided by thinner layers of connective tissue containing blood vessels and nerve fibres.

Skeletal muscles have a striped appearance, due to the microscopic fibres (called **myofibrils**) which they contain. These myofibrils are made up of alternating rows of two basic protein threads (or **filaments**) called **actin** and **myosin**, which resemble the teeth of interlocking combs. According to the **sliding filament theory**, small projections on the myosin filaments allow the protein filaments to slide past each other as the muscle changes in length.

Deltoids Triangular muscle split into three sections: front, middle and back. Causes abduction, flexion, extension, and rotation of the shoulder, depending on which section is shortened.

Pectorals Acts upon the shoulder joint, causing flexion, adduction and rotation.

Biceps These muscles have two heads at one end, which are attached to the humerus and scapula. When shortened, the biceps cause flexion at the elbow.

Obliques These muscles run diagonally, causing rotation and lateral (sideways) flexion of the spine.

Abdominals A group of muscles providing support for the front of the abdominal wall, and for flexing the spine. Also known as the **rectus abdominus**.

Quadriceps Group made up of four muscles (**rectus femoris, vastus lateralis, vastus intermedius**, and **vastus medialis**) which all meet at the patella. Responsible for flexion of the hip and extension of the knee.

Trapezius Elevates (raises) the shoulder girdle when shortened.

Triceps This muscle has three heads at one end, two attached to the humerus and one attached to the scapula. It mainly causes extension of the elbow joint, but also helps with extension and abduction of the shoulder joint.

Latissimus dorsi Also acts upon the shoulder joint, but causes extension, adduction and rotation.

Gluteals This muscle group has three main sections: The **gluteus maximus** is the largest part of the buttocks, and is the strongest muscle in the body. It mainly causes extension of the hip joint. The **gluteus medius** and **gluteus minimus** help with hip adduction and rotation.

Hamstrings Group made up of three muscles which extend the hip and flex the knee: *biceps femoris, semimembranous*, and *semitendinosus*.

Calf Formed by two muscles, the *gastrocnemius* and *soleus*. These muscles cause **plantarflexion** (pointing the toes) of the ankle joint.

Skeletal muscles – front and back view

1) Below is a selected list of skeletal muscles. Complete the table by filling in which movement is caused by the muscle contracting, and at which joint the movement occurs.

Muscle	Movement caused	Joint involved	Joint type
Biceps	?	Elbow	Hinge
Trapezius	Elevation	?	?
Abdominals	Flexion	?	?
Gastrocnemius	?	Ankle	?

2) Now add the other major muscles to this table. Can you work out the movement caused by each muscle contracting and the joint(s) affected?

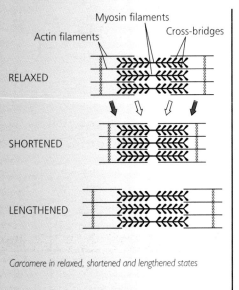

Carcomere in relaxed, shortened and lengthened states

TENDON
Cord of strong tissue attaching muscle to bone

MUSCLE FIBRE TYPES

There are two major types of skeletal muscle fibres in the human body known as **fast twitch** and **slow twitch**. These are described in the table below.

Most people will tend to have a balance of about 50% of each of these two fibre types in their muscles. Experiments have shown that top-class sports people have varying levels of each fibre type in specific muscles. For instance, swimmers tend to have a higher percentage of fast twitch fibres (68%) in their shoulder muscle, whereas long distance runners tend to have a higher percentage of slow twitch fibres (74%) in their calf muscles.

Muscle attachment and levers

Muscles are usually attached to two or more different bones, so that when they shorten, movement occurs. The fibrous connective tissues that make this attachment are called **tendons**, and are fairly elastic.

The longest tendon in the body is the **Achilles tendon**. Do you know which muscle this connects to the heel bone?

	Fast twitch	Slow twitch
Size	Large	Small
Colour	White	Red
Speed of contraction	Contract quickly	Contract slowly
Force generated	Large	Small
Ability to maintain contraction	Tire quickly	Tire slowly
Used in	Fast, explosive sports (sprinting, weightlifting)	Endurance-type sports (marathon running, swimming)

Swimmers have a high percentage of fast twitch fibres in their shoulder muscles

Runners have a high percentage of slow twitch fibres in their calf muscles

Points of origin and insertion

The points at which the tendons connect the muscle to bone are known as the **point of origin** and the **point of insertion**. In simple terms, when a muscle shortens, the point of origin stays still, whilst the point of insertion moves. For example, the abdominals are attached to the pelvis and the sternum. When the abdominals shorten (for example, when we perform a sit-up), it is the sternum which moves the most – this is the point of insertion.

> **POINT OF ORIGIN/INSERTION**
> *Points at which tendons connect muscle to bone*

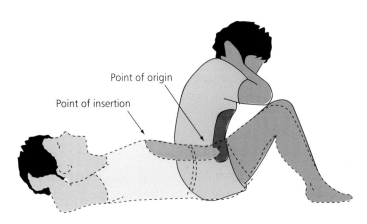

Point of origin

Point of insertion

Levers

Wherever a muscle is attached to a bone, a **lever system** is formed. In the case of tools such as a spanner or a pair of scissors, levers comprise a **pivot (P)**, **load (L)**, **effort (E)**, and **bar**. In the human body these are replaced by joints, body weight (or an external weight such as a dumbbell), muscles and bones. These allow us to move.

QUICK QUIZ

1) What is unique about cardiac muscle?

2) Name three characteristics that are common to all muscles.

3) Which muscle group(s) cause flexion of the hip?

4) 'The biceps is the strongest muscle in the body.' True or false?

5) What is the name of the thick protein filament found inside a myofibril?

6) What colour is fast twitch muscle fibre?

> **LEVER**
> *System comprising pivot, load and effort, formed where muscle is attached to bone*

Lever systems in the body can be divided into three types:

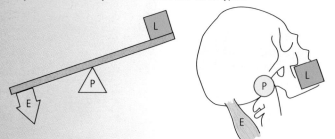

KEY
E = Effort (muscle insertion)
P= Pivot
L = Load

1st Order In this system the PIVOT is the middle, between the load and the effort, resembling the arrangement of a crowbar. This type of lever system can be found at the joint between the atlas and the skull.

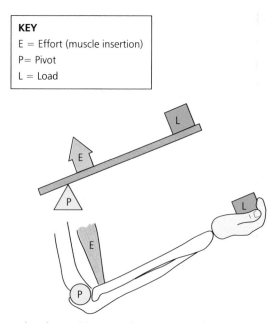

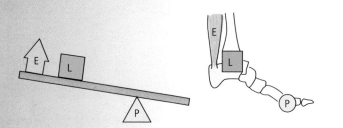

2nd Order In this system the LOAD is in the middle, similar to a wheelbarrow. This system can be found at the ankle joint when we are standing on tip toes.

3rd Order In this system the EFFORT is in the middle. This system is found at the elbow joint, but is the most common type of lever in the body. This arrangement is particularly useful in the limbs because the long bones allow a large range of movement and rapid movement with only a small amount of contraction by the muscle.

Three lever systems

CONCENTRIC CONTRACTION
Where a muscle shortens in length

ECCENTRIC CONTRACTION
Where a muscle increases in length

ISOMETRIC CONTRACTION
Where a muscle tenses but does not change in length

Muscle action

We are most interested in muscles when they are in a state of **contraction**. This means that they are developing tension. This can happen in a number of different ways:

- **Concentric contraction** occurs when a muscle shortens in length and develops tension. Most of the movements that we evaluate in sport involve contractions of this type

- **Eccentric contraction** involves the development of tension whilst the muscle is being lengthened. This contraction is taking place in our biceps as we lower ourselves while performing chin-ups. Plyometric exercises are an example of eccentric contractions

- **Isometric contraction** occurs when the muscle develops tension but does not change in length. If we were to examine this contraction in microscopic detail, we would see that in the myofibril, the myosin filaments connect to the actin filaments. Activities which involve this type of contraction include arm-wrestling, tug-of-war and a rugby scrum (where there is no noticeable movement)

- **Isokinetic contraction** is a special situation in which the muscle is changing in length (either shortening or length-ening), but at a constant rate (isokinetic means 'same speed'). Normally this state of contraction is achieved using expensive machinery.

The muscles in action – movement analysis

Muscles usually work in **antagonistic** pairs to control movement, as they are only able to pull bones closer together (by contracting), not push them apart. For example, the biceps flexes the elbow joint, whilst the triceps extends the elbow joint. Many of our movements, therefore, involve a number of different muscles.

In the arm curl (i.e. during elbow flexion), the biceps is the muscle that is contracting (concentrically) to move the joint and raise the weight. This muscle is known as the **prime mover**. To allow elbow flexion to occur, the triceps must cooperate and relax. This is known as the **antagonist**, and sometimes exerts a 'braking' influence to help control the movement. As the weight is lowered, these two muscles swap roles: the triceps becomes the prime mover, and the biceps becomes the antagonist.

There are two other connected movement terms which you should know:

- **Fixators** are any other muscles situated near the point of origin (the still end) of the prime mover, which act to stabilise the body part so that only the end at the point of insertion will move. In the elbow curl, the deltoid performs this role

- **Synergists** are any other muscles that are actively working to help the prime mover to cause a movement. In the elbow curl, a muscle in the forearm, the **brachialis,** acts as a synergist. Sometimes the synergist and the fixator are the same muscle.

ANTAGONISTIC MUSCLES
Muscles which work in pairs to control movement

PRIME MOVER
Muscle which contracts in order to perform a movement

QUICK QUIZ

1) *'Tendons connect muscle to bone.' True or false?*

2) *Name a point of insertion for the triceps muscle.*

3) *Which component is in the middle of a second-class lever – the bar, pivot, effort, or load?*

4) *Which muscle works eccentrically as we lower the body during chin-ups?*

5) *Which muscle acts as the antagonist during a leg curl?*

QUICK TASK

1) *Using the information given above, complete the following table:*

	Arm curl	**Leg extension**
Prime mover	Biceps	?
Antagonist	?	Hamstrings
Synergist	Brachialis	?
Fixator	?	Gluteus Maximus

2) *Carry out a similar analysis using two further exercises, the toe raise and the bench press.*

S P O R T   I N   A C T I O N

Refer back to the information about Emma in Chapter 2, page 13.

1) Take the table you completed and add three columns headed as follows:

- Muscle acting as the prime mover
- Type of contraction
- Muscle acting as the antagonist

2) Complete the table.

✓ KEY WORDS

Tick each box when you understand the word

INVOLUNTARY MUSCLE ☐
 (SMOOTH AND CARDIAC)

VOLUNTARY ☐
MUSCLE (SKELETAL)

EPIMYSIUM ☐

MYOFIBRILS ☐

ACTIN AND MYOSIN ☐

FAST AND SLOW ☐
TWITCH FIBRE TYPES

TENDON ☐

POINT OF ORIGIN/ ☐
INSERTION

LEVER ☐

CONCENTRIC ☐
CONTRACTION

ECCENTRIC ☐
CONTRACTION

ISOMETRIC ☐
CONTRACTION

ANTAGONISTIC ☐
MUSCLES

PRIME MOVER ☐

FIXATORS ☐

SYNERGISTS ☐

M A T C H   I T

TERM	DEFINITION
Quadriceps	Muscle that works in opposition to the prime mover
Origin	Microscopic fibres within a muscle
Isometric	Muscle group located at the back of the thigh
Antagonist	Muscle group that causes flexion at the hip joint
Hamstrings	Muscle that develops tension but remains the same length
Myofibril	Attachment point of muscle that remains stationary

✓ R E V I S E   I T !

For your exams you will need to know:

☐ That muscles can be classified as voluntary (skeletal) or involuntary (cardiac or smooth)

☐ The structure of skeletal muscle and the location of the major muscle groups

☐ The function of tendons

☐ The movements produced by the muscle groups when they contract (shorten)

☐ That muscles work as antagonistic pairs (one as the prime mover, and one as the antagonist)

☐ The role of synergists and fixators in sporting actions

☐ The difference between fast twitch and slow twitch muscles, and their relevance to sporting actions

☐ The meaning of the key words for this chapter

The Cardiovascular System

CHAPTER 04

The aim of this chapter is to help you:

- Understand the **structure** and **function** of **blood** and its components

- Explain the different **blood vessels**

- Identify the structures of the **heart**

- Explain the **double circulatory system**

- Understand the relationship between **heart rate, stroke volume** and **cardiac output**

- Understand the importance of **blood pressure**

The cardiovascular system has a very important role to play in human physiology, as it provides the main means of transporting oxygen around the body. Our muscles require energy to contract and to enable us to play sport. There are energy supplies in the working muscles, but these are used up very quickly. Therefore, we require a method of transporting the oxygen into these muscles.

Cardio- refers to the heart, whilst **vascular** refers to the network of blood vessels: together, these make up the **double circulatory system**. However, a third important element is **blood**, the substance in which various materials are transported around the body.

BLOOD

Blood is classified as a connective tissue. The average total blood volume is about 5 litres (about 9 pints), making up approximately 8% of our body weight. It consists of the following elements:

> BLOOD
> *Classified as a connective tissue. Average total blood volume is about 5 litres*

- **Blood plasma** makes up 55% of the total blood volume, and is a pale yellow fluid which consists mainly of water. The remainder contains dissolved food substances, gases, chemicals and waste products

- **Red blood cells** make up the majority of the remaining 45% of total blood volume. These small red disks contain a substance called **haemoglobin**, which carries oxygen. When the blood contains oxygen it is said to be **oxygenated**, and when it has no oxygen it is **deoxygenated**

- **White blood cells** protect the body from disease and infection by attacking any foreign substances

- **Blood platelets** are microscopic cells that normally appear at the site of a cut, forming a platelet plug in small blood vessels, and forming a clot in larger wounds in order to stop bleeding. This clot is known as a **thrombus**.

HAEMOGLOBIN
Substance contained within red blood cells, giving them their colour. Its main function is to carry oxygen

OXYGENATED BLOOD
Blood that contains oxygen

DEOXYGENATED BLOOD
Blood that does not contain oxygen

The circulatory system showing the heart and blood vessels

PULMONARY CIRCULATION
The circulatory system that transports deoxygenated blood from the right ventricle to the left atrium via the lungs in order to oxygenate the blood

SYSTEMIC CIRCULATION
The circulatory system that transports oxygenated blood from the left ventricle to the cells of the body

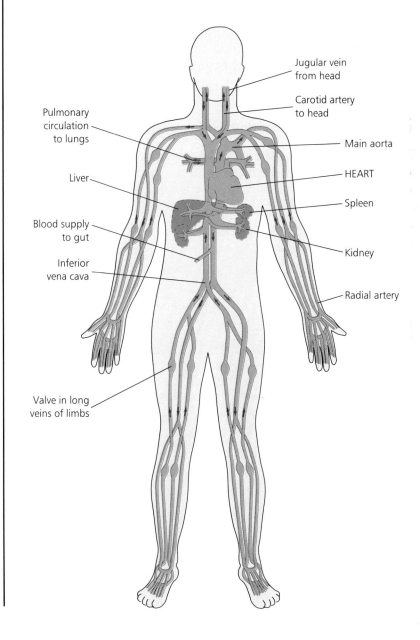

Labels: Jugular vein from head · Carotid artery to head · Pulmonary circulation to lungs · Main aorta · Liver · HEART · Spleen · Blood supply to gut · Inferior vena cava · Kidney · Radial artery · Valve in long veins of limbs

BLOOD VESSELS

Blood is transported around the body in a series of blood vessels. There are three main types:

- **Arteries** carry blood away from the heart. They consist of three layers: an inner lining, a layer of smooth muscle and a fibrous outer covering. Artery walls are thick, as the blood is travelling under high pressure; yet we can detect the surge of blood through arteries located close to the surface of the skin. This pulse can be felt at the wrist (the **radial artery**) and in the neck (at the **carotid artery**)

- Once the arteries begin to spread out, the blood passes through a network of smaller vessels called **capillaries**. These are thin vessels through which a red blood cell can barely squeeze. The walls of capillaries are only one cell thick, which enables gases and nutrients to be exchanged between the blood and the cells. This process is known as **diffusion**

- **Veins** are blood vessels which carry blood back to the heart. They also have a wall with three layers, but the walls are thinner. Veins also prevent the backflow of blood through a system of valves.

STRUCTURE OF THE HEART

The **heart** is at the centre of the circulatory system. It consists of four chambers and is almost entirely made out of cardiac muscle. Its main function is to pump blood around the body. It consists of two muscular pumps separated into a left-hand side and a right-hand side by a solid muscular wall called the **septum**. In adults, the heart is about the size of a closed fist.

ARTERIES
Vessels which carry blood away from the heart

QUICK QUIZ

1) Name three functions of blood.

2) How much of our blood is plasma?

3) Name two places where you can feel a pulse.

4) What is the function of the valves in veins?

5) What is the function of arteries?

CAPILLARIES
Network of small vessels through which blood passes

DIFFUSION
Process whereby gases pass through a membrane from an area of high concentration to an area of lower concentration

VEINS
Blood vessels which carry blood back to the heart

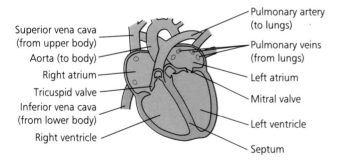

Superior vena cava (from upper body)
Aorta (to body)
Right atrium
Tricuspid valve
Inferior vena cava (from lower body)
Right ventricle

Pulmonary artery (to lungs)
Pulmonary veins (from lungs)
Left atrium
Mitral valve
Left ventricle
Septum

Right atrium Blood enters the right-hand side of the heart through the vena cava. Here, the blood is deoxygenated.

Tricuspid valve This valve has three flaps and prevents blood from flowing back into the right-hand side of the heart.

Right ventricle This larger chamber pumps the blood around the pulmonary circulation system. Blood passes through semi-lunar valves before passing into the pulmonary artery.

Left atrium Blood enters the right-hand side of the heart through the pulmonary vein. The blood here is oxygenated.

Bicuspid valve This valve has two flaps to prevent blood from flowing back into the left-hand side of the heart.

Left ventricle This is the largest and strongest chamber in the heart, which pumps the blood around the systemic circulation system. Blood passes through semi-lunar valves before going into the aorta (the thickest blood vessel in the body).

HEART RATE AND BLOOD PRESSURE

Heart rate (HR)

> *HEART RATE (HR)*
> *Number of pulses or heart beats per minute. Average resting HR is 75 beats per minute (bpm)*

As we saw earlier, the heart is made from cardiac muscle. This muscle tissue has a number of unique characteristics. As well as never tiring, it also has the ability to contract and relax in a natural rhythm. This produces the heart beat, which is started by an electrical impulse from an organ on the surface of the right atrium called the sino-atrial (SA) node. This is the 'pacemaker' of the heart.

Stroke volume (SV)

> *STROKE VOLUME (SV)*
> *Volume of blood ejected from the heart in one beat, measured in ml/beat*

The volume of blood ejected from our heart in one beat is known as our **stroke volume (SV)**. In most instances, this refers to the volume of blood ejected from the left ventricle (measured in ml/beat).

Whilst we can easily measure our HR, assessing our SV is not so easy. However, there is another concept that can help us to estimate this:

Cardiac output (Q̇)

> *CARDIAC OUTPUT*
> *Volume of blood ejected from left ventricle in one minute, measured in l/min*

This refers to the volume of blood ejected from the left ventricle in one minute (measured in l/min).

Heart rate, stroke volume and cardiac output are linked in the following way:

$$\text{HR} \times \text{SV} = \dot{Q}$$

QUICK TASK

1) Starting at the left ventricle, trace the route that a drop of blood would follow around one lap of the double circulatory system. Note the various vessels, chambers and valves through which the blood passes.

2) Comment on whether the blood is oxygenated or deoxygenated, and indicate when it changes from one to the other.

QUICK QUIZ

1) How big is the adult heart?

2) What is the sino-atrial node?

3) What type of valve is the aortic valve?

4) Is the blood that passes through the pulmonary valve oxygenated or deoxygenated?

5) Which blood vessel supplies the heart with oxygenated blood?

Exterior view of the heart

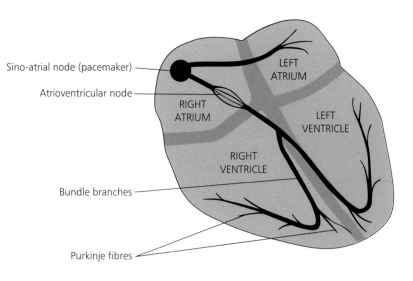

Sino-atrial node (pacemaker)

Atrioventricular node

RIGHT ATRIUM

LEFT ATRIUM

LEFT VENTRICLE

RIGHT VENTRICLE

Bundle branches

Purkinje fibres

Thus, if we know two of these values, we can calculate the third. If we look at our average values, we know that resting HR is 75 bpm. Resting cardiac output is 5 l/min, as it takes blood a full minute to complete one lap of the double circulatory system at rest, and we have a blood volume of 5 litres.

Therefore:

$$75 \times SV = 5$$

$$SV = \frac{5}{75} \qquad = 0.066 \text{ l/beat} \qquad = \textbf{66 ml/beat}$$

Blood pressure (BP)

Whilst we can measure our HR by locating an artery near the surface of the skin, we have to use a slightly different method to measure our BP. One way is to use a **sphygmomanometer** (the technical term for a BP meter) to measure the pressure needed to stop blood flowing through an artery.

The average BP reading for an adult is 120/80 mmHg. The first number represents **systolic BP**, whilst the second figure represents **diastolic BP** (The unit of measurement is millimetres of mercury). If the values obtained are greater than 140/90 mmHg, and similar high values are shown after several tests (all performed by a qualified medic), then the person has high BP. This is a condition known as **hypertension**, and it can become a problem if left untreated. The heart has to work too hard and becomes inefficient, and this can commonly lead to a number of cardiovascular diseases including stroke and heart attack.

QUICK TASK

1) *While in a sitting position, locate your pulse. Use either your carotid or radial pulse. Count it for 60 seconds (don't include the first pulse of blood). Is your score above or below average resting HR? Can you explain why?*

2) *Repeat the above process a further two times, once standing up, and once lying down. Does your resting HR change? Can you explain why?*

BLOOD PRESSURE (BP)
Pressure needed to pump blood around the human body

SYSTOLIC BP AND DIASTOLIC BP
Systolic BP is measured when the heart forcefully ejects blood. Diastolic BP is measured when the heart relaxes. Systolic BP is normally higher than diastolic BP

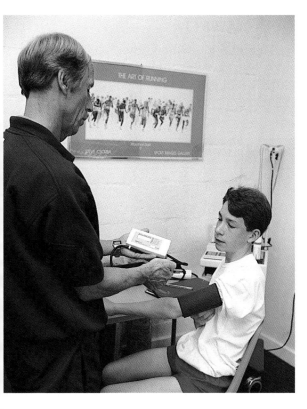

Left: *Measuring blood pressure*

Below: *apparatus for testing blood pressure*

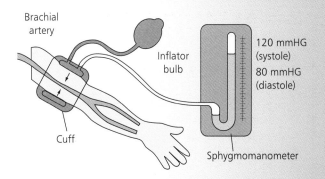

Brachial artery

Inflator bulb

120 mmHG (systole)
80 mmHG (diastole)

Cuff

Sphygmomanometer

QUICK QUIZ

1) Where is the pacemaker of the heart located?

2) What is average resting HR?

3) Define cardiac output.

4) What device is used to measure BP?

5) Name two factors that can affect blood pressure.

6) Define the term 'hypertension'

FAST FORWARD ▷▷

ADRENAL GLAND   see page 44

MAXIMUM HR
The maximum number of heart beats per minute of which a person is capable

Factors affecting blood pressure

BP values can be affected by a number of factors:

● **Age** As we get older, our arteries do not stretch as much when blood is pumped through them

● **Stress and tension** When we are under stress, our body's natural response is to raise our blood pressure. Sometimes, having our blood pressure measured (particularly by a doctor) can be stressful in itself!

● **Diet** High levels of fat and salt cause the arteries to stiffen and become clogged up. This will increase blood pressure

● **Exercise** Blood pressure will increase dramatically during physical activity, as the heart is forced to work harder to supply oxygen to the muscles. However, with regular exercise, resting BP can be reduced, thus preventing cardiovascular disease

THE CIRCULATORY SYSTEM IN ACTION

When we take part in physical activity, a number of changes occur in the cardiovascular system:

● The increased demand for oxygen to the working muscles causes an increase in heart rate (this is helped by the release of the hormone **adrenaline**)

● This increase in heart rate depends upon how strenuous the activity is. There is a guideline which lets us estimate our **maximum HR**: simply subtract your age (in years) from the number 220. For example a fifteen-year-old would have a maximum HR of 205 bpm (220 – 15).

● The heart is able to pump more blood more quickly around the double circulatory system. As more blood returns to the left atrium, the left ventricle will eject more blood per beat. Therefore SV will increase:

S P O R T   I N   A C T I O N

Measure your resting HR (it is best to do this before you get up in the morning). Then ask a friend to help you record the results as you perform the following physical activities:

● Walk slowly for 1 minute (use a flat surface – an athletics track is ideal)
● Measure your HR (count your pulse for 10 seconds and then multiply it by 6)
● Rest for 3 minutes, measuring your HR every minute
● Walk quickly for 1 minute. Measure your HR. Rest for 3 minutes
● Jog at a steady pace for 1 minute. Measure your HR. Rest for 3 minutes
● Run at a fast pace for 1 minute. Measure your HR. Rest for 3 minutes

Plot the results on a graph, with time on the horizontal axis and heart rate on the vertical axis.
Be sure to note when you performed the different physical activities. Can you explain the results?

● If both HR and SV increase, Q will also increase. If we assume that HR increases from 75 bpm to 120 bpm, and that SV increases from 66 ml/beat to 100 ml/beat, we can calculate cardiac output as follows:

$$\dot{Q} = 120 \times 100 \qquad = 12,000 \text{ ml/min} \qquad = \textbf{12 l/min}$$

● BP will also increase since the heart is under more strain than normal

● Blood flow will be re-directed to the working muscles, since they require more oxygen, whereas other areas of the body (the stomach and gut, for example) do not require the oxygen as urgently

● The blood vessels leading to the skin become **dilated**, allowing excess heat to escape from the body. However, when we are going at maximum intensity ('flat out') we require more blood for the muscles, so the vessels leading to the skin are constricted. This causes body temperature to rise, which can lead to fatigue, dehydration and over-exhaustion

SPORT IN ACTION

Bill is a cyclist. Before he began competing seriously, his resting HR was 70 bpm and his resting SV was 70 l/min.

1)   Calculate Bill's resting cardiac output.
2)   Six months later Bill's resting stroke volume has increased to 100 l/min.
     Can you explain this change and work out his resting heart rate and cardiac output?

MATCH IT

TERM	DEFINITION
SA node	The surge of blood through an artery felt close to the skin
Capillaries	The amount of blood ejected from the left ventricle in one minute
Pulse	Fight infection and disease
White blood cells	A group of cells responsible for our heart beat
Pulmonary circulation	Oxygenates blood
Cardiac output	Thin blood vessels where diffusion occurs

✓ KEY WORDS

Tick each box when you understand the word

BLOOD ☐

OXYGENATED AND DEOXYGENATED BLOOD ☐

ARTERIES ☐

CAPILLARIES ☐

VEINS ☐

DIFFUSION ☐

LEFT AND RIGHT VENTRICLE ☐

LEFT AND RIGHT ATRIUM ☐

PULMONARY CIRCULATION ☐

SYSTEMIC CIRCULATION ☐

HEART RATE (HR) ☐

STROKE VOLUME (SV) ☐

CARDIAC OUTPUT (Q) ☐

BLOOD PRESSURE (BP) ☐

SYSTOLIC BP AND DIASTOLIC BP ☐

MAXIMUM HR ☐

✓ REVISE IT!

For your exams you will need to know:

☐ The structure and functions of blood (red cells, white cells, platelets and plasma)

☐ The differences in structure and function between arteries, capillaries and veins

☐ The names of the four major blood vessels attached to the heart

☐ The parts identified in a diagram of the heart, including the names of the chambers and the valves

☐ How the heart acts as a pump in a double circulatory system

☐ How heart rate can be measured

☐ The definitions of stroke volume and cardiac output, how they are related to heart rate, and how they vary due to physical activity

☐ The importance of blood pressure, and how it can be recorded

☐ The meaning of the key words for this chapter

The Respiratory System

CHAPTER 05

The aim of this chapter is to help you:

- Identify the various structures that help us to **breathe**

- Recognise the different **volumes of air** that enter and leave our lungs

- Understand why the air we breathe in is different from the air we breathe out

- Explain how breathing is affected by **physical activity** and **exercise training**

- Understand the three main **energy systems**

Breathing is a very important function of the respiratory system which supplies the body (via the circulatory system) with oxygen. Air is taken into the lungs by a process known as **inhalation** (breathing in), and expelled from the lungs by a process known as **exhalation** (breathing out). The body uses the **oxygen** we inhale for energy and to keep the cells working. Without oxygen we could only survive a few minutes at most, as organs such as our brain would stop working. Also, by exhaling, we get rid of the gas **carbon dioxide**, a waste product produced by the body's cells.

STRUCTURE OF THE RESPIRATORY SYSTEM

In order to get oxygen into our circulatory system, we first need to inhale air. This air ends up in our lungs, two spongy elastic air bags in the thoracic (chest) cavity which extract the oxygen from the air. As the air enters the body, it passes through a number of structures:

INHALATION AND EXHALATION
Process of breathing in and out

OXYGEN
Gas which, together with carbon dioxide, forms the air we breathe

CARBON DIOXIDE
Gas forming 0.04% of inhaled air and 4% of exhaled air

RESPIRATION
The process of transporting oxygen to the cells of the body, where it can be used, and the removal of waste products such as carbon dioxide

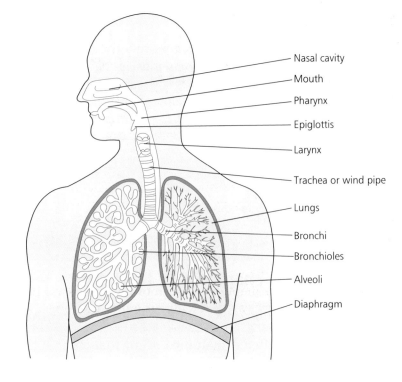

The human respiratory system

- The nasal cavity contains tiny hairs called **cilia** that filter out dust particles, and blood vessels close to the surface that warm the air. Mucus in the cavity also helps to moisten the air

- The mouth is also known as the **oral cavity**. We can inhale through our mouths, but breathing through our nose is more efficient. A bony plate called the **palate** separates the nasal and oral cavities

- The **pharynx** forms the throat and is shared by air and food. The end of the passage divides into the wind pipe, or **trachea**, and the food pipe or **oesophagus**

- The **epiglottis** is a flap of cartilage (can you remember which type?) which prevents food from going down the trachea

- The **larynx** is the voice-box, a structure made of cartilage (fibrocartilage). It contains the **vocal cord**s which help us to speak as air passes over them

- The **trachea** or **wind pipe** is made up of 20 'C'-shaped pieces of cartilage which keep the airway open. The opening in the cartilage at the back allows the food pipe to expand when swallowing food

- At the end of the trachea, the airway splits into two branches or **bronchi**. One enters the right lung and one the left

- Inside the lungs, the bronchi divide again and again like the branches of a tree. The smallest branches are less than 1 mm in diameter and are called **bronchioles**

- At the end of the bronchioles there are tiny hollow sacs called **alveoli**, which are filled with air when we inhale. There are millions of these sacs in each lung.

BRONCHI
Two small branch-like passages at the end of the trachea

BRONCHIOLES
Small branch-like passages formed by the division of the bronchi inside the lungs

ALVEOLI
Tiny hollow sacs at the end of the bronchioles which fill with air when we breathe in

The mechanics of breathing

When we are resting, breathing is a process that occurs automatically. As we inhale, the only muscle that contracts is the **diaphragm**. This dome-shaped muscle flattens, increasing the volume of the thoracic cavity and causing air to rush into the lungs. As the diaphragm relaxes, it returns to its original shape, reducing the volume of the thoracic cavity and forcing air out of the lungs.

During exercise we need to get more oxygen to the muscles, and so we need to use extra muscles to help us to breathe. The **external intercostal** muscles, which are located between the ribs, contract, causing the rib cage to move upwards and outwards. During exhalation, the **internal intercostal muscles** contract, causing the rib cage to move downwards and inwards. The abdominals also contract, squeezing our organs upwards towards our diaphragm. Both of these decrease the volume of the thoracic cavity, forcing air out of the lungs.

> **DIAPHRAGM**
> Dome-shaped muscle in the thorax which regulates the flow of air in and out of the lungs

> **INTERCOSTAL MUSCLES**
> Extra muscles located between the ribs which help us to inhale and exhale

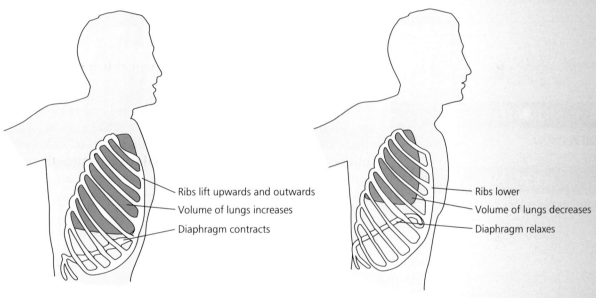

- Ribs lift upwards and outwards
- Volume of lungs increases
- Diaphragm contracts

- Ribs lower
- Volume of lungs decreases
- Diaphragm relaxes

Breathing in (inhalation)   Breathing out (exhalation)

LUNG VOLUME

Lung capacity varies according to age, sex, body type and fitness level. Smoking can also affect the capacity of the lungs, reducing their volume and efficiency. Normally, our lungs are capable of holding approximately 6 litres of air (about 10 pints).

When we breathe normally (i.e. when we are at rest), we inhale and exhale between 12–16 times a minute. This is known as our **respiratory rate**. Each time we breathe, about 500 ml (just under a pint) of air is moved. This is called our **tidal volume (TV)**. We can measure these amounts using a **spirometer**. The amount of air we breathe in one minute is known as **minute ventilation**, and can be calculated by multiplying tidal volume and respiratory rate.

> **RESPIRATORY RATE**
> The rate at which we inhale and exhale when breathing normally – usually between 12 and 16 times a minute

> **TIDAL VOLUME (TV)**
> The amount of air moved each time we breathe, usually about 500ml

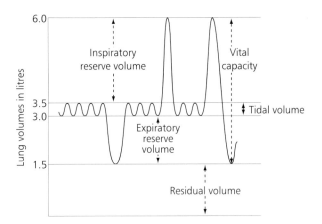

A spirometer trace showing lung volumes and capacities

QUICK TASK

Trace the route of a molecule of oxygen from the air via the lungs to any cell in the body. List the major structures through which it passes.

◀◀ **REWIND**

DIFFUSION   see page 25

◀◀ **REWIND**

RED BLOOD CELLS   see page 24

When we breathe in as deeply as possible (**inspiratory reserve volume – IRV**) or blow out as much air as possible (**expiratory reserve volume – ERV**), this makes the spirometer trace increase in size (*see above*). The resulting two volumes can be added to our tidal volume and make up our **vital capacity**. Every time we exhale, even when we try to force out as much air as possible, some air remains in our lungs. This is known as the **residual volume**, and prevents the lungs from collapsing.

Gaseous exchange

When the air enters the alveoli, oxygen is removed from it. The oxygen **diffuses** through the thin walls of the alveoli, which are only one cell thick. Each alveolus is connected to its own blood capillary, so there is an abundant supply of **red blood cells** which are available to pick up the oxygen. (Can you remember the name of the substance which combines with the oxygen?). At the same time, carbon dioxide is released from red blood cells back into the alveoli, where it is removed as we exhale.

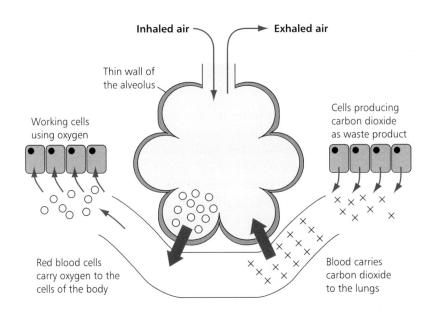

The process of gaseous exchange

What is air made of?

The air around us, which we inhale, contains a number of different gases. The main gas is nitrogen, which makes up 79 per cent of the air. The percentage of oxygen and carbon dioxide in the air we inhale and exhale is shown below:

Gas	Inhaled air	Exhaled air
Oxygen	21%	16%
Carbon dioxide	0.04%	4%

QUICK QUIZ

1) What is meant by the term **inhalation**?

2) How is the air we breathe filtered, warmed and moistened?

3) What shape is the diaphragm when relaxed?

4) Tidal volume + ERV + IRV = ?

5) Define the term **diffusion**.

6) How much of the oxygen that we inhale do we use?

S P O R T   I N   A C T I O N

1)   While you are resting, count your respiratory rate, then repeat the Sport In Action activity on page 28, but this time concentrating on your respiratory rate.
Ask a friend to help you record the results.

NB During rest periods, count for 30 seconds and then double this score – it is more accurate than counting for 10 seconds.

2)   Plot your results on a graph, showing time on the horizontal axis and respiratory rate on the vertical axis. Be sure to note when you performed the different physical activities. Can you explain the results? Do they show a pattern similar to your heart rate responses?

THE RESPIRATORY SYSTEM IN ACTION

There are a number of changes that occur in the respiratory system when we take part in physical activity. The most obvious is that we breathe much more frequently. Also, as we inhale and exhale more deeply, our tidal volume increases.

Oxygen uptake

Because the demand for oxygen increases as we take part in physical activity, so does our capacity to use it. This capacity increases up to a point known as **maximal oxygen uptake** (or **VO$_2$ max**). This is the amount of oxygen we can transport and use in one minute, and is expressed relative to body weight. Typical values will be in the range of 30–60 ml/kg/min, depending upon fitness levels. (The cyclist Miguel Indurain's VO$_2$ max was 88 ml/kg/min.)

QUICK TASK

1) Calculate minute ventilation for a person at rest (assume average build and fitness level).

2) What happens to minute ventilation during physical activity? Explain your answer.

3) What happens to residual volume during physical activity? Explain your answer

VO$_2$ MAX
The maximum amount of oxygen we can transport and use in one minute, measured in ml/kh/min

Sprinting 100m uses our creatine phosphate system

Running the 400m uses our lactic acid system

FAST FORWARD ▷▷

GLYCOGEN   see page 74

LACTIC ACID
Substance which can build up in the muscles, causing pain and heaviness

AEROBIC
System providing long-term energy for low-intensity physical activity

Running the Marathon uses our aerobic system

ENERGY SYSTEMS

The muscles of the body needs energy to contract, and this is provided by a substance called **adenosine triphosphate (ATP)**. This is made up of a molecule of adenosine which has three phosphate molecules attached to it (**tri-** means 'three'). ATP can be broken down, and the chemical reaction that causes this produces adenosine diphosphate (ADP) and energy. This is explained by the following equation:

$$ATP \rightarrow ADP + Energy$$

There is not a large store of ATP in the body, and most will be used up in about five seconds. In order to produce energy for physical activity which lasts longer than this, there are three main systems that the body can use:

1 Creatine phosphate system
Creatine phosphate (CP) is a naturally occurring substance in the muscle tissue which is used to generate energy. When combined with ADP, it forms ATP. As it is stored in the muscles, CP is available for *immediate* use and produces energy for high-intensity activity – i.e. quick bursts of explosive speed and strength. The supply of CP in the body only lasts for 15–20 seconds. This process occurs **anaerobically ('without oxygen')**, and is summarised in the table on page 37.

2 Lactic acid system
Once the CP has been used up, the muscles are able to use a substance called **glycogen**. This glycogen combines with ADP to form ATP, producing a substance called **pyruvic acid**. If there is no oxygen present, the pyruvic acid will turn into **lactic acid (LA)**. A build-up of this substance in the muscles causes pain, and makes the affected limbs feel heavy. This system can be used for short-term energy, and lasts for about 60 seconds.

3 Aerobic system
Aerobic means 'in the presence of oxygen'. If pyruvic acid combines with oxygen (O_2), it breaks down to produce water (H_2O), carbon dioxide (CO_2) and heat. The water can be used by

the body, whilst the carbon dioxide is taken up by the blood and transported to the lungs, where it is exhaled. The aerobic system provides long-term energy, and is useful for physical activity at a low intensity. The aerobic process is shown in the following table.

THE THREE ENERGY SYSTEMS	
Creatine phosphate system	$ADP + CP \rightarrow ATP + Creatine$ $ATP \rightarrow ADP + Energy$
Lactic acid system	$ADP + Glycogen \rightarrow ATP + Pyruvic Acid$ $ATP \rightarrow ADP + Energy$ Pyruvic acid (without oxygen) $\rightarrow$ Lactic acid
Aerobic system	$ADP + Glycogen \rightarrow ATP + Pyruvic acid$ $ATP \rightarrow ADP + Energy$ Pyruvic acid $+ O_2 \rightarrow H_2O + CO_2 + heat$

THE RECOVERY PROCESS

As we start to exercise, it takes time for our breathing to adjust to the rate we require. This is shown in the diagram below. For a short period, the demand for oxygen is greater than the supply, and the energy we need is supplied anaerobically (i.e. by the CP and LA systems). This is known as the **oxygen debt**.

Once we stop exercising, the reverse happens – the supply of oxygen is greater than the demand, and this is known as the **oxygen deficit**. This continues into the recovery period until the oxygen debt has been repaid. It is also used to rid the body of any lactic acid in the muscles.

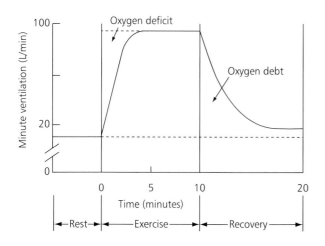

Oxygen consumption during rest, exercise and recovery

QUICK TASK

When we play sport, our body uses three different systems to create energy. Which system provides the majority of the energy in the following sports?

1) 400m
2) Long-distance cycling
3) Long jump
4) Hockey

QUICK QUIZ

1) What happens to the tidal volume when we exercise?

2) How many molecules of phosphate are there in ATP?

3) Define the term **VO$_2$ max**.

4) Where is glycogen stored?

5) What happens to pyruvic acid when it is mixed with oxygen?

6) Define the term **oxygen debt**.

OXYGEN DEBT
Where the demand for oxygen is greater than the supply

OXYGEN DEFICIT
Where the supply of oxygen is greater than the demand

✓ KEY WORDS

Tick each box when you understand the word

INHALATION AND EXHALATION ☐

RESPIRATION ☐

BRONCHI AND BRONCHIOLES ☐

ALVEOLI ☐

DIAPHRAGM ☐

EXTERNAL AND INTERNAL INTERCOSTAL MUSCLES ☐

RESPIRATORY RATE ☐

TIDAL VOLUME ☐

MINUTE VENTILATION ☐

OXYGEN ☐

CARBON DIOXIDE ☐

MAXIMAL OXYGEN UPTAKE (VO₂ MAX) ☐

ADENOSINE TRIPHOSPHATE (ATP) ☐

CREATINE PHOSPHATE (CP) ☐

LACTIC ACID (LA) ☐

ANAEROBIC AND AEROBIC ☐

OXYGEN DEBT AND OXYGEN DEFICIT ☐

MATCH IT

TERM	DEFINITION
Lactic acid	Muscles between the ribs that help with inhalation
Cilia	The air that remains in our lungs following forced exhalation
ATP	Small sacs in the lungs where gas exchange occurs
Alveoli	Substance that produces pain in muscles
Residual volume	Substance that produces energy
External intercostal	Small hairs in the nasal cavity

✓ REVISE IT!

For your exams you will need to know:

☐ The structure, function and location of the nasal passages, larynx, trachea, bronchi, bronchioles and alveoli

☐ The action of the diaphragm and intercostal muscles and the movement of the ribs during breathing

☐ Definitions and values of the lung capacities (in particular, vital capacity, tidal volume, inspiratory reserve volume, expiratory reserve volume and residual volume), and how they vary during physical activity and exercise training

☐ The process of gaseous exchange in the alveoli

☐ The composition of air (inhaled and exhaled)

☐ The differences between aerobic and anaerobic respiration, and their role in the production of energy

☐ The effect of lactic acid on physical activity, and the role of the oxygen debt

☐ The meaning of the key words for this chapter

The Nervous System

CHAPTER 06

The aim of this chapter is to help you:

- Understand how the brain controls **voluntary movements**
- Identify the structure and function of **nerve cells**
- Recognise the role of the **involuntary nervous system**
- Understand how **reflex actions** occur and their importance in sporting movement

The **nervous system** enables us to coordinate and control our movements. At the higher levels, it enables performers to produce high-precision movements time and time again, making them appear **skilful**.

THE NERVOUS SYSTEM

The nervous system consists of the brain, spinal cord, nerve fibre, and **effector** and **receptor** organs. It is responsible for all of our conscious (or voluntary) actions and has two main parts:

1 The central nervous system

This consists of the **brain** and the **spinal cord**. The brain has two main parts:

- The **cerebrum** is the largest part of the brain and controls thought, speech and movement. The left-hand hemisphere controls the right-hand side of the body, and influences logical thought and reasoning. The right-hand half controls the left-hand side of the body, and influences imagination and creativity. This is believed to explain why left-handed people are sometimes more creative than right-handed people

- The **cerebellum** or 'little brain' is located at the back underneath the cerebrum. It is responsible for maintaining balance and coordinating body movements.

FAST FORWARD ▶▶

SKILFUL PERFORMANCE   See page 83

EFFECTOR ORGANS
Organs that receive information and instructions from the brain

BRAIN
The control centre for most of our actions

CEREBRUM
Largest part of the brain, which controls thought, speech and movement

CEREBELLUM
The 'little brain' located under the cerebrum, responsible for balance and coordination

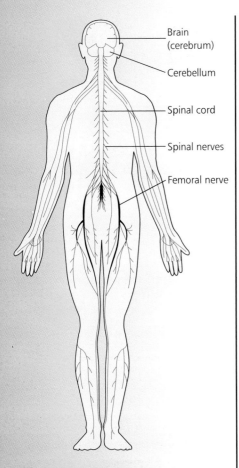

The brain, spinal cord and peripheral nerves

> **SPINAL CORD**
> *conducts nerve impulses to and from the brain*

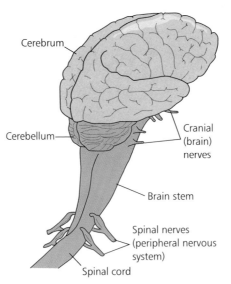

The **brain** is the control centre for most of our actions. It is made up of spongy tissue suspended in a fluid inside the flat bones of the skull which protect it. It is a highly complex and delicate organ.

The **spinal cord** emerges from the base of the brain, passing through a hole about 1cm wide in the base of the skull. It extends all the way down the spine through gaps in the centre of the vertebrae, and is made up of spinal nerves which are able to transmit messages both to and from the brain.

The **peripheral nerve fibres** branch out between the gaps in the vertebrae, extending to nearly every part of the body.

2 The peripheral nervous system

The **peripheral nervous system** consists of the nerve fibres that branch out from the spinal cord, and the various organs to which they are connected.

- **Brain** This is the control centre for most of our actions. It is made up of spongy tissue suspended in a fluid inside the flat bones of the skull which protect it. It is a highly complex and very delicate organ

- **Spinal cord** This emerges from the base of the brain, passing through a hole about 1 cm wide in the base of the skull. It extends all the way down the spine through gaps in the centre of the vertebrae, and is made up of **spinal nerves** which are able to transmit messages both to and from the brain

- **Peripheral nerve fibres** These branch out between the gaps in the vertebrae, extending throughout the body

STRUCTURE OF NERVE CELLS

Nerve cells or **neurones** carry the information to and from the spinal cord and brain. They have three main sections:

- **Dendrites** receive messages in the form of nerve impulses

- The **nucleus** is the main body of the cell

- The **axon** transmits the impulse away from the nucleus

Neurones are not actually connected to each other but are separated by a microscopic gap. This is called the **synaptic gap**. Impulses are able to cross this gap via the release of a chemical substance called **acetylcholine**, which allows an impulse to travel through the nervous system at great speed.

There are two main types of nerve:

- **Motor neurones** transmit impulses from the brain to the effector organs, where the instructions are carried out.

- **Sensory neurones** receive information from receptor organs and transmit impulses to the brain, where the information is processed

THE INVOLUNTARY NERVOUS SYSTEM

This part of the nervous system is responsible for functions over which we have no control – for example, our heart beat and digestion. These actions are 'controlled' by the **medulla oblongata**, an area that forms the top of the spinal cord. This is divided into two sections:

- The **sympathetic nervous system** is responsible for 'preparing' the body for action. It stimulates the **adrenal gland** and causes our heart rate to increase, our bronchi to dilate and our breathing rate to increase. It also slows down the functioning of organs that are not essential for physical activity. This is known as the **'fight or flight'** response.

- The **parasympathetic nervous system** is responsible for 'slowing' the body down, and functions in opposition to the sympathetic nervous system.

The role of receptors and reflex actions

While the brain is continually making decisions and sending out instructions, it also receives information from three main types of **receptor organs**:

- **Exteroceptors** receive information from outside the body. They include the eyes, ears and touch

- **Interoceptors** receive information from inside the body, such as chemical changes in the blood or lungs

- **Proprioceptors** receive information from within muscles, tendons and joints. The main organs are **golgi tendon organs** which detect the amount of stretch in a tendon; **muscle spindles**, which detect stretch in muscles; and **joint receptors** which tell the brain at what angle our joints are positioned. The information picked up by these organs enables us to move our limbs quickly without the need to watch them.

Reflex actions

Although we constantly process the information picked up by effector organs, there are times when we want to be able to act on information straight away. For instance, if we touch something hot, we want to be able to remove our hand instantly without having to think about it. This is where our **reflexes** come into play.

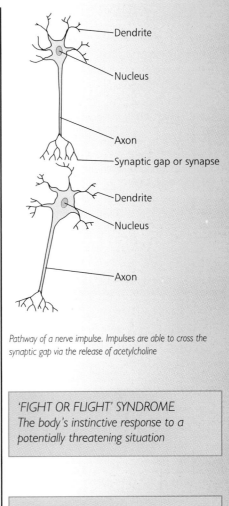

Pathway of a nerve impulse. Impulses are able to cross the synaptic gap via the release of acetylcholine

---

'FIGHT OR FLIGHT' SYNDROME
The body's instinctive response to a potentially threatening situation

---

RECEPTOR ORGANS
Organs that transmit information to the brain

EXTEROCEPTORS
Organs that receive information from outside the body. They include the eyes, ears and sense of touch

---

INTEROCEPTORS
Receive information from inside the body, e.g. chemical changes in the blood or lungs

---

PROPRIOCEPTORS
Organs that receive information from within muscles, tendons and joints

QUICK TASK

Work with a partner to try out the knee-jerk reflex. Sit on a chair with one leg crossed over the other. Get your partner to tap you gently on the uppermost leg just below the kneecap. Your leg should shoot forwards and upwards.

Can you describe this movement? Can you remember the name of the muscle action that occurs when two opposing muscles are working together?

QUICK QUIZ

1) *What does the central nervous system consist of?*

2) *Which part of the brain coordinates movement?*

3 *What is the name of the chemical that flows into the synaptic gap?*

4) *Does the parasympathetic nervous system 'speed up' or 'slow down' heart rate?*

5) *Where would you find a proprioceptor?*

6) *Name one type of reflex action.*

We use our eyes (effector organs) to detect an approaching tennis ball

FAST FORWARD ▷▷

DECISION-MAKING AND ANTICIPATION   see page 88

In the basic reflex response, a nerve impulse is sent from the receptor organ to the spinal cord. Rather than travelling all the way to the brain (and back again), the impulse is returned to the appropriate effector organs to take evasive action – in this case, to move our hand from the source of heat. This is known as the **withdrawal reflex**. It is similar to the reflex actions that occur when blinking or sneezing as a response to a foreign object in the eye or nose.

Another example is the **knee jerk reflex**, also known as the **stretch reflex**. Here, a bang on the knee results in the leg extending. This occurs as a result of the quadriceps being forcefully stretched and then contracting. The knee jerk is helped by the hamstrings relaxing. This type of reflex occurs almost all the time when we are walking and running, as we have muscles working together to maintain our balance.

THE NERVOUS SYSTEM IN ACTION

When we take part in physical activity, the movements we produce are voluntary, and are under the control of the central nervous system. This is capable of coordinating enormously complex movements involving many different muscle groups. When we perform a skill 'automatically', it is still controlled by the central nervous system – we just give less conscious thought to it. In the same way, we learn to rely more on the information picked up by our proprioceptors than our exteroceptors.

As we have seen, reflex actions are very important in sports performance. However, to say that somebody has 'good reflexes' is often incorrect. Very often, the reason why sportspeople are able to make rapid movements is that they have good decision-making and anticipation skills.

MATCH IT

TERM	DEFINITION
Left hemisphere	Control centre for involuntary actions
Sensory neurones	Our eyes and ears
Exteroceptors	Creative side of the brain
Medulla oblongata	Transmit impulses from the brain
Motor neurones	Transmit impulses to the brain

✓ REVISE IT!

For your exams you will need to know:

☐ How the central nervous system coordinates voluntary movement

☐ The role of the autonomic nervous system in the control of unconscious functions within the body

☐ The importance of reflex actions in sport, particularly in helping us maintain our balance and avoid danger

☐ The meaning of the key words for this chapter

✓ KEY WORDS

Tick each box when you understand the word

CENTRAL NERVOUS SYSTEM ☐

BRAIN ☐

CEREBRUM ☐

CEREBELLUM ☐

SPINAL CORD ☐

PERIPHERAL NERVOUS SYSTEM ☐

SYMPATHETIC AND PARASYMPATHETIC NERVOUS SYSTEM ☐

EFFECTOR ORGANS ☐

MOTOR NEURONES ☐

SENSORY NEURONES ☐

RECEPTOR ORGANS ☐

EXTEROCEPTORS ☐

INTEROCEPTORS ☐

PROPRIOCEPTORS ☐

'FIGHT OR FLIGHT' SYNDROME ☐

WITHDRAWAL AND STRETCH REFLEX ACTIONS ☐

The Endocrine and Digestive Systems

The aim of this chapter is to help you:

⊘ Recognise the **glands** that make up the endocrine system

⊘ Understand the role of **hormones** in physical activity

⊘ Describe the structure of the **digestive system**

⊘ Identify how **food** is broken down and used by the body

When we study the anatomy and physiology of the body in sport, we tend to focus mainly on body parts and systems that directly influence and control our movements. We looked at these in Chapters 2–6. In this chapter, we shall look at two systems that affect our sporting performance to a lesser extent.

THE ENDOCRINE SYSTEM

There are a number of bodily functions that are not coordinated by the nervous system, but are controlled by various chemical substances released into the body. These chemical substances are called **hormones**. The organs responsible for producing and releasing the hormones (sometimes called **glands**) make up the **endocrine system**. Each produces its own unique hormone which affects particular functions of the body *(see opposite)*.

HORMONES
Chemical 'messengers' normally released into the bloodstream by the glands of the endocrine system

The endocrine system in action

When we begin to exercise, a number of hormones are released into the body. As we saw in Chapter 6, **adrenaline** has a number of effects in preparing the body for action:

◀◀ **REWIND**

'FIGHT OR FLIGHT'   see page 41

● Heart rate is increased

● Blood is diverted away from non-essential areas such as the digestive system and towards the muscles

● The release of energy is increased

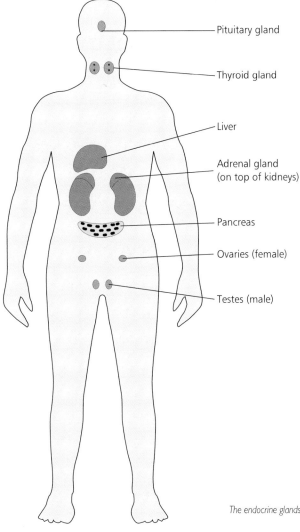

The endocrine glands of the body

- **Pituitary gland**
- **Thyroid gland**
- **Liver**
- **Adrenal gland** (on top of kidneys)
- **Pancreas**
- **Ovaries (female)**
- **Testes (male)**

- The **pituitary gland** is located under the base of the brain, where it interacts with the nervous system. It is regarded as the control centre of the endocrine system, releasing nine different hormones, some of which control other glands.

- The **thyroid gland** is located next to the trachea, just below the larynx. It produces **thyroxine**, a hormone which controls the speed at which oxygen and food nutrients are used to produce energy.

- The **pancreas** is located beneath the stomach and produces a hormone called **insulin**. This helps to control the level of sugar in the blood, and is the substance which is lacking in diabetes sufferers. The pancreas also helps in the digestion of food.

- The two small **adrenal glands** are located above the kidneys. They are responsible for producing adrenaline, which causes the **fight or flight** syndrome.

- **Ovaries** help to control the development of secondary sexual characteristics in women. The ovaries produce a hormone called **oestrogen** and also play an important role during pregnancy.

- The **testes** help to control the development of secondary sexual characteristics in men, producing a hormone called **testosterone**.

Other hormonal effects include the following:

- Glucose (a food substance that produces energy) is broken down much more rapidly
- Stroke volume is increased
- Blood pressure is increased
- Respiratory rate is increased
- Fluid levels are controlled to prevent **dehydration** (*see Chapter 10*)

THE STRUCTURE OF THE DIGESTIVE SYSTEM

Digestion means breaking down food into smaller molecules called **nutrients**, which are absorbed into the body and used by the cells. Food provides us with a source of energy. The job of the digestive system is to extract these nutrients from the food.

QUICK QUIZ

1) What is the function of hormones?

2) Where is the thyroid gland located?

3) What hormone is lacking in someone suffering from diabetes?

4) Which hormone causes the 'fight or flight' syndrome?

5) Name the gland which releases nine different hormones.

6) List four effects of hormones that help us when we exercise

FAST FORWARD ▷▷

DEHYDRATION   see page 71

FAST FORWARD ▷▷

COMPONENTS OF DIET
see page 68

ENZYME
Substance that helps to speed up chemical reactions. Saliva is an enzyme which aids the digestion of food

EXCRETION
The process of removing waste substances from the body

The digestive system in action

The food that we digest has three main components which are broken down into nutrients which the body can use:

- **Carbohydrates** are a valuable source of food and provide the body with readily available energy supplies. Carbohydrates are broken down into glucose (a simplified form of sugar), and stored in muscles and the liver as glycogen

- **Fats** are energy-giving food components that are broken down into fatty acids

- **Proteins** help to build cells and tissues in the body. In order to make them more easily absorbed, they are broken down into amino acids

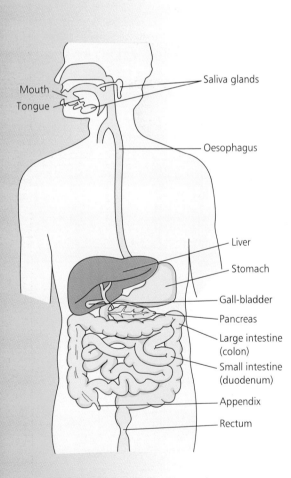

The digestive system

Saliva glands

Mouth
Tongue

Oesophagus

Liver

Stomach

Gall-bladder

Pancreas

Large intestine (colon)

Small intestine (duodenum)

Appendix

Rectum

1 The process of digestion begins in the **mouth**, where the food is broken into smaller pieces by the teeth. The chewing of food also helps to mix it with **saliva**, an enzyme released from the **saliva glands** which are located under the tongue.

2 The **oesophagus** is a tube at the back of the throat lined with smooth muscle which contracts to produce a wave-like movement. This is known as **peristalsis**, and is so efficient that some people can eat and drink whilst standing on their head (this is not recommended!).

3 The **stomach** is a sack-like structure at the end of the oesophagus. Here the food is mixed with a number of acidic substances called **gastric juices** that destroy any harmful bacteria. In the stomach, some of the nutrients (including some sugars, alcohol and drugs) and water contained in the food are absorbed into the bloodstream. The stomach has a capacity of about a litre and also acts as a storage tank, holding food for up to four hours.

4 Slowly, food is released into the tube-like **small intestine**, also known as the **gut**. In the first section of the intestine called the **duodenum**, a number of other enzymes produced by the **gall-bladder**, the **liver** and the **pancreas** are mixed with the food. The majority of the nutrients are absorbed in the remainder of the small intestine (which can range from 4.5 – 9 metres in length). Food passes through the small intestine in 4–6 hours.

5 The **gall-bladder** is a small organ which stores an enzyme called **bile**, which neutralises the acid leaving the stomach. Bile also helps to break down any fats in the small intestine.

6 The **liver** is the largest internal organ of the body, and is located underneath the diaphragm. It produces bile which helps with the digestion of carbohydrates and proteins. It also acts as a filter, maintaining the balance of nutrients in the blood.

7 The **pancreas** produces insulin and also other enzymes which help with the digestion of food.

8 The remaining undigested food travels into the **large intestine** or **colon** where it remains for about 12 hours, while most of the water is absorbed. Any remaining fluids are taken to the kidneys via the blood. Here they are filtered, and the waste fluid (now in the form of urine) travels into the bladder before it is excreted.

9 The solid waste which has passed through the large intestine travels to the last part of the system, the **rectum**, before being excreted out of the anus.

Digestion and exercise

The process of digestion requires the stomach to break down the food, which travels through the gut. In order to provide energy for the smooth muscles to contract, and to absorb the nutrients, a large volume of blood is needed. It is therefore important to keep physical activity to a minimum after eating. Generally, it is best to avoid exercising until at least three hours after a meal.

QUICK QUIZ

1) What are nutrients?

2) Name the type of muscle that surrounds the oesophagus.

3) Where is the duodenum located?

4) Which organ stores bile?

5) How long does it take for food to pass through the entire digestive system?

6) What are amino acids?

M A T C H   I T

TERM	DEFINITION
Insulin	Organ located in the brain which releases hormones
Adrenal gland	Largest internal organ of the body
Saliva	Enzyme produced by the liver that is stored in the gall bladder
Liver	Enzyme produced by the pancreas that regulates blood sugar levels
Pituitary gland	Organ located above each of the kidneys
Bile	Enzyme that aids digestion, released in the oral cavity

✓ KEY WORDS

Tick each box when you understand the word

HORMONES ☐

PITUITARY GLAND ☐

ADRENAL GLANDS ☐

OVARIES/TESTES ☐

ENZYME ☐

STOMACH ☐

LIVER ☐

PANCREAS ☐

LARGE INTESTINE (COLON) ☐

✓ R E V I S E   I T !

For your exams you will need to know:

☐ How the hormones of the body affect physical activity and exercise training

☐ How the food we eat is digested and used by the body

☐ The meaning of the key words for this chapter

Exam questions: Anatomy and physiology

The questions below are typical of those that you might have to answer in your examination.
Try answering each, remembering that the number of marks available for each question gives
you a clue to the type of answer required.

Maximum possible marks

1   What are the main functions of the **cardiovascular system?**   [2]

2   Name the three types of muscle tissue found in the human body.   [3]

3   What are the features of the human skeleton system that allows it to carry out
its numerous functions?   [4]

4   Describe, using examples, how the role of ligaments differs from that of tendons.   [4]

5   Sketch a diagram of a synovial joint, identifying the following structures: [6]

   a Cartilage

   b Synovial fluid

   c Synovial membrane

   d Joint capsule

6   List **two** examples of **each** of the following joints in the human body: [6]

   a Immovable joints

   b Ball and socket joints

   c Hinge joints

7   Explain what is meant by the terms **fast** and **slow twitch muscle fibres** and
comment on their relevance to particular types of sporting activity.   [4]

8   What is meant by the term **posture** and why is it important for performers   [3]
to have good posture?

9   The heart plays an essential role in the working of the body.

   a Explain the following terms related to the function of the heart: [3]

     Heart rate

     Stroke volume

     Cardiac output

   b What happens to heart rate, stroke volume and cardiac output when the body
starts undertaking physical exercise?   [3]

10   Sketch a basic diagram of the respiratory system, labelling the following structures: [5]

   a Trachea   *b* Alveoli

   c Intercostal muscles   *d* Diaphragm

11 What role do the intercostal muscles play in the mechanics of breathing? [3]

12 Most sports require energy produced by either the aerobic or anaerobic energy systems.

   a Describe what is meant by the terms **aerobic** and **anaerobic** in relation to physical exercise and energy production. [2]

   b Suggest ways of testing the aerobic and anaerobic fitness of a performer. [3]

13 Explain the part lactic acid plays in energy production and its effect on the body. [4]

14 **Minute volume** is defined as the amount of air we breathe in one minute.

   a What happens to minute ventilation during physical activity? [1]

   b What does the body do with air inhaled by the respiratory system? [3]

15 **Adrenaline** is an important hormone which prepares the body for action. What physiological effects does adrenaline have on the body? [4]

16 Explain the terms **origin** and **insertion** in relation to muscles in the body. [2]

17 Give four functions of the human skeleton. [4]

18 What is the role of the **endocrine system** in the body, and what role may this system play when we are playing sport? [3]

19 What three parts make up the network of blood vessels in the cardiovascular system? [3]

20 Where would you find an example of the following type of muscle in the body? [3]
   a Smooth
   b Cardiac
   c Skeletal

21 Describe how the three different types of **lever system** are used in the body. [3]

22 Some muscles act as **fixators**. Can you explain what is meant by this term and give an example of a fixator in the body. [3]

23 What are the functions of the **tendons** in the body? [2]

24 What essential role does **haemoglobin** play in the body and specifically when we are taking part in physical exercise? [3]

Revision guide: Anatomy and physiology

These pages summarise the most important areas covered in chapters 1–7 on anatomy and physiology. By fully understanding everything below you will be better prepared to succeed in your examination.

Body structure and function

There are three key aspects to understanding how the human body works:

- **Anatomy** is the structure of the body, and how it is put together.
- **Physiology** is the function of the body or how it works.
- **Cells** are the basic structure of the body. These form tissues that are specialised to perform particular functions. These in turn join to form organs such as the heart or kidneys.

The skeletal system

The bones and joints make up the **skeletal system**. The function of the skeleton includes:

- to provide support for our bodies
- to keep the body in the correct posture
- to support the internal organs
- to protect the vital organs of the body
- to provide sites for muscle attachment
- to produce blood cells
- to allow the body to move

The **skeleton** is split into two parts:

- **Axial**: central part, skull, spine, ribs and sternum
- **Appendicular**: the remaining parts

Bones

There are four main types of bone in the body:

- long bones
- short bones
- flat bones
- irregular bones

Other components include ligaments and cartilage:

- **Cartilage** is found at the ends of bones and helps to protect and/or support them
- **Ligaments** are strong, non-elastic tissues that connect bone to bone, usually at a joint.

The skeleton in action – movement terms

There are six distinct types of joint movement:

- **Flexion**: where the angle between two bones is reduced (bending)
- **Extension**: where the angle between two bones is increased (straightening)
- **Abduction**: movement of a limb away from the midline of the body
- **Adduction**: movement of a limb towards the midline of the body

- **Rotation**: circular movement
- **Circumduction**: a combination of all the above

The muscular system

The muscular system allows us to maintain our body position and move body parts.

Muscle types

There are three main type of muscle:

- **Smooth**: involuntary muscle mainly in digestive and cardiovascular system
- **Cardiac**: automatic, found only in heart
- **Skeletal**: voluntary muscles responsible for bodily movement

Skeletal muscles

Muscles are elastic tissue that consist of bundles of fibres that give strength and allow the muscle to change in shape and length.

Tendons attach muscle to bone, allowing the body to use bones as levers and so create movement.

Muscle fibre types

There are two types of muscle fibre:

- **Fast twitch**: white fibres that are used in fast explosive sports and movement
- **Slow twitch**: red fibres that are used in endurance-type sports and movement

Muscles in action

Movement occurs when muscles contract. They may contract in the following ways:

- **Concentric contraction**: when tension develops, muscles shorten in length
- **Eccentric contraction**: when tension develops, muscles increase in length
- **Isometric contraction**: when tension develops, muscle length remains unchanged
- **Isokinetic contraction**: when tension develops, the muscle is changing in length but at a constant rate

Movement analysis

Muscles usually work in pairs, one acting as a **protagonist** or **prime mover** and the other acting as a **brake** or **antagonist.** Muscles may also work as **fixators** – stabilising a joint – or as **synergists** helping a prime mover produce movement.

The cardiovascular system

The cardiovascular system is made up of the heart and blood vessels. The **heart** is the pump that drives the system. It sends blood around the body through a double circulatory system. The pathway follows the pattern shown below.

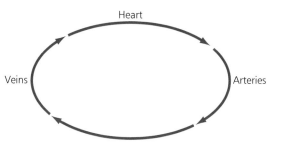

Heart rate and blood pressure

Heart rate (HR) determines how many times the heart beats in a minute. Each beat forces blood into the circulatory system and is generated by the cardiac muscle in the heart.

Stroke volume(SV) is the amount of blood ejected from the heart in one beat.

Cardiac output (Q̇) is the volume of blood ejected from the left ventricle in one minute. We can calculate this with the equation **HR x SV = Q̇**.

Blood pressure (BP) is the force with which blood is moving around the body. It is affected by the friction of the blood vessel walls.

Other factors that affect blood pressure are age, stress, diet and exercise.

The respiratory system

The body breathes in order to take in oxygen which is used in energy production and also to expel carbon dioxide from the body cells.

– **Inhalation**: breathing in
– **Exhalation**: breathing out

The respiratory system is made up of the airway, trachea, lungs and alveoli. The **diaphragm** and **intercostal muscles** provide the mechanical force to allow breathing.

Respiratory terms

There are three key technical terms to remember:

– **Respiratory rate**: normal breathing rate of 12–16 times per minute
– **Tidal volume**: the amount of air that is removed each time we breathe
– **Minute ventilation**: the amount of air we breathe in one minute, calculated by the formula **Tidal Volume x Respiratory Rate**

The respiratory system in action

As we exercise, our demand for oxygen increases. The amount of oxygen we can use increases up to a point called **VO_2 max** – the maximum amount of oxygen we can transport and use in a minute. For most people this is between 30–60ml/kg/min.

Energy systems

Energy in the body is created from **adenosine triphosphate (ATP)**:

$$ATP \rightarrow ADP \text{ (adenosine diphosphate)} + ENERGY$$

The body uses three main systems to produce ATP and ENERGY:

Creatine phosphate (CP) system – for short bursts of energy (anaerobic)

$$ADP + CP = ATP + CREATINE$$

Lactic acid system – short-term energy for up to 60 seconds (anaerobic)

$$ADP + GLYGOGEN = ATP + PYRUVIC ACID$$

Aerobic system – long-term energy for low intensity exercise with oxygen

$$ADP + GLYCOGEN = ATP + PYRUVIC ACID$$

The recovery process

Oxygen debt – where the demand for oxygen is greater than the body can supply

Oxygen deficit – after exercise, the supply of oxygen is greater than the demand. Oxygen is used to rebuild the ATP stores and get rid of lactic acid from the muscles.

Further reading

● Davis, D., Kimmer, T., and Auty. M., *Physical Education: Theory And Practice*, Macmillan, 1986

● Esbuys, J., Guest, V., and Lawrence, J., *Fundamentals Of Health And Physical Education*, Heinemann, 1987

● Honeybourne, J., Hill, M., and Moors, H., *Advanced Physical Education And Sport*, Stanley Thornes, 1996

● Rowett, H.G.Q., *Basic Anatomy And Physiology*, John Murray, 1975

● Wirhead, R., *Athletic Ability And The Anatomy of Motion*, Wolfe Medical Publishers, 1989

CHAPTER 8

Defining Fitness

The aim of this chapter is to help you:

- Understand what is meant by **physical fitness**

- Recognise the health-related and skill-related components of fitness

- Understand the importance of **cardiovascular fitness**

- Identify the components of **muscular fitness**

- Describe the methods used in **fitness testing**

'Physical fitness' means different things to different people. Fitness for an office worker is different from fitness for an Olympic high-jumper, and both will differ from the kind of fitness that you need as a PE student on a GCSE course! However, most people would agree that their level of physical fitness does have a major effect on their performance in sport.

COMPONENTS OF FITNESS

One definition of **physical fitness** is *'the ability of the body to meet the demands of the environment'*.

When we are physically fit, the body systems work efficiently and are able to cope with the physical tasks that we perform every day. This concept of physical fitness is very similar to that of **health**.

According to another definition, fitness is *'the ability of the body to carry out everyday activities without excessive fatigue and with enough energy left over for emergencies'*.

This means that, as well as performing our normal daily tasks, we can also perform additional physical activities, including sport.

In order to cope with this, we have to improve the efficiency of the body and develop our fitness levels. However, before we can do this, we need to know what makes up physical fitness.

PHYSICAL FITNESS
The ability of the body to meet the demands placed on it

FAST FORWARD ▶▶

HEALTH   see page 106

Health-related fitness

The following components of fitness are important if the human body is to work efficiently:

- **Cardiovascular endurance** The ability of the heart, blood vessels, blood, and respiratory system to supply fuel and especially oxygen to the muscles

- **Muscular strength** The ability to exert an external force or to lift a heavy weight

- **Muscular endurance** The ability of the muscles to repeatedly exert themselves

- **Flexibility** Having a wide range of motion in a joint

- **Body composition** The relative percentage of muscle, fat, bone and other tissues of which the body is composed

An additional component, which is increasingly important in modern life, is the ability to cope with **stress**.

Skill-related fitness

The following are of great importance when we play sport:

- **Agility** The ability to rapidly and accurately change the direction of the entire body in space

- **Balance** The ability to maintain equilibrium while standing or moving

- **Coordination** The ability to use the senses and body parts in order to perform motor tasks smoothly and accurately

- **Power** The ability to transfer energy swiftly into force

- **Reaction time** The ability to respond quickly to stimuli

- **Speed** The ability to perform a movement quickly

CARDIOVASCULAR FITNESS

Cardiovascular fitness refers to a person's ability to exercise the whole body for prolonged periods of time. This is achieved by the cardiovascular and respiratory systems working efficiently to transport oxygen to the muscles, which is then used to produce energy. As we saw in Chapter 5, the ability to use oxygen is known as **VO₂ max** (maximum aerobic capacity), and indicates our cardiovascular fitness levels.

Sub-maximal activity

The cardiovascular element of fitness is important when we take part in sports that involve **sub-maximal activity**, such as cycling, running, and swimming. Other terms commonly used to describe this type of fitness include **cardio-respiratory fitness**, **aerobic fitness**, **stamina** and **endurance**.

HEALTH-RELATED FITNESS
Combination of cardiovascular endurance, muscular strength and endurance, flexibility, body composition and ability to cope with stress

FAST FORWARD ▷▷
BODY see page 64
COMPOSITION

FAST FORWARD ▷▷
STRESS see page 97
MANAGEMENT

SKILL-RELATED FITNESS
Combination of agility, balance, coordination, power, reaction-time and speed

QUICK TASK
List the components of skill-related fitness. Next to each one, describe why it is important, and name a sport in which the component is expecially vital.

◁◁ **REWIND**
VO₂ MAX see page 35

SUB-MAXIMAL
A physical activity carried on at a low intensity, often over a long time period

STAMINA
*The ability of the body to carry on working without becoming tired. General stamina is called **cardiovascular fitness**, while local stamina is called **muscular endurance***

Cardiovascular fitness is important in long distance running

MUSCULAR FITNESS

I Muscular strength

When we think about muscles, we normally think in terms of strength. The ability to produce force in our muscles is very important in sports.

There are three main types of strength:

- **Static strength** This is the greatest amount of force that the muscles can generate. This occurs in sport when the resistance we are trying to overcome is great – for example, when we push in a rugby scrum

- **Explosive strength** This is when we use our muscles to produce a very quick movement. Examples of this would be when a sprinter leaves the starting blocks, or when we perform the vertical jump test (ask your teacher about this test). This is very similar to the fitness component of power

- **Dynamic strength** This type of strength is used by a sportsperson to support their own body weight over a period of time. For example, on a downhill run, a skier requires a large amount of dynamic strength in their quadriceps in order to keep their balance. This is similar to the fitness component of muscular endurance

> **MUSCULAR STRENGTH**
> *The ability to exert an external force or to lift a heavy weight*

2 Muscular endurance

The ability of a muscle to work for a sustained period of time is also important in most sports. Not having a good level of muscular endurance leads to muscle fatigue, causing our arms and legs to feel tired and heavy. This often means that our performance becomes worse, and some cases we may have to stop playing.

Muscular endurance is also important for maintaining our body **posture.** Even when we are sitting, we constantly use muscles to keep us upright, and it is these muscles that must maintain their **muscle tone**.

3 Flexibility

This third component of muscle fitness is linked to the muscular and skeletal systems. Muscles that are not stretched regularly become tight, causing pain when we stretch them. A loss of flexibility can also be caused by problems in the joints, such as worn-down cartilage or lack of synovial fluid.

Flexibility is important in most sports as it helps to reduce the risk of injury. Swimmers, javelin throwers and tennis players all need good shoulder flexibility, while gymnasts need a high level of all-round flexibility. Flexibility is often called **suppleness** or **mobility**.

General fitness and specific fitness

So far we have examined the components needed for **general fitness**. If certain fitness components are more important than others in a sport, then people playing that sport also need a level of **specific fitness**. For instance, a sprinter needs a high level of strength, speed and power, but cardiovascular fitness and agility are less important.

Similarly, the standard of competition will affect fitness levels: an Olympic athlete will have greater levels of fitness than a club athlete. Training to achieve specific fitness is described in Chapter 15.

FITNESS TESTING

Now that we know which components of fitness are important for our own particular sport, it is useful to find out how each of these components can be measured. By carrying out a number of fitness tests, we can get a picture of our current state of fitness. From this we can identify strengths and weaknesses and then work to improve the weaker areas.

Also, by repeating fitness tests after completing a training programme (at least a few months later) and comparing them with tests carried out earlier, it is possible to see how fitness levels have improved.

Performing press-ups requires a good level of muscular endurance

◀◀ REWIND

POSTURE see page 8

QUICK TASK

1) Can you think of three examples of sports requiring static, explosive and dynamic strength?

2) Re-read the section on muscle fibre types on page 18, Chapter 3. Which of the muscle fibre types is mainly used when we apply maximum strength?

3) Which of the muscle fibre types is mainly used when we rely on our muscular endurance to produce repeated movements?

QUICK QUIZ

1) Define the term 'physical fitness'.

2) Name three health-related components of physical fitness.

3) What is meant by the term **aerobic**?

4) What type of strength do we use when we push in a rugby scrum?

5) Which sports require good shoulder flexibility?

6) In what way is fitness 'specific'?

FAST FORWARD ▶▶

TRAINING FOR FITNESS see page 112

ASSESSING CARDIOVASCULAR FITNESS

There are three main methods that can be used to measure cardiovascular fitness:

NCF Multi-stage Fitness Test

This involves running back and forward along a 20-metre track. The speed of running is controlled by a cassette tape, which beeps at the moment when you should be turning at the end of the track. The aim of the test is to run for as long as possible, continuing until you are unable to keep up with the beeping sound (i.e. if you are unable to get to the end of the track three times in a row).

The level at which you stop running gives you your cardio-vascular fitness score – for example, Level 11, Shuttle 4 – which can be converted into a VO_2 max value. The higher your level of cardiovascular fitness, the longer this test will take to complete.

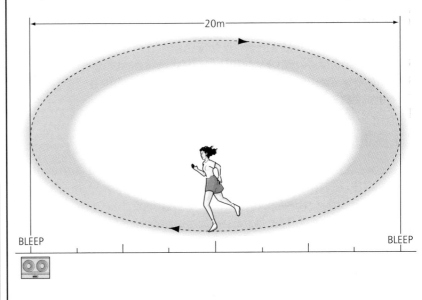

The Multi-Stage Fitness Test measures cardiovascular endurance, and is both maximal and incremental

> **NCF MULTI-STAGE FITNESS TEST**
> Designed to test for cardiovascular endurance

> **MAXIMAL AND INCREMENTAL**
> The Multi-Stage Fitness Test is **maximal** in that it measures the maximum time for which you can keep up with the beeps. It is **incremental** because it begins at a very gentle pace and quickens for every level

> **HARVARD STEP TEST**
> Involves stepping on and off a bench for 5 minutes, after which heart rate is recorded

Harvard Step Test

To complete this test, you need a bench (or a step) that is 45 cm high. You step on and off this bench for 5 minutes at a rate of 30 times a minute. In order to step at the right pace it is useful either to use a metronome or to ask a friend to count every two seconds. On each step up (the same foot first each time), the knee is fully extended.

After 5 minutes of stepping, heart rate is recorded. This is measured for 30 seconds on 3 occasions: 1 minute after the end of the exercise; 2 minutes after the end of the exercise; and 3 minutes after the end of the exercise.

The Harvard Step Test

This test takes into account your **recovery rate**, which is calculated using the following formula:

Score =

$$\frac{\text{Duration of exercise in seconds } (= 300) \times 100}{2 \times (\text{HR after 1 minute} + \text{HR after 2 minutes} + \text{HR after 3 minutes})}$$

> RECOVERY RATE
> *The speed at which the heart rate returns to its normal resting value following exercise*

12-Minute Cooper Test

This is a simple test that can be performed on any flat area that is marked out at 25-metre intervals. The only equipment needed is a stopwatch. The object is to run, jog or walk as far as possible in 12 minutes. As you increase your cardiovascular fitness, you should be able to cover a greater distance.

> 12-MINUTE COOPER TEST
> *Test involving running, walking or jogging as far as possible within 12 minutes*

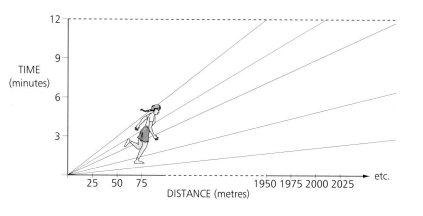

The 12-Minute Cooper Test

Harvard Step Test and 12-Minute Cooper Test Scores for 16-year-olds

	Excellent	Above average	Average	Below average	Poor
Harvard Step Test					
Males	Above 90	80–90	65–79	55–64	Below 55
Females	Above 86	76–86	61–75	50–60	Below 50
12-Minute Cooper Test					
Males	Above 2,800m	2,500–2,775m	2,300–2,475m	2,200–2,275m	Below 2,200m
Females	Above 2,300m	2,000–2,275m	1,900–1,975m	1,800–1,875m	Below 1,800m

Copy the table below, and write in the first column **ten** *sports that you have played or watched. For each of these sports develop a fitness profile, identifying whether each fitness component is:* **4**) *Highly important;* **3**) *Important;* **2**) *Not so important;* **1**) *Unimportant*

FITNESS PROFILES FOR SPORTS

Sport	1 Cardio-vascular endur-ance	2 Muscle endur-ance	3 Muscular strength	4 Flexi-bility	5 Body composi-tion	6 Agility	7 Balance	8 Coordi-nation	9 Power	10 Reaction time	11 Speed

ASSESSMENT OF MUSCULAR FITNESS

There are a number of different tests that can be used to measure muscular fitness.

The Hand Grip Dynamometer Test

Most schools and colleges will have an item of equipment known as a **dynamometer**. This is held in the hand with the arm raised, and the handle is squeezed as hard as possible in order to measure grip strength. Three attempts are made and the best score recorded.

HAND GRIP DYNAMOMETER
A device used for measuring strength. A hand grip dynamometer has a handle which is squeezed, and a display records the pressure exerted in kilograms

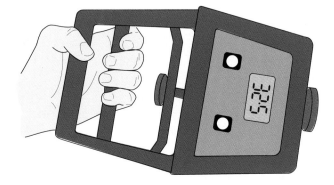

A hand grip dynamometer is used to measure grip strength

The Bent-Knee Sit-Up Test

This is a simple test for measuring the muscular endurance of the abdominal muscles. The aim is to complete as many sit-ups as possible in 30 seconds, with knees bent and arms folded across the chest. Subjects must start each sit-up with their back on the floor, and raise themselves up to 90 degrees. Their feet can be held in place by a partner.

Sit and Reach Test

The aim of this test is to measure the flexibility of the lower back and hamstrings. It can be carried out with the help of a 'sit and reach box', or you can simply use a bench with a ruler.

The starting position is sitting on the floor with shoes removed, feet flat against the box, and legs straight. Reaching as far forward as possible, the object is to push the ruler on the box. The distance from the ruler to the edge of the overhanging plate represents the score for that person. As the 'sit and reach' box has an overhang of 15 cm, a person who reaches 10 cm past their toes scores 25 cm. It is important to have several warm-up attempts first, and to record the best score.

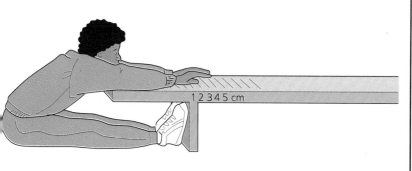

1 2 3 4 5 cm

Sit and Reach Test

QUICK TASK

A number of fitness tests are described in this chapter. Can you think of different tests that you might use to test people who play different sports? Use the fitness profiles you created earlier to identify fitness components that are very important.

QUICK QUIZ

1) Name two benefits of fitness testing.

2) Describe the Harvard Step Test.

3) How long is the track used in the NCF's Multi-Stage Fitness Test?

4) How long does it take to complete the Cooper Test?

5) The Bent-Knee Sit-up Test measures the muscular endurance of which muscles?

6) What type of fitness is measured by the Sit and Reach Test?

Hand Grip Test, Bent-Knee Sit-up Test and Sit and Reach Test Scores for 16-year-olds

	Excellent	Above average	Average	Below average	Poor
Hand Grip Test					
Males	Above 56 kg	52–56 kg	48–51 kg	43–47 kg	Below 43 kg
Females	Above 37 kg	34–37 kg	32–33 kg	29–31 kg	Below 29 kg
Bent-Knee Sit-up Test					
Males	Above 26	25–26	23–24	21–22	Below 22
Females	Above 23	21–23	19–20	17–18	Below 17
Sit and Reach Test					
Males	Above 28 cm	24–28 cm	20–23 cm	17–19 cm	Below 17 cm
Females	Above 35 cm	32–35 cm	30–31 cm	25–29 cm	Below 25 cm

SPORT IN ACTION

Complete the fitness tests described on pages 56–59 (remember to warm up thoroughly first).

Which tests did you score best and worst on? Can you give reasons for your results?

Look at the fitness profiles you created earlier. Using the fitness profile of your preferred sport, compare the fitness requirements with your personal fitness test scores.

✓ KEY WORDS

Tick each box when you understand the word

PHYSICAL FITNESS ☐

HEALTH-RELATED FITNESS ☐

CARDIOVASCULAR ENDURANCE ☐

MUSCULAR STRENGTH ☐

MUSCULAR ENDURANCE ☐

FLEXIBILITY ☐

BODY COMPOSITION ☐

SKILL-RELATED FITNESS ☐

FITNESS TESTING ☐

NCF MULTI-STAGE FITNESS TEST ☐

HARVARD STEP TEST ☐

12-MINUTE COOPER TEST ☐

HAND GRIP DYNAMOMETER ☐

SIT AND REACH TEST ☐

MATCH IT

TERM	DEFINITION
Cardiovascular fitness	A component of skill-related fitness
Dynamometer	A component of health-related fitness
Static strength	A component of muscular fitness
Flexibility	The ability of the heart, blood and lungs to supply oxygen to the muscles
Agility	A device used to measure strength

✓ REVISE IT!

For your exams you will need to know:

☐ Definitions of physical fitness

☐ The components of health-related fitness and skill-related fitness

☐ The importance of cardiovascular fitness, muscular strength, muscular endurance and flexibility for sport

☐ The tests used to measure cardiovascular fitness

☐ How to measure muscular strength, muscular endurance and flexibility

☐ The meaning of the key words for this chapter

Physique

CHAPTER 9

The aim of this chapter is to help you:

- Explain how **body size** can affect which sports we play
- Describe Sheldon's three main body types
- Understand the importance of **fat** in the body
- Identify anatomical and physiological differences between males and females
- Recognise the effect of **age** on sports performance

The human body comes in a variety of shapes and sizes, and we can see this in sport. We only have to look at a rugby team to see that there are major differences in the height and weight of the players. It is also clear that differences exist between the abilities of men and women, and that in some sports this difference is significant. Also, age can be an important factor that can affect our performance in sport, particularly as we grow older.

THE EFFECTS OF HEIGHT AND WEIGHT

Our **physique** is of great importance when we play sport. Not only does our body provide us with a means of moving objects around, but it must also be able to move itself around. The size of the body can influence the sports we choose to play and also our playing position. For instance, the ideal physique for a basketball player would be over 2 metres (6 feet 6 inches) tall, but this would be much too tall for a gymnast.

Physical height is normally linked with weight, as taller people generally tend to be heavier. The relationship between height and weight has been investigated in great detail, and there are a number of different charts based on a score called the **Body Mass Index (BMI)** that can be used to match height with ideal body weight.

PHYSIQUE
The size and weight of the body, and its composition in terms of tissues such as muscle and fat.

BODY MASS INDEX (BMI)
This is calculated by dividing weight in kilograms by the square of height in metres. The unit of measurement is kg/m^2

Competitors in different sports vary greatly in body shape and size

However, this does not take into account the fact that our bodies are made up of different tissues, which vary in proportion from person to person. For instance, muscle is denser than fat, and so a muscular person will almost certainly weigh more than a fatter person of the same height.

BODY TYPES

Whilst the human body comes in a number of different shapes and sizes, some scientists have attempted to classify it according to certain basic types. In the 1940s a scientist called Sheldon identified three main shapes representing extreme versions of the human form, which he labelled **somatotypes**:

- The **endomorph** body type is mainly pear-shaped. People at this extreme have a rounded head, narrow shoulders and wide hips. They have a lot of fat on their body, upper arms and thighs

- The **mesomorph** body type is wedge-shaped. People at this extreme have wide shoulders and narrow hips. They tend to have a lot of muscle mass on their arms and legs and relatively little body fat

- The **ectomorph** body type is linear. People at this extreme tend to be thin, with narrow shoulders and narrow hips. Their arms and legs are also very thin, and they tend to have little fat or muscle on their body

---

SOMATOTYPES
System of classifying the human body according to certain basic types of shape and build

QUICK TASK

Weigh yourself (in kilograms) and measure how tall you are (in metres), and then calculate your Body Mass Index (kg/m². A score of 20–25 kg/m² is 'ideal', 25–30 kg/m² is 'overweight', whilst above 30 kg/m² is 'extremely overweight'.

These three somatotypes can be scored on a scale of 1 to 7, with the most common body types scoring in the mid-range of the three scales (i.e. 3–4–4, or 4–3–4, or 3–4–3, etc.). A score of 5–6–2 indicates high endomorphy (5), high mesomorphy (6), and low ectomorphy (2) – ideal for a prop in rugby!

One advantage of this method is that it allows comparison of people even if they are different in height. We can see in the following table that people near the three extremes tend to play the same sports:

QUICK TASK

Using the information on somatotypes, can you identify suitable body types for the following sports?

a) *Volleyball*
b) *Sumo wrestling*
c) *Cycling*
d) *American football*

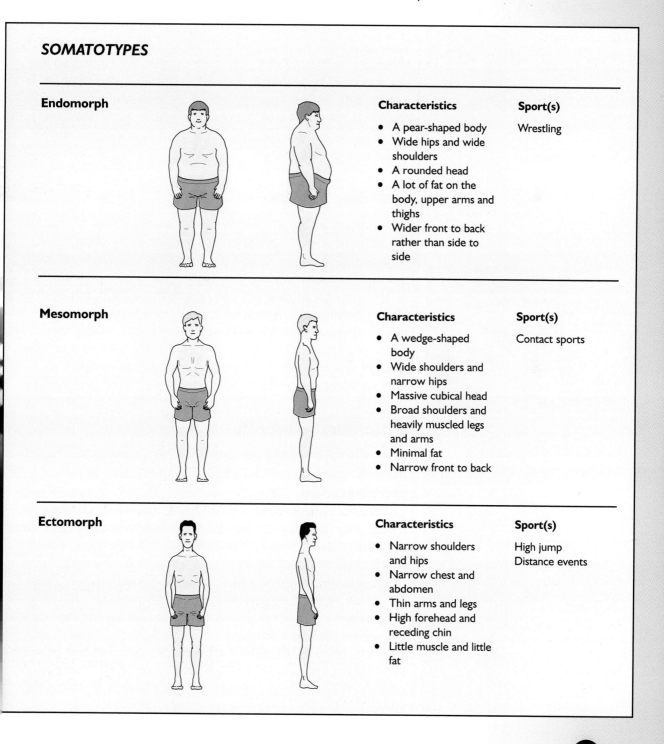

SOMATOTYPES

		Characteristics	Sport(s)
Endomorph		• A pear-shaped body • Wide hips and wide shoulders • A rounded head • A lot of fat on the body, upper arms and thighs • Wider front to back rather than side to side	Wrestling
Mesomorph		• A wedge-shaped body • Wide shoulders and narrow hips • Massive cubical head • Broad shoulders and heavily muscled legs and arms • Minimal fat • Narrow front to back	Contact sports
Ectomorph		• Narrow shoulders and hips • Narrow chest and abdomen • Thin arms and legs • High forehead and receding chin • Little muscle and little fat	High jump Distance events

◀◀◀ REWIND

BODY COMPOSITION see page 53

> **FAT-FREE WEIGHT**
> The weight of the body excluding fat but including the organs, blood and other connective tissue

Skinfold callipers can be used to estimate percentage body fat

QUICK QUIZ

1) Which is denser, fat or muscle?

2) Describe the physique of an extreme mesomorph.

3) Which somatotype would be represented by the score 7–1–1?

4) Where do we find body fat?

5) Name three sites at which skinfold measurements are taken.

6) What are the two most accurate methods of measuring percentage body fat?

BODY COMPOSITION

Body composition refers to *'the relative percentage of muscle, fat, bone and other tissues of which the body is composed'*. The body tissues can be split into two main groups:

- **Body fat** is the amount of fat that we have stored in our body. It is mainly found in two places: surrounding the internal organs and directly underneath the skin. It is the fat found beneath the skin which is of most importance

- **Fat-free weight** is the rest of the weight of the body, including the organs, blood and other connective tissues

Bone and muscle are important components. The density of the bones can vary from one person to another, depending on age, sex and race. Bone density can affect our ability to swim, as a person with denser bones will tend to sink rather than float! Muscle mass can also affect performance in sport. Muscle is a dense tissue and too much of it can be a disadvantage in endurance events.

Controlling body fat

It is important to control body fat as this is a tissue which does not help us in most sports, except perhaps cross-Channel swimming. Too much body fat puts a strain on the heart and muscles, and performance can suffer as a result.

It is possible to measure our height and weight, so calculating BMI is very easy. However, a person with a high level of muscle mass might be classified as being 'overweight', so this method is not necessarily the best one to use. Similarly, assessing somato-types is very difficult, as there are a number of complex measurements and calculations which need to be performed.

Measurement of body fat

Scientists have worked out that if we can measure fat beneath the skin at several sites we can make an estimate of our **percentage body fat**.

The most common sites for these measurements include the triceps, biceps, sub-scapular (shoulder-blade), chest, abdomen (stomach), iliac (waist), thigh and calf. The thickness of a skinfold (i.e. a double layer of skin and fat) is measured by using skinfold callipers, and the sum of the selected skinfolds can be converted into percentage body fat from a chart.

Having measured our percentage body fat, we are classified as being **overweight** if we have over 20% body fat (males), and over 30% body fat (females). **Obesity** is when we have over 25% body fat (males) and over 35% body fat (females). These two conditions can seriously disadvantage us when we play sport, and can also cause a variety of health problems.

SEX DIFFERENCES

Gender is perhaps one of the most important factors in sport. It affects not only our **participation in sport**, but also our level of sporting performance.

Pre-pubescence

For about the first ten years of life, girls and boys develop at a similar rate. They have similar body shapes, and their percentage body fat and muscle mass are also very similar. This means that up to the age of ten, competition between boys and girls is fairly evenly matched.

Before puberty girls and boys are evenly matched

Puberty

At puberty, females develop much faster than males. However, after a short period, males start to gain a distinct advantage over females in most sports.

The main physical differences are as follows:

- Body shape and size
- Percentage body fat
- Muscular strength
- Oxygen uptake capacity
- Flexibility

FAST FORWARD ▷▷

***PARTICIPATION
IN SPORT***   see page 155

QUICK TASK

1) *Look at the world records for men and women in track and field athletics (you may need to ask your teacher to help you find the relevant information). Give reasons for the gender differences in performance for each event.*

2) *The physical differences between men and women mean that they rarely compete against each other in sport during and after puberty. Can you name any sports in which they compete on equal terms? How could you make other sports open to both men and women?*

*PUBERTY
Growth spurt that occurs between the ages of 10 and 20. In females the process is normally complete by the age of 16*

QUICK TASK

1) List five sports that you consider to be suitable for young people (16-30 years old) and five sports that you consider to be for older people (over 40 years old). What physiological reasons would you give for excluding certain age-groups from playing these sports?

2) If you were to let young children take part in any of the 10 sports you listed, what changes would you make to the rules and playing conditions?

◄◄ **REWIND**

OSSIFICATION   see page 11

QUICK QUIZ

1) At what age does puberty end for males?

2) Name three physical differences between males and females.

3) At what age do we reach our physiological peak?

4) What is arthritis?

5) List five physiological changes that occur as we enter our forties and beyond.

AGE DIFFERENCES

Performance in sport can also be affected by age. The two main groups who need to be aware of their limitations are:

- Young children and adolescents
- Middle-aged and senior citizens

Among the first group, we need to ensure that sports are introduced safely and gradually. It is important that agility, balance and coordination are developed, and that motor skills are practised.

As young people's bones are still in the process of ossification, it important to avoid placing too much strain on the body until physical maturity has been reached. In some sports it is also important to ensure that age restrictions are enforced, particularly in team games.

The ageing process

Most sporting records are set by people in their twenties and thirties, when the body is at its physiological peak. As we move into our forties and beyond, our performance starts to decline. This is particularly apparent in strength and endurance sports. The reasons for this are:

- Bones become more brittle
- Joints stiffen and movement becomes painful (called **arthritis**)
- Muscles and tendons lose their elasticity
- Reduction of cardiac output
- Arteries lose elasticity
- Slower recovery rate
- Increased blood pressure
- Decreased lung capacity
- Decreased VO_2 max
- Increased body fat
- Increased chance of disease

However, the ageing process can be slowed down if we ensure that we remain active as we get older.

S P O R T   I N   A C T I O N

Collect the results of the fitness tests from all the members of your class.

1) Calculate the overall average scores for each test, and the average scores for males and females.

2) Are there any people who seem to perform particularly well in certain tests (i.e. falling into the 'excellent' category)? Why do you think this is?

MATCH IT

TERM	DEFINITION
Oestrogen	A thin and narrow person
Arthritis	The weight of our body, excluding fat
Ectomorph	The end of puberty
Skinfold callipers	Painful stiffening of the joints
Physical maturity	Hormone produced in females
Fat-free weight	Instrument used to measure the thickness of fat under the skin

✓ KEY WORDS

Tick each box when you understand the word

PHYSIQUE ☐

BODY MASS INDEX ☐

SOMATOTYPES ☐

ENDOMORPH ☐

MESOMORPH ☐

ECTOMORPH ☐

PERCENTAGE BODY FAT ☐

FAT-FREE WEIGHT ☐

OVERWEIGHT ☐

SKINFOLD CALLIPERS ☐

PUBERTY ☐

✓ REVISE IT!

For your exams you will need to know:

☐ The effects of height and weight on sports performance

☐ The characteristics of endomorphs, mesomorphs and ectomorphs

☐ How to measure body composition, and why it is important

☐ The physiological differences between males and females

☐ How our body is affected as we grow older

☐ The meaning of the key words for this chapter

Diet and Exercise

The aim of this chapter is to help you:

○ Understand how **foods** can be divided into various groups

○ Understand how much of each **food group** should be contained within a normal diet

○ Recognise the importance of **balancing** the intake of food with the energy we use

○ Understand how sportsmen and women can alter their diet in order to **maximise performance**

○ Identify ways to maintain **fluid levels** in the body

The food we eat and the liquids we drink help to keep us alive and functioning properly. They also provide the body with fuel for energy. However, most of us would accept that our diet is sometimes less than ideal. It is vital to be aware of what we eat, and also how food can affect our body weight. We also need to understand how to adapt our diet when playing particular sports in order to ensure that our energy levels are as high as they need to be.

COMPONENTS OF DIET

◀◀ **REWIND**

DIGESTIVE SYSTEM see page 46

In Chapter 7 we looked at the role of the digestive system, and how it breaks down the food we eat into different nutrients. These nutrients provide us with energy and also help to keep the body functioning efficiently. In order to remain fit and healthy, the human body needs 46 nutrients. These can all be found in the 7 major food groups that we eat:

● Carbohydrates   ● Fats   ● Proteins
● Vitamins   ● Minerals   ● Fibre
● Water

Carbohydrates

There are two main types:

- **Simple carbohydrates** are known as **sugars**, and are found in fruits, honey, jam, biscuits, sweets and cakes

- **Complex carbohydrates** are known as **starches**, and are found in fruits, vegetables, whole-grain breads and cereals (such as rice and wheat). It is better for us to eat most of our carbohydrate in this form.

Carbohydrates give us the energy we require for our muscles. This energy is stored in the blood in small amounts as **glucose**. Greater amounts are stored as **glycogen** in the skeletal muscle and in the liver. High-intensity sport and exercise uses up the glycogen stores quickly, so we need to make sure that we have an adequate supply before we start. Any extra carbohydrate that we do not use is stored as fat around our body.

Fats

Fats are divided into two main types:

- **Unsaturated fats** are found in fish and plant products such as nuts, corn, soya beans and olive oil

- **Saturated fats** are found in animal products such as meat, milk, cheese, cream and butter and also in biscuits, chocolates and cakes. If we eat too much saturated fats we can increase our **cholesterol** to unhealthy levels

Fats are used by the body as an energy source, especially when we are asleep or at rest. Fat is broken down into fatty acids. However, in order for us to use fatty acids efficiently, they must be combined with oxygen. This means that we must exercise at a lower intensity (i.e. work aerobically). Any excess fat that we eat is stored just under the skin. Whilst this can keep us warm and protect internal organs, too much body fat is a disadvantage when playing sport.

Proteins

Proteins are found in meat, fish and in animal and fish products. During digestion, they are broken down into amino acids. We need 21 types of amino acid in our body:

- **Non-essential amino acids** are the 13 amino acids which the body is able to make itself

- **Essential amino acids** are the remaining 8 amino acids which we must obtain through our food

Protein is a material found in large amounts in our body. It includes skin, bones and muscles. The protein we eat in our diet provides material to build and repair cells and tissues in the body. Any excess protein that we eat is not stored.

CARBOHYDRATES
Nutrients which provide energy for our muscles

These foods contain carbohydrate

FATS
Used by the body as an energy source, especially when we are asleep or at rest

These foods contain fat

PROTEINS
Vital nutrients for building and repairing cells and tissues in the body

These foods contain protein

VITAMINS
Essential nutrients for the body's growth and healthy functioning

Vitamins

Vitamins are found in a wide variety of fresh fruit and vegetables. They help many of the body's chemical reactions to take place, including the important reactions which allow body cells to grow and repair themselves. Each vitamin performs a different function:

Vitamins and their function

Vitamin	Function	Found in
A	Helps with vision, keeps tissues healthy	Dairy products, fresh green vegetables, fish oil
B	Helps with growth	Milk, eggs, fish
C	Helps to heal wounds, protects against germs	Oranges, lemons, potatoes, tomatoes
D	Builds up bones and teeth	Dairy products, fish oil
E	Not yet known	Vegetable oils, wholemeal bread, dairy products
K	Helps to clot the blood	Fresh green vegetables, liver

There are two types of vitamins:

● **Water-soluble vitamins** dissolve in water, so boiling food means these vitamins are lost. Also, water-soluble vitamins which are not used are not stored in the body, but are passed in the urine. Water-soluble vitamins need to be eaten every day, and include Vitamins B and C

● **Fat-soluble vitamins** dissolve in fat, rather than in the water in the body. They include vitamins A, D, E and K. Fat-soluble vitamins can be stored in the body

MINERALS
Substances found in a wide range of foods which are essential for the healthy functioning of the body

Minerals

Minerals are also found in a wide range of foods. They are essential for the functioning of the body, and perform a variety of roles:

Minerals and their function

Mineral	Function	Found in
Calcium	Hardens the bones and teeth	Milk, cheese, green vegetables
	Used during muscle contraction	
Zinc	Keeps the skin healthy	Nuts, fish
Iron	Helps produce haemoglobin in red blood cells	Liver, egg yolk, green vegetables
Sodium	Helps the contraction of muscles and the transmission of nerve impulses	Fish, meat, eggs, salt
Potassium	Helps with the contraction of muscles	Most foods
	Controls many chemical reactions inside cells	

Fibre

Fibre is found in vegetables, fruits and nuts. It does not contain any nutrients, as it forms part of our diet that is not digested. However, fibre is important because it adds bulk to our food, helping it to move through the digestive system. It is also called **roughage**.

Water

Water is a vital part of our diet and is essential for survival. It accounts for about 60% of our body weight and is found within most of the tissues of the body – even in bones. It also enables us to keep our bodies cool, transferring heat away from the centre of the body to the skin. Because we are constantly losing water (in sweat, urine, faeces and the air we exhale), it must be replaced to prevent **dehydration**.

A BALANCED DIET

What we eat varies from day to day, but on average it is recommended that we eat a diet made up as follows:

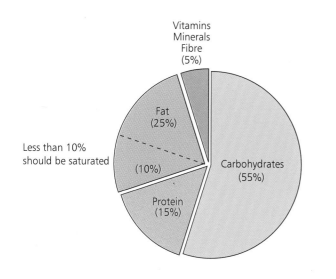

When it comes to improving our diet, a good general rule to apply is **'Minus Three, Plus One'**. Roughly translated, this means we should eat:

● **Less fat** Fat contains twice as many **calories** per gram as carbohydrates and proteins. We should also eat less saturated fat in order to lower the risk of heart disease

● **Less salt** This will lower the risk of high blood pressure

● **Less sugar** Eating less simple carbohydrates can help protect our teeth from decay and avoid overfat

● **More fibre** Fibre contains bulk rather than calories, and is often combined with complex carbohydrates

QUICK TASK

1) Write down all the food and drink you have consumed in the last 24 hours. Can you name the basic food groups contained within each item?

2) Using your list, compare your diet to the 'ideal balanced diet' shown in the diagram below. Which food groups are you eating too much of, and which are you not eating enough of? Can you give reasons for this?

DEHYDRATION
Occurs when we lose a volume of fluid greater than 1% of our body weight. Results include decreased cardiac output and muscular strength

How balanced is your diet?

CALORIE
Amount of energy needed to increase 1 cm³ of water by 1°C. One kilocalorie (kcal) is equal to 1,000 calories, and is the same as 4.2 kilojoules (kJ)

QUICK QUIZ

1) Name the two energy-producing components in the diet.

2) What is glucose, and where is it found in the body?

3) What are proteins broken down into?

4) Which vitamins must we eat every day?

5) How much protein should we have in our diet?

QUICK TASK

Look at the nutritional information on the packaging of a number of food products that you have eaten recently (chocolate bar wrappers, crisp packets, etc.). How many calories does each product contain? Can you convert these into kilojoules?

THE ENERGY EQUATION

Energy

The carbohydrates and fats that we eat are converted to energy and used when we make bodily movements. Energy is normally measured in kilojoules (kj). One kilojoule is equal to 1,000j.

On average, we need between 9,000 and 12,000 kj (2,200 to 2,800 kcal) every day. The lower value is for females, the higher value for males. Different activities require different amounts of energy for each hour of their duration:

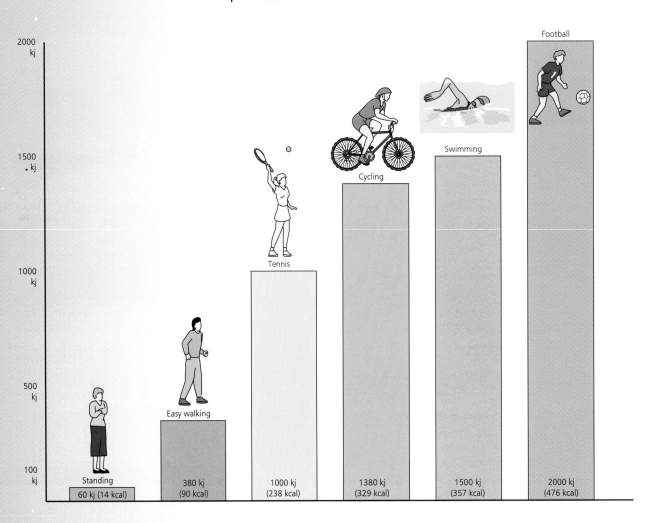

Standing	Easy walking	Tennis	Cycling	Swimming	Football
60 kj (14 kcal)	380 kj (90 kcal)	1000 kj (238 kcal)	1380 kj (329 kcal)	1500 kj (357 kcal)	2000 kj (476 kcal)

THE ENERGY EQUATION
Energy Intake = Energy Expenditure

Maintaining weight – the energy equation

In order to control our body weight, there is a simple formula that we must remember:

Energy intake = Energy expenditure

For instance, if we take in 10,000 kj of energy, and we expend 10,000 kj of energy, our body weight will remain stable. In other words, we must *balance* the amount of food that we eat with the amount of energy we use in physical activity.

To gain weight, our energy intake must be greater than our energy expenditure. This can occur in two ways:

- By decreasing the amount of physical activity we do (i.e. reducing our energy expenditure)

- By increasing the amount of food we eat (i.e. increasing our energy intake)

Most people will choose the second approach. However, it can lead to overfatness if continued for too long.

Another cause of overfatness may be our **basic metabolic rate (BMR)**. This is very high during our teenage years, but slows down as we get older. If we do not reduce our food intake or increase our energy expenditure, the result will be fatness. This is also known as **creeping obesity** or **middle-age spread**, because it often happens without us noticing!

Losing weight

There are three main ways to lose body weight:

1 Reduce energy intake
In effect, this means going on a calorie-controlled diet. When dieting, it is important to maintain a balance between the main food groups. Only a moderate reduction of calories per day is needed, otherwise BMR may be affected.

It is now widely recognised that diets on their own are not a very effective way to lose weight, as people tend to get bored with them and give up. Some people get into pattern of starting and stopping diets every few months. This kind of 'yo-yo' dieting causes the BMR to become very unstable and is not recommended.

2 Increase energy expenditure
This occurs when we start to increase our level of daily physical activity. Exercise burns up both fat and carbohydrate. The more intensively we exercise, the more carbohydrates we use.

3 Reduce energy intake and increase energy expenditure
Combining regular exercise and physical activity with a sensibly controlled diet is the most effective way of losing fat.

Measuring weight loss

In order to lose body weight, it is best to aim for a fat loss of no more than 1 kg per week. As we saw in Chapter 9, by taking skinfold measurements, it is possible to calculate the effect of dieting and exercising on overall body fat percentage. However, from the point of view of motivation, it is probably better to measure the skinfold thickness itself, as the effect of the diet will tend to show up more dramatically.

BASIC METABOLIC RATE
The minimal level of energy needed by the body when resting. This varies from person to person depending on sex, physique, age, etc.

Maintaining body weight
Kilojoules eaten each day **equal** kilojoules burned up each day

Gaining body weight
Kilojoules eaten each day **exceed** kilojoules burned up each day

Losing body weight
Kilojoules eaten each day are **less than** kilojoules burned up each day

◀◀ **REWIND**

MEASURING BODY FAT
see page 64

NUTRITION FOR SPORT

Having gained a knowledge of the basic food groups and methods of weight control, we can use our understanding to help us when we are preparing to exercise or play sport. If we eat the 'best' diet possible, we can gain the edge over opponents who are of a similar skill level.

There are three time phases that we need to be aware of:

1 Before exercise

Before taking part in endurance events (or any sport that lasts for more than 60 minutes), it is vital that our glycogen stores are as full as possible. We can achieve this by what is known as **carbohydrate loading.**

The pre-exercise or **pre-match meal** should ideally be eaten at least 3–4 hours beforehand, and consist of food that you know and are used to. As we saw in Chapter 7, it takes this length of time for a meal to pass through the stomach. The main points to follow are:

- **Eat complex carbohydrates**: these release energy slowly

- **Avoid simple carbohydrates**: these release energy quickly, but trigger the release of insulin which can soon make you feel tired

- **Avoid fats and proteins**: these take longer for the stomach to digest

2 During exercise

Normally, it is best to avoid solids during exercise (although a banana at half-time may give you an extra rush of energy). However, 'sports nutrition drinks' that contain glucose are permissible if the activity lasts for more than a couple of hours.

3 After exercise

The first two hours after exercise are crucial, as this is the time to replace the stocks of **glycogen** that have been used up during the activity. It is important to do this even if you do not feel hungry and to continue to replace your glycogen stores up to a day or two after the event

FLUID REPLACEMENT

To avoid dehydration, it is vital to replace fluid regularly. During normal day-today activity we lose fluid from our body constantly in the air we exhale, in our sweat, etc. During exercise, we lose even more. It has been estimated that marathon runners at the 1996 Atlanta Olympics lost as much as five litres of water through sweat!

CARBOHYDRATE LOADING
Eating more carbohydrates (up to 60%) and reducing physical activity on the three days leading up to a competition in order to build up stocks of glycogen in the body

PRE-MATCH MEAL
Normally eaten 3–4 hours before a sporting fixture or endurance event

GLYCOGEN
A source of energy stored in the muscles and liver, glycogen is a converted form of glucose which we have (as sugar) in our diet

FLUID REPLACEMENT
Drinking at regular intervals in order to replace lost fluid

It is important for athletes to drink water regularly while they are running

QUICK QUIZ

1) What are calories?

2) Explain the energy equation.

3) How can we lose body weight?

4) How many days before competition should we start carbohydrate loading?

5) Why is fluid replacement so important?

6) How do isotonic sports drinks work?

Avoiding dehydration

There are three key guidelines:

- Make sure that you are fully hydrated before you play sport

- Drink water at regular intervals during exercise, even if you do not feel thirsty

- Always replace any water you have lost after you have finished playing sport

Most sports authorities now recognise the need for fluid replacement, and water should always be available to players either by the side of the pitch or at designated 'feeding' stations (e.g. for long-distance runners and cyclists). Fluid replacement is particularly important in hot climates, but all sportsmen and women should ensure that they remain hydrated even when performing in colder environments.

ELECTROLYTES
Minerals such as sodium, potassium, and chloride which are contained within a fluid. These help to control the body so that various reactions may take place. During exercise, the body loses electrolytes in sweat

Sports nutrition drinks

There are a number of fluids (and powders that can be mixed with water) that can aid the process of fluid replacement. These are known as **isotonic drinks**, and are available for sale in most shops and sports centre vending machines.

The term **isotonic** means that the drink is in a solution of **electrolytes** with a concentration similar to that of body fluids. These drinks increase the rate at which water is absorbed by the body, helping to promote body cooling and to avoid dehydration. However, if a drink contains too much glucose (more than 6%), the body recognises it as a food, and the fluid is less likely to be absorbed, leaving you more dehydrated.

Sports nutrition drinks help the process of fluid replacement

S P O R T   I N   A C T I O N

Dave is preparing to run a half-marathon in six months' time. Using the information in this chapter, how would you suggest he plans his diet in the build-up to the run?

✓ K E Y   W O R D S

Tick each box when you understand the word

CARBOHYDRATES ☐
(SIMPLE AND COMPLEX)

FATS (SATURATED AND ☐
UNSATURATED)

PROTEINS ☐

VITAMINS ☐

MINERALS ☐

FIBRE ☐

WATER ☐

CALORIE ☐

THE ENERGY ☐
EQUATION

BASIC METABOLIC ☐
RATE

PRE-MATCH MEAL ☐

CARBOHYDATE ☐
LOADING

FLUID REPLACEMENT ☐

M A T C H   I T

TERM	DEFINITION
Sodium	The building component of our diet
Cholesterol	Helps food pass through the digestive system
Fibre	Fat that is deposited in the walls of arteries
Vitamin A	Found in chocolate, sweets, and cakes
Simple carbohydrate	Mineral that helps transmit nerve impulses
Protein	Helps with vision

✓ R E V I S E   I T !

For your exams you will need to know:

☐ The basic components which can be found in food

☐ The composition of a healthy balanced diet

☐ The effects of dietary intake and exercise on body weight

☐ The specific dietary requirements of sportspeople

☐ The meaning of the key words for this chapter

Drugs and Sport

CHAPTER 11

The aim of this chapter is to help you:

⊘ Discuss the use of **drugs** in sport

⊘ Understand the effect that **different types of drugs** can have on sports performers

⊘ Understand the effects of **smoking** on the body

⊘ Understand the effects of **alcohol** on the body

Drug abuse or **doping** has been one of the main areas of cheating in sport over the last few years. Sports authorities now spend huge amounts of money testing athletes and publicising the dangers of drug-taking. Some drugs are legal, such as those that help recovery from illness or injuries. However, others – usually called **performance-enhancing drugs** – are banned substances.

> DOPING
> Illegal use of a drug to enhance sports performance

> PERFORMANCE-ENHANCING DRUG
> Drug often developed to treat illnesses but misused by athletes in order artificially to boost performance

THE FIGHT AGAINST DRUGS

The UK **Sports Council** has been at the forefront of the fight against drugs in sport. It works with regional, national and international bodies such as the International Olympic Committee to enforce anti-doping programmes and promote drug-free sport and ethical sporting practices. As a result, top-level athletes are now **randomly tested** during sporting events, and many competitors at other levels may be called for out-of-competition testing at any time.

> RANDOM TESTING
> Sports bodies can require any sports performer to have a drug test at any time. In a sprint race, for example, three out of the eight athletes can be randomly selected for a drugs test

Drug abuse in sport is a major problem that all sports organisations have to confront

WHAT IS A DRUG?

A **drug** is any substance that may affect a person's emotional state, body function or behaviour. In this sense, alcohol, caffeine and over-the-counter medicines are all drugs. However, many drugs which are legally available contain substances which are prohibited by sport governing bodies. Also, drugs which are banned in one sport may not necessarily be prohibited in others. For this reason, the Sports Council now issues cards which list the banned drugs and the medicines that contain them, as well as permitted medicines for certain common conditions.

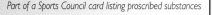

Part of a Sports Council card listing proscribed substances

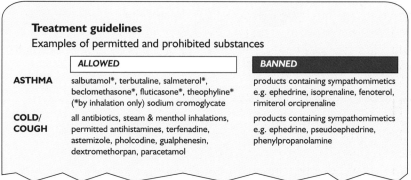

Treatment guidelines

Examples of permitted and prohibited substances

	ALLOWED	BANNED
ASTHMA	salbutamol*, terbutaline, salmeterol*, beclomethasone*, fluticasone*, theophyline* (*by inhalation only) sodium cromoglycate	products containing sympathomimetics e.g. ephedrine, isoprenaline, fenoterol, rimiterol orciprenaline
COLD/ COUGH	all antibiotics, steam & menthol inhalations, permitted antihistamines, terfenadine, astemizole, pholcodine, gualphenesin, dextromethorpan, paracetamol	products containing sympathomimetics e.g. ephedrine, pseudoephedrine, phenylpropanolamine

Drug-taking in sport is cheating. It can also be harmful to health. The vast majority of athletes compete drug-free. However, the huge increases in the rewards of winning have meant that the temptation to take drugs has become ever greater. Possibly the most famous example was at the 1988 Olympics, when Canadian sprinter Ben Johnson was disqualified and banned after winning the gold medal. He failed the drugs test but still made money from his fame.

Ben Johnson, a famous Olympic athlete, was banned for taking an illegal drug

THE EFFECTS OF DRUGS

A variety of drugs can be used to improve performance. Most have been developed by scientists and doctors to treat people who are sick or injured. However, athletes and their coaches have found out about their properties and misuse them in order gain an unfair advantage over other competitors.

Tranquillisers

Some drugs help performers by calming them down and helping them to concentrate more easily. These are called **tranquillisers** and include drugs such as benzodiazipanes and beta blockers. In sports such as snooker there have been cases of misuse.

Stimulants

Other drugs called **stimulants** reduce feelings of fatigue and increase feelings of competitiveness and aggression. These drugs, such as amphetamines, have been used illegally in events that require a lot of energy, such as cycling.

In long distance events such as cycling, some competitors have illegally used amphetamines to boost performance.

Anabolic steroids

These are man-made hormones that have the effect of artifically helping athletes build up muscular power and strength.

Narcotic analgesics

Narcotic analgesics are used by athletes to raise their pain threshold so that they can continue to compete while recovering from injury. This can often make the underlying injury worse and may cause permanent damage.

Diuretics

Other drugs called **diuretics** are used to get rid of fluid from the body. In sports where weight is important such as horse racing and boxing, performers have taken diuretics in order to reduce body weight. Swimmers have also tested positive for diuretics. Diuretics can also be used to mask the presence of other banned substances.

THE DANGERS OF DRUGS

All the drugs discussed above may have positive effects on performance. However, in the long term there will also be a number of negative effects on both health and performance. In many cases – particularly with drugs such as anabolic steroids – the effects can be fatal. In the table below and on page 80 we summarise some of the effects drug-taking can have.

ANABOLIC STEROID
Man-made hormone used illegally by sports performers to increase strength, power and aggression

---

NARCOTIC ANALGESIC
Narcotic *means sleep-inducing, and* ***analgesic*** *means pain-killing*

QUICK QUIZ

1) When can an athlete be drug-tested?

2) Why might drug-taking be increasing in sport?

3) Which body leads the campaign for drug-free sport in the UK?

THE EFFECTS OF DRUGS

Drug type	Examples	Effects	Associated sports
Stimulant	Amphetamine Caffeine	Raise heart rate and blood pressure Increase alertness, mask fatigue	Cycling, running Contact sports

Depressants /Tranquillisers	Beta blockers
	
	Benzodiazepine
		Reduce anxiety
		Reduce heart rate
		   and blood pressure
		Improve concentration
		   and control
			Snooker, archery
			Target shooting
			Motor racing, skiing

Narcotic analgesics (painkillers)	Codeine Morphine Heroin	Drowsiness Deaden pain Relax	Cycling Contact sports
Anabolic agents	Anabolic steroids	Increase strength/power Increase aggression	Contact sports Weight lifting Boxing Athletics – sprinting/throwing
Diuretics		Get rid of fluid from body Help reduce body weight Increase flow of urine Mask presence of other drugs	Horse racing Motor racing Boxing/wrestling/judo

THE HARMFUL EFFECTS OF DRUGS

Drug type	Harmful effect
Stimulants	Overuse of body – can lead to tissue damage, heat exhaustion, liver and brain damage Over-aggressive behaviour
Narcotic analgesics	All are addictive – can lead to dependence Injuries are made worse by continued use Lower blood pressure
Anabolic steroids	Heart problems Increased risk of cancer Infertility in males Development of male characteristics in females Aggressive behaviour
Depressants	Overuse can lead to depression Can be very addictive Lack of energy and lethargy
Diuretics	Essential salts are also lost in fluid – this can lead to muscle damage Heart damage

DIURETIC
A substance that withdraws fluid from the body

BLOOD DOPING
The process of artificially increasing the number of red blood cells in the body

ALTITUDE
Height above sea level. **At high altitude** *means 'high up' where there is less oxygen to breathe*

BLOOD DOPING

Blood doping is also a banned practice. If athletes train at altitude, the body responds by making the blood carry more oxygen. This is beneficial to athletes who compete in endurance-type events as it means they can work harder for longer.

Blood doping involves artifically increasing the number of red blood cells by injecting stored blood into the athlete's body. The extra red blood cells increase the amount of oxygen carried to the muscles, thus improving performance.

Blood doping is very difficult to detect. Recently scientists have also discovered a chemical which simulates the effects of altitude training. This in turn may become a banned substance.

The risks of blood doping

Blood doping involves the same process as blood transfusion, and the same risks apply. These are:

- Infection with hepatitis or AIDS
- Allergic reaction if incorrect blood type is used
- Blood clots
- Kidney damage
- Strain on the circulatory system

THE EFFECTS OF 'SOCIAL DRUGS'

So-called **social drugs** such as tobacco and alcohol are widely used, although alcohol is now banned by some sports such as motor sports and fencing. However, social drugs have harmful effects on the body and anyone who wants to be fit and healthy should think carefully before using them.

Smoking and health

Smoking has been popular in the UK for several hundred years but it is only fairly recently that we have discovered the harm that smoking does to our bodies. Over 100,000 people a year die of smoking-related diseases, and all cigarettes and tobacco products now have to carry a health warning issued by the government.

Smoking reduces fitness, and no sports performer who smokes can expect to be able to perform to their full potential. The only cure is to give up smoking – or better still, not to start. Nor is it just smokers who are affected. Non-smokers can suffer the same harmful effects through **passive smoking**.

The effects of smoking on the body are as follows:

- Decrease in lung capacity

- Increase in the risk of developing cancer, especially lung and throat cancer

- Reduction in the amount of oxygen the blood can carry

- Increased risk of heart disease and damage

The effects of alcohol

Alcohol is another very popular drug. Over 90% of the UK population drink, and alcohol is one of the oldest drugs known to man. Most people drink to help them relax and socialise. In moderate amounts, alcohol does little harm to the body, but if large quantities are consumed, permanent and serious damage can result.

Sport is often associated with alcohol, and 'a drink after the match' is an accepted part of the social side of sport. However, alcohol can have a detrimental effect on sports performance and many top sports performers are now either reducing the amount of alcohol they consume or cutting it out altogether.

Some sports actually list alcohol has a banned substance. Since alcohol is a depressant it can help people calm their nerves. In sports such as **modern pentathlon**, fencing and shooting this could be an advantage.

As alcohol is a diuretic, it can have a negative effect on sports performance. If athletes drink before an event – even the night before – this could lead to dehydration and impair their performance.

QUICK TASK

1) How might smoking affect the fitness of a runner?

2) What physiological changes which are the results of smoking will make it harder for the runner to run at his or her best?

PASSIVE SMOKING
Effects of smoking on non-smokers. People who do not smoke but are in a smokey environment actually breathe around 20% of the smoke exhaled by smokers

QUICK QUIZ

1) Approximately how many people die each year from smoking-related diseases?

2) What effect does smoking have on a person's physical fitness?

3) What effect does smoking have on a person's lung capacity?

Fencing is one of a number of sports that have now banned alcohol altogether

Effects of alcohol on the body

- Liver damage (alcohol is toxic and is sent to the liver where it is broken down and expelled from the body)

- Damage to the digestive system

- Depression and possibly brain damage

- Reaction time slows down

- Damage to the body's immune system, increasing the risk of illnesses

- Dehydration

- Alcohol is very high in calories and can lead to increase in body weight

✓ KEY WORDS

Tick each box when you understand the word

DRUG ☐

PERFORMANCE-ENHANCING DRUG ☐

RANDOM TESTING ☐

ANABOLIC STEROID ☐

NARCOTIC ANALGESIC ☐

DIURETIC ☐

ALTITUDE ☐

BLOOD DOPING ☐

PASSIVE SMOKING ☐

MATCH IT

DRUG	NEGATIVE EFFECT
Depressant	Heart damage
Anabolic steroid	Depression
Diuretic	Liver and brain damage
Stimulant	Infertility in male athletes
Narcotic analgesic	Further injury, and aggravation of existing injuries

✓ REVISE IT!

For your exams you will need to know:

☐ The effects on performance of: stimulants, narcotic analgesics, growth hormones/steroids, diuretics, betablockers/benzodiazipanes, and their side-effects

☐ The short- and long-term effects of smoking on the body

☐ The short- and long-term effects of alcohol

☐ The dangers of using drugs to improve performance

☐ The meaning of the key words for this chapter

Learning Skills

CHAPTER 12

The aim of this chapter is to help you:

⊘ Find out what is meant by **skilful movement**

⊘ Understand that there are different classifications of skills

⊘ Look at **open** and **closed** skills in more detail

⊘ Find out about the different ways in which we **learn** skills

⊘ Understand how to **teach** different skills

⊘ Look at other influences, such as our personalities and how aggressive we are

Before we can learn the correct skills for our sport, or teach skills correctly, we need to find out more about these skills. This chapter will look in detail at skills that we need to have and how we learn them. We will then look at other personal factors which affect the way we learn and perform skills.

A 'skilful' gymnast has balance and coordination

COMPONENTS OF SKILFUL MOVEMENT

A **skill** is a movement that some of us can do in some sports. For instance, you might be able to curl the ball during a free kick in football or flick the ball in hockey. Skill is something that we learn: we are not born with any particular skills.

Someone who is **skilful** completes the movement or set of movements correctly almost every time and is in control. For example, a skilful archer will be able to fire an arrow and hit the target accurately almost every time.

A skilful player also has agility, coordination, power, quick reactions, balance and speed. Let us look at each of these in turn.

A 'skilled' archer will hit the target accurately every time

QUICK TASK

1) Time yourself against a partner.
    In two minutes, see how many team
    skills you can name, e.g. passing in
    football. Write them down. Do the
    same with skills that you might
    perform on your own, e.g. throwing
    the javelin.

2) Do the same as above, but for one
    particular team sport and one
    particular individual activity.

SKILL
The term 'skill' is used in different ways:

— To describe a movement that is good.
   For example, we might describe a
   tricky manoeuvre in football or ice-
   skating as 'skilful'

— To describe a particular action in a
   particular sport, e.g. the 'skill' of
   bowling in cricket

AGILITY
The ability to move quickly and change
direction at speed

A skilful goalkeeper is agile

Agility

A skilful performer in sport has good **agility**. This means that he
or she is quick and nimble, can move well and change direction
at speed. A goalkeeper has to be agile to save the ball by diving
to catch it.

Testing for agility

This can be done by running around obstacles and then
recording the time it takes to complete a set course. When you
use this course – or if you test yourself against others –
remember to set the course out in exactly the same way each
time. An alternative is the **Illinois Agility Run**. To perform
this, lie face-down behind a starting line. When the 'tester'
shouts 'go', get up as fast as you can and run around an obstacle
course of four cones, each cone spaced two metres apart. The
start line is four metres away from the first cone.

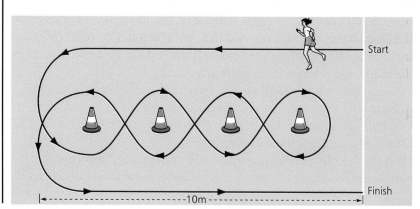

The Illinois Agility Run

You may like to compare your time against someone else who is of a similar body shape to you. A much more useful way of using this type of test is to test yourself at the beginning of a training period or the beginning of the season, and then to test yourself again at the end.

Coordination

A skilful performer's movements are nearly always smooth, with no waste of effort. You will have seen top-class sports people who seem to be able to perform without effort. They are in fact trying extremely hard but because they know what to do and when to do it, it seems easy!

Tennis is one sport where **coordination** is important. In a match, the player has to coordinate the swing of the racket with the bounce of the ball and the position of the opponent.

Testing for coordination
A useful and easy test that you could try would be to throw a tennis ball against a wall with one hand and then catch it with the other hand. Stand two metres away from the wall and keep throwing and catching, using both hands. Time yourself over two minutes and record how many catches you make.

Power

A skilful sports person will have **speed** and **strength**. Power is only short-lived. A sports performer can only produce maximum power over a short period of time. Power is very important in explosive events like the throws in athletics or in weightlifting.

Testing for strength
The pull-up test is a useful way to test strength. You will need a **chinning bar**, which is often found attached to weight-training equipment or multigyms. Hold the bar in an 'overgrasp' position and lift yourself up, keeping your body straight. Now lower yourself until your arms are straight. Repeat the movement as many times as you can and record your results.

One way to measure the strength of your grip is to use a **hand grip dynamometer** *(see page 58)*. But perhaps the most effective and easiest way is to try to lift as heavy a weight as possible, such as in a bench press lift. You must ensure, however, that you have warmed up and that your teacher or coach is present to advise you. Lifting weights can be dangerous if you do not know what you are doing.

Reaction time

This is very important in many sports, the most obvious being those where you have to react to a starting pistol, such as sprinting. A skilful athlete will be able to react very quickly to try to get that split-second edge over opponents.

> COORDINATION
> The ability to perform movements smoothly and with no waste of effort

Power means having both speed and strength

Your strength can be measured by how much you can lift

REACTION TIME
The time it takes for us to think about what needs to be done and then begin to do it. For example, a sprinter will hear the gun and instantly drive off the blocks

QUICK TASK

1) Standing opposite a partner, hold a metre rule at one end, grasping it between your thumb and first finger. As soon as you drop it, your partner attempts to catch the ruler by clapping his or her hands and trapping the ruler between them. Have five goes each and see whether your reactions get quicker

2) Do the Ruler Drop Test ten times each and record your results. Plot a graph to show your results.
Talk to your partner about your results. How can you explain them?

SPEED
Ability to move quickly

INHERITED CHARACTERISTICS
Physical factors that are genetically transmitted

Speed of **reaction** depends upon muscle fibres that we are born with but also on practice. A sprinter gets quicker at reacting to the gun with practice, just as a young person might get quicker at reacting to a computer game.

Balance

Skilful performers in sport will keep very steady or balanced when they need to. For example, skilful gymnasts will be very steady or balanced when doing a handstand. To achieve this, they need to distribute their weight evenly. Balance is also important when playing team sports. A netball player must have balance when shooting, and a rugby forward must be balanced in a scrum.

Testing for balance

You can test your balance by standing on one foot on a balance beam or on a bench with your eyes closed. Get a partner to time how long you can stand on one foot without losing your balance.

Speed

Speed of movement is often very important in sport. As we found with reaction time, skilful sports people are able to make decisions quickly, but they also need to move quickly. A skilful hockey forward is one who can get to the ball quickly and take a shot. An athlete doing the long jump must be able to sprint fast before take-off.

How fast you are depends on the muscle fibres you are born with. These are called **inherited characteristics**.

Testing for speed

You can test how quick you are by timing yourself or getting someone else to time you while you perform a 30-metre sprint. Make sure that you have clear start and finish lines and use a stopwatch. Compare your time with your partner's time.

Balance is important for both team and individual sports

We classify skills depending on what they involve. Some involve opponents, some are easy, some more difficult

QUICK QUIZ

1) Give an example of a skill in which agility is important.

2) How could you test for levels of coordination?

3) What are the two essential elements of power?

4) What does a hand grip dynamometer do?

5) Some people are quicker at reacting in sport than others. Why?

TYPES OF SKILLS

There are many different types of skills in sport. Some are more difficult to learn and perform than others. For example, dribbling in hockey is more difficult than just running.

● More difficult skills are called **complex skills**

● Very easy skills are called **basic skills**

● When we put skills into different groups, this is called **skill classification**

Open and closed skills

If a skill is affected a lot by what is going on around the player or performer, then it is said to be more **open**. If the skill is not affected much by what is going on around, it is said to be more **closed**. Although a skill can be mostly open or mostly closed, it is never completely open or closed, but can always be put on a scale between the two, called a **continuum**. Because both the basketball player and the windsurfer are affected by other factors, they are both performing open-type skills. A weightlifter does not have to bother with the weather or any direct opponent, therefore weightlifting can be seen as not having many **environmental influences** and is therefore a more closed skill.

OPEN/CLOSED SKILLS
*Skills which are more affected by surrounding events are **open**, while those which are less affected are **closed***

ENVIRONMENTAL INFLUENCES
Actions or events that are happening around you as you perform a skill

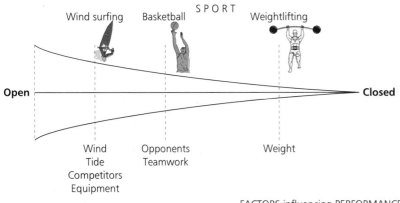

FACTORS influencing PERFORMANCE

In windsurfing, environmental influences can include the action of the wind and tides

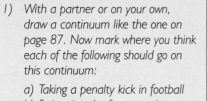

QUICK TASK

1) With a partner or on your own, draw a continuum like the one on page 87. Now mark where you think each of the following should go on this continuum:

    a) Taking a penalty kick in football
    b) Swimming the front crawl
    c) Dribbling in hockey
    d) Cycling

2) Write down reasons why you have placed these skills where you have on your continuum.

3) Draw another continuum, but this time instead of open/closed, make it for **difficult** (complex) and at the other end **easy** (basic) skills

M A T C H   I T

TERM	DEFINITION
Reaction time	Keeping very steady and in control
Balance skills	Skills that are not affected by surrounding factors
Basic skills	Grouping skills together, depending on what they are like
Skills classification	Skills which are affected by surrounding factors
Open skills	Simple skills like running
Closed skills	How quickly you can think about what to do

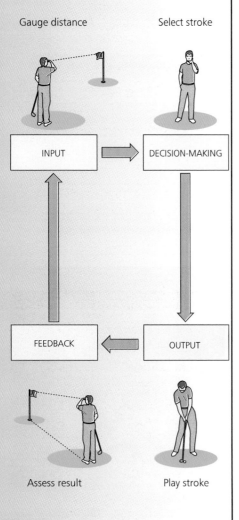

The stages of information processing

THE LEARNING AND PERFORMANCE OF SKILLS

Each time you practise a skill it is known as a **performance**. Before you can perform a skill, you have to learn it. Learning involves understanding and then being able to perform the skill over and over again. There are many different ways in which you can learn a skill depending on how difficult the skill is, how you are taught and your own ability and eagerness to learn.

Information processing

To learn a skill our brain has to take in information about what to do and how to do it. It then recalls how to perform the skill and tells our muscles to move in a particular way. We then perform the skill. This is called **information processing**.

The first step is to receive information through our senses. This information is called **input**. For example, the input for returning a serve in tennis is the sight of the ball and the net, the sound of the opponent who has just hit the ball and the feel of the racket in our hand. Of course, a lot more information is coming to us as well – like the noise of the crowd or the sound of an aircraft passing overhead.

Once the brain has taken in information, it sorts it and makes sense of it by comparing it with information already stored in our **memory**. This is the process we call **perception**. It then makes a decision about what to do next – for instance, in tennis, to play a forehand. This is called **decision-making**.

After decisions have been made, messages are sent to our muscles to move in a particular way, and we then move. The part of the information processing system when we put our decisions into action is called **output**.

During the performance of a skill and after it is completed, we get information about how we are doing – this is known as **feedback**. We cannot, however, deal with all the information that comes to us at any one time. This is because we have what is called **limited channel capacity** – the inability of the brain to process too much information at any one time.

Selective attention

The more skilful we are, the more we are able to shut out information which is of no use to us. This ability to shut out information and just concentrate on what is important is known as **selective attention**. If we are beginners at a sport, we do not have very good selective attention. We therefore pay too much attention to things going on around us that are irrelevant to performing the skill.

Memory

The brain's ability to store information is known as **memory**. We would not be able to perform skills well in sport unless we had a memory. We remember how to do the skill and this forms part of our decision-making.

There are said to be two parts to our memory: the **short-term** and the **long-term** memory store.

● When information passes into the brain, it is held in the short-term memory store

● Here it only stays briefly until it is used to make a decision about what to do. For example, a table tennis player seeing the ball come over the net will only think about the ball very briefly before hitting it

● Information that we do not need is forgotten, as we have seen with selective attention

● Our long-term memory holds memories of how to perform the skill if we are a skilful performer

> **PERCEPTION**
> The process of interpreting information taken in via the senses

> **SELECTIVE ATTENTION**
> The ability to concentrate on what is important when performing a skill

Golf skills demand selective attention

> **MEMORY**
> The brain's ability to store information

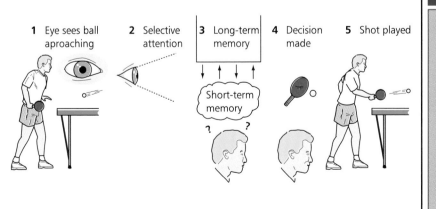

1 Eye sees ball aproaching   **2** Selective attention   **3** Long-term memory   **4** Decision made   **5** Shot played

Short-term memory

How memory helps us perform a skill

QUICK QUIZ

1) Give an example of a basic skill and a complex skill.

2) Give a reason why windsurfing involves open skills.

3) What is it called when our brains sort out what needs to be done before we perform a sports skill?

4) What is limited channel capacity and why do we have it?

5) Name a sport where selective attention is important.

PROPRIOCEPTION
The feeling or awareness of your own body which tells you how well you are performing a certain action or skill

◄◄ **REWIND**

PROPRIOCEPTION   see page 41

QUICK TASK

1) Pretend that you are a coach of your chosen sport. Choose one particular skill and then demonstrate it to your partner.

   While you are demonstrating, draw attention to the information that your partner will have to select in order to be able to do the skill. Then watch your partner perform the skill.

   Is your partner's selective attention effective? If not, then perhaps he or she is concentrating on the wrong things.

2) Think of a skill in your favourite sport, e.g. the smash in badminton. List all the items of information which you need to concentrate on in order to perform it well. Make a list of information that you do **not** want to concentrate on.

QUICK QUIZ

1) Name two stores which make up our memory.

2) How do we make sure we remember how to perform a skill?

3) Give an example of feedback in a sport of your choice.

4) What is proprioception?

TRANSFER
The influence of learning or performing one skill on the learning or performance of another

Feedback

As we saw earlier, feedback is the process which tells us how we are getting on as we perform a skill and afterwards tells us how well we did. For example, when we throw the discus in athletics we *feel* how well we are throwing.

A top-class golfer will know how a drive has gone just by the 'feel' of the swing, even though he or she may be unaware of where the ball has been hit. These are both examples of what is called **proprioception**.

Feedback that we feel (proprioception) is called **internal feedback**, while the feedback which shows us how we got on is **external feedback**. For example, if a swimming coach shouts to the swimmer that his or her legs are bent, this is external feedback. The swimmer can then do something about it!

Effective use of feedback

External feedback from a coach or teacher must be as positive as possible. A coach should tell the performer what is going well and suggest ways of making it even better. A coach who only concentrates on what is going wrong will make the sports performer miserable and undermine their will to carry on and improve. Too much advice can be unhelpful – remember limited channel capacity!

The following tasks are based on football or netball skills, but you can adapt them to your own sport if you prefer.

Football: heading the ball

● Demonstrate to a partner how you would head the ball, both in attack and defence

● Name three coaching points that you would include for either an attacking or a defensive header

● How would you make sure that your partner remembered your advice?

Netball: passing

● Demonstrate either a shoulder, underarm, bounce or chest pass to your partner

● Name three coaching points that you would include for the particular pass you have chosen

● How would you make sure that your partner remembered your advice?

Types of practice

The teaching of skills can only work well if the training or practice session is cleverly and thoughtfully structured. Practice sessions should include activities which allow for the maximum amount of **transfer** to take place.

Practice sessions must allow transfer of skills

For example, if you want to teach a beginner the serve in tennis, you may start by getting the beginner to throw the ball over-arm over the net. This throwing action is similar to the serving arm action in the tennis serve. There may then be transfer of the skill of throwing to the skill of serving.

Part practice and whole practice

The teaching of skills in practice sessions often varies depending on the skills being taught. If a gymnastic routine is to be taught, for instance, each part of the routine has to be taught separately. This is called **part practice**.

Sometimes it is better not to split the skill up into parts. This is because it might confuse the learner or prevent them getting the true 'feel' of the skill. The type of practice when skills are not split up is called **whole practice**.

An example of a skill which you would teach as a whole would be a golf swing. It would be very difficult to split this skill up into parts because you would lose the flow and 'feel' of the swing.

Types of guidance

Guidance is a term used to describe the way we help people learn and perform skills. There are basically three main types of guidance:

- **Visual** – showing the performer what needs to be done
- **Verbal** – telling the performer what needs to be done
- **Physical** (manual or mechanical) – helping the performer to carry out the task

Visual guidance

The best way of showing someone how to perform a physical or motor skill is usually to give a **demonstration**.

Other forms of visual guidance include the use of video, either to show the learner how to perform a skill or to replay a performance, so that mistakes can be corrected.

QUICK TASK

1) Make a list of five skills that you would teach a beginner using the part method. Next, make a list of five skills that you would teach a beginner using the whole method.

2) Write a list of instructions for a beginner on how to perform a tennis serve. Number each instruction so that the beginner can practise each part separately.

A coach demonstrating a skill to a learner

QUICK TASK

Choose a skill from your favourite sport and plan how you would teach it using a demonstration. Who would do the demonstrating? Would you split the skill up into parts?

It is sometimes better for a coach to give verbal instructions during a break in play than during the game itself

QUICK QUIZ

1) What do we mean by the term **transfer**?

2) What should practice sessions allow for?

3) Give a skill for which part practice is more suitable than whole practice.

4) Why is it better sometimes **not** to split a skill into parts?

5) Name three types of guidance.

6) What are the requirements for effective demonstration of skills?

7) How can videos help in the teaching of skills?

EXTROVERT
Type of person who tends to be more noisy, lively and outgoing

INTROVERT
Type of person who is quiet and shy and prefers to spend time on their own rather than with others

Verbal guidance

Telling a sports performer what to do may sound straightforward, but the instructions that you give as a coach or a teacher must be clear and correct.

If instructions are given during the activity itself – for example, during a football match – the player may be concentrating so hard on the game they may find the guidance almost impossible to follow. It is often better to wait until a break in play – for example, at half-time.

Physical guidance

This involves the teacher or coach helping the performer, either by giving them physical support or by providing artificial help such as armbands in swimming.

This type of guidance is very useful because it can give confidence to the performer and help them conquer their natural fear of first trying a skill. This is particularly true when teaching young children.

FACTORS AFFECTING THE PERFORMANCE OF SKILLS

Personality has an important effect on how we perform skills in sport. A group of sports performers may have the same skill level, but in a match situation each one will perform differently. Some will simply try harder than others – something which we will investigate in the next chapter, under the heading of **motivation**. Other reasons include the type of personality that we have, and how aggressive or competitive we are.

Personality

By **personality** we mean what sort of person we are. We are all different, but there are certain characteristics that we may share with others. This affects our choice of sports. For instance, a sociable, confident person who likes to be the centre of attention will probably tend to choose sports that involve working with other people, such as team sports.

Types of personality

There are many different personality types. One of the most common ways of describing someone's personality is to say whether they are **extrovert** or **introvert**. Although research is inconclusive and there is much evidence to suggest that *all* personalities can be attracted to *all* sports, the general trends can be summarised as follows:

● **Extroverts** tend to prefer team sports, sports with aggression and action-packed, competitive sports

● **Introverts** tend to prefer sports which are solitary, less active and less competitive

Aggression

Aggression is often thought to be necessary in some sports. If you are a rugby forward, for instance, you will be expected to act aggressively and win the ball. Aggression, however, can be very destructive and can ruin performance. For instance, a rugby forward could give away a penalty by punching an opponent.

> **AGGRESSION**
> *This means you are very forceful in the way you behave*

Aggression can lead to unacceptable behaviour

M A T C H   I T

TERM	DEFINITION
Perception	A store of information about past experience
Memory	Process of sorting information from the senses
Feedback	Concentrating on what is important
Selective attention	Information about how well we are performing

QUICK TASK

1) Write down words that might describe your personality. Then write down the sports you particularly like to play and watch. Do your sports match up with your personality?

2) Write down the names of some top sports people. Next to each name identify what sort of people they are, e.g. loud/quiet, violent/gentle, lively/miserable, etc.
Can you see a connection between the personalities and their sports?

QUICK QUIZ

1) Which type of personality – extrovert or introvert – is most likely to play the following sports?

a) Rugby
b) Ice hockey
c) Marathon running
d) Weightlifting
e) Wrestling
f) Rock climbing
g) Tennis
h) Volleyball

2) State whether the following involve direct or indirect aggression:

a) Boxing
b) Vaulting in gymnastics
c) Karate
d) Bowling in cricket
e) Batting in cricket
f) Rugby scrum
g) Golf drive

✓ KEY WORDS

Tick each box when you understand the word

SKILL ☐

BALANCE ☐

POWER ☐

SPEED ☐

AGILITY ☐

COORDINATION ☐

OPEN AND CLOSED SKILLS ☐

PERCEPTION ☐

MEMORY ☐

SELECTIVE ATTENTION ☐

TRANSFER ☐

✓ REVISE IT !

For your exams you will need to know:

☐ How to identify different types of skills, especially basic, complex, open and closed skills

☐ How information processing can help to explain how we learn skills

☐ How memory can also help

☐ What is meant by feedback and how it helps us to perform skills

☐ The different types of guidance, and examples

☐ The definition of an introvert and an extrovert

☐ Examples of sports which suit either introverts or extroverts

☐ Examples of sports which involve indirect and/or direct aggression

☐ The meaning of the key words for this chapter

Mental Preparation

CHAPTER 13

The aim of this chapter is to help you:

- Find out what is meant by **motivation**

- Identify **intrinsic** and **extrinsic** motivation and give examples

- Find out what is meant by **arousal** and **anxiety** in sport

- Understand how sportsmen and women cope with anxiety and stress

- Find out about **goal-setting** and how it affects motivation and levels of stress

To be able to perform at our best in sport, we have to *want* to do well. Some players or performers seem to have the drive to succeed more than others. We refer to this drive to do well as **motivation**.

MOTIVATION

Motivation is often referred to in two ways:

1 Intrinsic motivation

This is the drive to do well that comes from inside yourself. You enjoy the activity and you want to experience the satisfaction and pride of winning, or just taking part.

2 Extrinsic motivation

This is the drive to do well that comes from the outside – in other words, someone or something else giving you the need to do well or just to take part. Extrinsic motivation usually comes in the form of a reward. Many people participate in sport to win something – a badge, trophy or money.

Motivation is the key to success in sport

> MOTIVATION
> The drive to do well. The more drive we have, the more motivated we are to be successful

QUICK TASK

*Think of a sport that you are involved in. Write down all the reasons why you participate in this sport. Then write next to the reasons **intrinsic** or **extrinsic**, depending on whether you feel that the drive to do this sport and to be successful comes from outside or inside yourself.*

Trophies and prizes provide extrinsic motivation

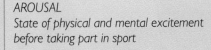

AROUSAL
State of physical and mental excitement before taking part in sport

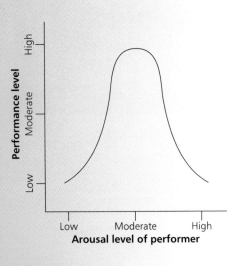

The Inverted U Theory

AROUSAL LEVELS IN SPORT

The more motivated we are, the more **aroused** we are said to be. Our arousal level, or how keen we are to do well, affects how well we do. If we are keen to do well, we are more likely to succeed. However, if we are over-keen to do well, we are said to be **over-aroused** and this can be harmful to our performance.

When we are aroused our bodies prepare for action by:

● Heart beating faster; sweating; slight shaking, breathing more rapidly than usual

Our minds react by:

● Feeling anxious, excited and nervous

Sometimes we have difficulty in getting ourselves physically and mentally ready for sport. Our arousal level is then said to be low. Sometimes we over-react and become too anxious about our sport. Here, our arousal levels may be too high.

If our arousal levels are just right, then we tend to do well in our sport. Finding the right arousal level to get the best possible performance is shown by the **Inverted U Theory** *(left)*.

The graph shows that to do our best in our sport we need to be aroused, but only up to a point. Beyond moderate arousal level, we do not do so well, and our performance level drops.

Factors affecting arousal

The following factors affect our levels of arousal:

- The coach/teacher giving praise or rewards
- The coach/teacher punishing or threatening to punish us if we do not succeed
- Other people watching us or cheering us on
- Other people booing or jeering us
- Being involved in an important competition

Coaches and teachers must be aware of appropriate ways of controlling arousal levels for particular sportsmen or women.

ANXIETY

Quite often, particularly before competitive sports events, we get **anxious** about how well we are going to perform. We often call this type of anxiety **stress.** Although it is quite normal to experience some anxiety, too much can cause us to perform badly and it is important to know how to control it.

Coping with anxiety

If you experience too much anxiety, then you need to find ways to cope with the pressures of your sport. As a coach, it is also important to help performers overcome their fear of failure.

One way to help to increase confidence is through **stress management**. Stress management means lowering your anxiety levels, or calming down. Coaches can do this by:

- **Verbal reassurance** Telling the performer that he or she will succeed, and not to worry
- **Ensuring success** For example, setting the performer a task that is easier to start with, e.g. lowering the bar in the high jump
- **Relaxation** Helping the performer to relax physically by controlled breathing exercises, and by relaxing the major muscle groups
- **Positive thinking** Encouraging the performer to concentrate on success and block out thoughts of failing
- **Imagery** Helping the performer to have calm, relaxing thoughts
- **Mental rehearsal** Encouraging the performer to run through what they need to do in their mind before attempting the real thing, e.g. imagining a perfect golf swing

The pressures of competitive sport can be intense

> ANXIETY
> When arousal levels are too high and we feel under threat, worried and apprehensive

QUICK TASK

List the things that cause you to experience anxiety in your sport, e.g. the risk of injury.

QUICK QUIZ

1) Give an example of **intrinsic** and an example of **extrinsic** motivation in a sport of your choice.

2) Generally, what level of arousal leads to the best performance?

3) What is the name of the theory underlying your answer to Question 2?

4) List three factors which affect arousal levels in a sportsman or woman.

5) Identify as many ways as possible of controlling anxiety in sport.

> **GOAL-SETTING**
> *Establishing aims or objectives to work towards*

GOAL-SETTING

When we say that we are going to achieve something in the future, we set a **goal** or an **aim** that we then work towards.

For example, in sport, we might work towards winning a netball or soccer match – this would be a **short-term goal**; or we might work towards winning the schools' league for our area – a **long-term goal**.

Why set goals?

Setting goals or targets in your sport is important because it helps to:

- Motivate us to try harder and to achieve more
- Control anxiety

Once we have identified what we are trying to do and what we are aiming for, we often feel more motivated to get the job done and to achieve our goal. It is also good for our confidence if we know that we have set a goal that we can eventually reach – even though it may take a lot of hard work to get there.

QUICK TASK

1) Write down some of the things that you want to eventually achieve in your sport, or for a team you play in.

2) The goals that you have mentioned are probably **long-term**, e.g. to be a skilful player. Now think about what you have to do now to achieve these goals – in other words, your **short-term** goals.

   For example, a team player may wish to improve his or her stamina (long-term goal). To achieve this, he or she will need to go running three times a week (short-term goal).

Goals must be challenging but also achievable

Goals set by a coach need to be carefully thought out and considered. Goals that are achievable will help sportsmen or women to control anxiety and stress because they know they are working towards something that is within their reach.

In a team sport it is important that all team members work towards the same goals. For instance, if one person is in the team just to have a good time and does not care about the result, while the rest of the team are keen to win, the team will not play well together and this may cause them to lose matches.

Goal-setting principles

The following points have been highlighted by the **National Coaching Foundation** to make goal-setting more worthwhile and effective. As a coach or player, you can improve by thinking about these points. You can remember them by thinking of the word SMARTER:

- **S** is for **Specific** Goals must be clear and understood by everybody. For instance, the goal *'to play a better basketball game'* is far too vague. The goal should be to improve a specific skill, such as shooting

- **M** is for **Measurable** You must be able to check or assess how well you are doing and so you must be able to measure your goals

- **A** is for **Agreed** Goals which have been shared between the coach and the performer are more likely to be achieved because both know what they are aiming for and have a common purpose. Coaches need to discuss what should be aimed for in the future. Once agreed, these goals can then be written down

- **R** is for **Realistic** As we have identified earlier, goals must be within reach of the performer, but they should not be made too easy, because this will result in the performer not trying very hard

- **T** is for **Time-phased** Short-term goals must be set which lead step-by-step to long-term goals. Each step should be more difficult than the last

- **E** is for **Exciting** Like all training strategies, goals must stimulate the performer and offer rewards, not be monotonous and boring

- **R** is for **Recorded** Goals that are agreed by both the coach and the performer must be written down, and progress recorded. As the short-term goals are achieved, they can be crossed off. This will help to motivate the performer

FAST FORWARD ▷▷

NATIONAL COACHING FOUNDATION   see page 171

QUICK TASK

Robert is really into athletics, especially track events.

1) *Choose one of the SMARTER points – e.g. 'Measurable' – and write down a goal that would meet this requirement.*

2) *Now write down all the other points for Robert: Specific, Agreed, Realistic, Time-phased, Exciting and Recorded.*

S P O R T   I N   A C T I O N

Kate is a discus-thrower. She has been involved in setting goals with her coach, Jane.
Here is how Kate and Jane are putting SMARTER principles into action:

Specific

Kate and Jane have agreed that Kate's long-term goal is to be picked for the All England Championships. The short-term goal is for Kate to improve her turning technique in the throwing circle.

Measurable

Kate's throws will be measured before her technique is refined, then measured again after a period of training.

Agreed

Kate and Jane carefully discuss what they are trying to achieve. It is agreed that Kate's throwing technique should be improved and that her throws will be assessed again after two weeks.

Realistic

Once Kate has mastered the technique, the aim is to produce a throw of a certain distance that is realistic considering her present performance level.

Time-phased

At each training session over the next few weeks, Kate will aim to throw gradually further.

Exciting

The challenge of perfecting a new technique and representing her county will provide the challenge and excitement needed to motivate Kate.

Recorded

The distances which Kate covers in her training throws will be recorded at the end of each session, so that her progress can be mapped. Kate's coach warns her that there may be a decline in performance at first, while she learns the new technique.

Kate and her coach Jane are following a goal-setting regime that should be successful. If after a period of time Kate's distances have not improved significantly, then new goals should be set with the possibility of a new long-term goal, e.g. to get into the All England Championships next season.

M A T C H   I T

TERM	DEFINITION
Extrinsic	When our body goes on the alert
Anxiety	Motivation that comes from outside
Intrinsic	State of worry or apprehension before a competitive event
Arousal	Motivation that comes from within
Goal-setting	Desire to do well
Motivation	Establishing objectives to work towards

✓ R E V I S E   I T !

For your exams you will need to know:

☐ Meaning and examples of intrinsic and extrinsic motivation

☐ Meaning of arousal in sport and its links with motivation

☐ The Inverted U Theory and the relationship between the level of arousal and the quality of performance

☐ About anxiety and its effect on performance

☐ How to control anxiety and stress, and the effects of anxiety on performance

☐ The meaning and different types of goal-setting

☐ The effects of goal-setting on motivation and mental preparation

☐ The SMARTER goal-setting principles, together with practical examples

☐ The meaning of the key words for this chapter

✓ K E Y   W O R D S

Tick each box when you understand the word

MOTIVATION ☐

AROUSAL ☐

ANXIETY ☐

GOAL-SETTING ☐

Exam questions: Factors affecting performance

The questions below are typical of those that you might have to answer in your examination. Try answering each, remembering that the number of marks available for each question gives you a clue to the type of answer required.

Maximum possible marks

1 What is meant by the term **cardiovascular fitness** and can you suggest types of exercises that can be used to improve it? [3]

2 Most sports performers and coaches now use fitness testing as part of a training programme. Give two benefits of regular fitness testing. [2]

3 Describe what the following terms mean in relation to body type: [3]

   a Endomorph

   b Mesomorph

   c Ectomorph

4 What effect does ageing have on the body's ability to perform physical exercise? [4]

5 A balanced diet is an essential part of a healthy lifestyle. Can you identify the **seven** major food groups that should be included in a balanced diet? [7]

6 In order to control our body weight, a simple formula can be used: **Energy Intake = Energy Expenditure**. Can you explain what is meant by these terms and how this formula is used in controlling body weight? [4]

7 What advice would you give a performer who needs to lose weight before the start of a new season? [4]

8 **Dehydration** can have a serious effect on performance. What guidelines should all performers follow during exercise to reduce the risk of dehydration? [3]

9 Why has there been an increase in the number of positive **drug tests** in recent years? [4]

10 What effect do **steroids** have on the body, and why do some performers take this type of drug? [3]

11 What are the negative effects that **alcohol** can have on the body? [5]

12 What problems do sports governing bodies have in trying to detect **drug abuse** amongst sports performers? [3]

Maximum possible marks

3 Name **four** parts of the body that benefit from regular, well-planned exercise. [4]

4 Name **four** different ways of training for fitness. [4]

5 *a* Briefly describe how you should take a person's pulse. [3]

   b What would you expect your **resting pulse** to be? [1]

   c How can knowledge of pulse rates help when planning a training routine? [3]

6 Explain fully the organisation and purpose of the **NCF Multi-stage Fitness Test**. [4]

7 **Skill** is an essential element in developing performance.

   a What is meant by the term **skill**? [2]

   b Why is it important to learn skills to play sport? [2]

8 What is meant by the term **selective attention** and how could a coach use knowledge of this term to help athletes prepare for competition? [4]

9 Explain how **open skills** differ from **closed skills** and give three examples of each. [8]

10 What does the term **transfer of training** mean, and how could a PE teacher use it in their approach to planning lessons? [3]

11 Give an example of each of the following and then explain how they differ: [4]

   a Basic skill

   b Gross motor skills

   c Fine motor skills

12 Suggest **four** factors that could affect a player's performance during a game. [4]

13 What are the **two** forms of memory we use, and how do they differ? [4]

14 What role does **feedback** play in the development and refinement of skills? [4]

Revision guide: Factors affecting performance

These pages summarise the most important areas covered in Chapters 8–13 on factors affecting performance. By fully understanding everything below you will be better prepared to succeed in your examination.

Components of fitness

There are five key components of fitness:
– Cardiovascular endurance
– Muscular strength
– Muscular endurance
– Flexibility
– Body composition

Skill-related fitness
The six components of **skill-related fitness** are:

Agility   Balance
Co-ordination   Power
Reaction time   Speed

Cardiovascular fitness is the ability to exercise for prolonged periods of time – linked to ability to supply oxygen to our muscles. **VO₂ max** is the key measure of cardiovascular fitness.

Tests include **NCF Multi-stage, Harvard Step Test** and **12-minute Cooper Test**.

Muscular strength is the ability to produce force.

Types of strength
There are three main types of strength:
– **Static strength**: e.g. the push in a scrum
– **Explosive strength**: e.g. when a sprinter pushes off from the blocks
– **Dynamic strength**: e.g. balance when skiing
Strength tests include the **hand grip dynamometer**.

Muscular endurance is the ability of a muscle to work for a sustained period of time, important in maintaining good posture. Tests for muscular endurance include the **Sit-up Test**.

Flexibility is the ability of muscles to stretch: important in all sports. Flexibility tests include the **Sit and Reach Test**.

Physique is the size and weight of the body and its composition in terms of tissue such as muscle and fat. Physique plays an important part in our choice of sports and activities.

Body types

There are three main shapes representing extreme versions of human form called **somatotypes**:

Endomorph – pear-shaped
Mesomorph – wedge-shaped and muscular
Ectomorph – linear shape

Body composition

Body tissue can be split into two main groups:

– Body fat
– Fat-free weight

The amount of body fat can be measured using **skinfold callipers.**

Body fat percentage should be controlled, and over 20% body fat (males), over 30% body fat (females) is defined as being **overfat.**

Obesity means over 25% body fat (males), over 35% body fat (females).

Gender differences after puberty
The main difference between the sexes are:

– Body shape and size: males bigger
– Percentage body fat: females have more
– Muscular strength: males stronger
– Oxygen uptake capacity: larger in males
– Flexibility: females more flexible

Age differences
Physiological affects of ageing include:

– Bones become more brittle and joints stiffen
– Muscles and tendons lose elasticity
– Cardiac output reduces and blood pressure increases
– Decrease in lung capacity and VO₂ max
– Increase in body fat

Diet

The food we eat and the liquids we drink help to keep us alive and functioning properly. There are seven major food groups:

– **Carbohydrates**: energy providers
– **Vitamins**: help body's chemical reactions take place
– **Water**: cools body, essential for survival
  Dehydration is lack of water
– **Fats**: another source of energy but only aerobic, also protects body
– **Minerals**: many roles in structure and function of a healthy body
– **Proteins**: building blocks of the body, help build and repair tissues
– **Fibre**: adds bulk to food, helping it pass through digestive system

Balanced diet
'Minus 3 + 1', i.e. *less* fat, *less* salt and *less* sugar, *more* fibre.

Energy Intake = Energy Expenditure – an important equation in maintaining body weight.

To lose weight: reduce energy intake + increase energy expenditure

To gain weight: increase energy intake + reduce energy expenditure

Nutrition for sport

Carbohydrate loading before exercise increases glycogen stores; need to replace fluid throughout exercise by drinking.

Drugs in sport

Substances that chemically or artificially aid performance are called **performance-enhancing drugs**.

The **International Olympic Committee** lists banned drugs and the UK Sports Council carries out drug tests on all performers.

Performers can be tested at any time – at competitions, during training, outside season.

Blood doping: artificially increasing the blood's ability to carry oxygen to the muscles – an advantage in sports that require cardiovascular endurance.

The effects of smoking on the body

– Decrease in lung capacity
– Increase in risk of cancer
– Reduction in the amount of oxygen the blood can carry
– Increased risk of heart disease and damage

The effects of alcohol on the body

– Liver damage
– Damage to digestive system
– Depression and brain damage
– Reaction time slows down
– Damage to body's immune system
– Dehydration
– Increase in body weight

Further reading

● Davis, D., Kimmer, T., and Auty. M., *Physical Education: Theory and Practice*, Macmillan Australia, 1986

● Dick, F., *Sports Training Principles*, A & C Black, 1989

● Esbuys, J., Guest, V., and Lawrence, J., *Fundamentals of Health And Physical Education*, Heinemann, 1987

● Hazeldine, R., *Fitness For Sport*, Gowood Press, 1985

● Honeybourne, J., Hill, M., and Moors, H., *Advanced Physical Education And Sport*, Stanley Thornes, 1996

● Sharp, R., *Acquiring Skill In Sport*, Sports Dynamics, 1992

● Parish, W., *Training For Peak Performance*, A & C Black, 1991

Health-related Exercise

The aim of this chapter is to help you:

○ Define the term **health**

○ Understand what makes up a healthy lifestyle

○ Define the term **exercise**

○ Be able to use the **FITT** principles of exercise planning

○ Know about the importance of **warming up** before exercise and **cooling down** after exercise

Keeping fit has now become a very popular pastime. Large amounts of money are spent on various different ways of getting fit. Aerobics, step aerobics, aqua-aerobics and jogging have all been recent health fashions. All of these types of activities help improve people's health and fitness, but all do it differently. Everybody has different needs in terms of health and fitness.

HEALTH

In Chapter 8 we defined and discussed what we meant by the term **fitness**. Although the terms **health** and **fitness** are often used together, they are actually two different concepts. To be healthy means to feel well and be free from disease. Fitness is one way of developing a healthy lifestyle, but there are also many other ways of getting healthy.

A healthy lifestyle

In order to keep healthy, we have to look after our bodies and minds. Feeling good and looking good will make our lives more enjoyable. There are four main components that make up a healthy lifestyle:

HEALTH
A state of physical, mental and emotional well-being in which we are free from illness or injury

◀◀ **REWIND**

FITNESS   see page 52

---

1 Exercise

Exercise keeps the body in good physical condition. Unlike most machines, the body's main motor, the heart, actually works better the more it is worked. Other organs and body systems also work better if the body is exercised regularly. The minimum amount of exercise recommended is three times a week for approximately 20 minutes. The **intensity** of the exercise needs to be enough to make you breathless.

2 Diet

The key is maintaining a balance, or having a **balanced diet**. In order to stay healthy, our bodies need:

- Carbohydrates (e.g. from potatoes or pasta)
- Protein (e.g. from meat, fish or soya beans)
- Vitamins (e.g. from fresh fruit)
- Minerals (e.g. from milk)
- Fats (e.g. from margarine, cheese and oils)

If this balance is not right, there may be important consequences for health. Serious under-eating may lead to a condition known as **anorexia**, causing severe loss of weight and ill health. Alternatively, a high-fat diet or lack of exercise may cause people to be overweight for their age and height. The extreme form of this condition is **obesity**, where people eat far too much of all or some dietary elements.

The actual amount of food we need depends on our individual **body type**. It will also depend on how much – and what sort of – exercise we take. Most sports performers need to eat more since they burn off a lot of energy. For example, an Olympic rower needs up to 6,000 **kilocalories** a day.

3 Hygiene

Hygiene involves keeping yourself clean. **Personal hygiene** has an important effect on how your body functions and how you perform in sporting activities.

When we exercise or exert ourselves, our bodies sweat. After playing sport, it is important to wash away this sweat, and also the grime and dirt we pick up when we fall! Sweat can create body odour, which can be unpleasant for our friends and family.

There are also two specific hyiene problems often associated with sport:

- A **verruca** is a viral infection usually affecting the feet, and often associated with swimming pools. If you get a verruca, your chemist will be able to suggest an appropriate treatment. If the problem persists, or more verrucas appear, see your doctor straight away

---

EXERCISE
Physical activity that improves health and fitness

INTENSITY
How hard we exercise or exert ourselves

BALANCED DIET
Diet that provides all the necessary nutrients, or things our bodies need, in the right amounts

◀◀ **REWIND**

NUTRIENTS   see page 69

◀◀ **REWIND**

BODY TYPES   see page 62

◀◀ **REWIND**

KILOCALORIE   see page 71

PERSONAL HYGIENE
Keeping your body clean and healthy – for example, washing after exercise

QUICK QUIZ

1) Approximately how many kilocalories does an Olympic rower need in one day?

2) What is the main symptom of the disease anorexia?

3) On average how many hours of sleep do most people need?

● **Athlete's foot** is a fungal infection, which makes the skin between the toes white, flakey and uncomfortable. As with verrucas, it needs curing immediately, since it can spread very quickly. Many chemists now sell products both to prevent and treat athlete's foot

4 Rest

Lack of sleep, or feeling tired, is another factor that can affect our performance. On average most people require at least eight hours sleep to function properly. Sports performers may need more than this. Insufficient sleep can reduce our performance in sports. Since we have less energy, our skill level falls and we cannot concentrate on the task in hand.

DEFINING EXERCISE

Exercise can improve both our health and fitness, and should involve using as much of the body as possible. Exercise involves the use of **gross motor skills**.

Exercise has two benefits:

● **Short-term** These are effects that happen during the activity itself. For example, the heart rate will increase, which in turn increases the flow and pressure of the blood. Although these will return to normal at the end of the exercise, they will contribute to the long-term benefits of exercise

● **Long-term** These are lasting changes that take place in response to regular physical activity. All these effects help the body to work more efficiently and deal better with the demands that we place on it when we take part in sport

SHORT-TERM EXERCISE EFFECTS
Temporary changes which take place in the body during physical activity

LONG-TERM EXERCISE EFFECTS
Lasting changes which result from regular exercise

Regular aerobic exercise can benefit the body system in the long term

Many people now regularly visit fitness centres

For example, if you train three times a week for twelve weeks as suggested above, you will find yourself able do to the training more easily towards the end of the period. This is because your body has adapted to the exercise and improved its performance.

Long-term adaptations to exercise include the following:

- The heart becomes stronger, bigger and capable of pumping more blood around the body

- The lungs get more oxygen to the muscles

- Blood volume increases, so more oxygen can be carried

- Muscles increase in size and strength

EXERCISE PLANNING

In order to reap the full benefits of exercise, you need to train in a specific way. The whole point of training is to improve your level of fitness. But you will only improve your level of fitness if you **overload** your body.

If you overload your body it will gradually adapt to the new level of work and your level of fitness will improve. However, remember it is dangerous to overload the body too much. The increase in workload needs to be gradual – a little at a time.

FITT principles

To reach this overload, when planning your training programmes, use the **FITT** principles:

- **F** is for **Frequency** – This means the number of times you train (for example, three times a week)

- **I** is for **Intensity** – How hard you work.

- **T** is for **Time** – How long you train. Increasing the duration of exercise increases the overload on your body.

- **T** is for **Type** of activity – Some training is very specific to certain kinds of sport. The problem here is that it may be boring, so many people practise **cross training**.

Warming up and cooling down

An essential part of any training sessions should be the **warm up** and **cool down**. These not only reduce the risk of injury but may help you to concentrate better on the activity as well.

The warm up
The warm up helps to prepare the body for the physical exercise to come. By gently raising your pulse rate, it prepares the heart for more strenuous activity. The body starts to transport more oxygen and other fuels to the muscles, which become warm and ready for exercise.

OVERLOAD
To make your body work harder than normal

In weightlifting, overload is achieved by lifting progressively heavier weights

WARM UP/COOL DOWN
Necessary routine before and after exercise or physical activity

Skills practice should be included in the warm up

The warm up should have three phases:

● **Pulse raiser** This is normally a gentle movement such as jogging or skipping that will gently raise the pulse rate

● **Stretch** Stretching the joints and muscles to be used in the exercise warms them and reduces the risk of injury

● **Skills practice** This involves practising some of the individual skills needed in the activity. Footballers, for example, often finish their warm up by practising passing skills or taking shots at the goal

The cool down

The purpose of the **cool down** is to help the body return to its normal state as quickly as possible. Generally it should involve exercise using the whole body, as in the pulse raiser in the warm up, followed by gentle stretching. A thorough cool down routine will help keep the blood flow high, wash out all the waste products the muscles have produced and replenish the fuel stores. A cool down also allows the muscles to return to their normal temperature slowly, and reduces the risk of damage due to a sudden drop in temperature.

QUICK TASK

1) Tariq is hoping to become a sprinter. He is reasonably fit but would like to train over the summer holidays, specifically for sprinting 100m and 200m.

Can you suggest a training programme he could follow to achieve this?

2) Now apply the FITT principles to your particular sport.

After strenuous exercise, a cool down helps the body get back to normal

SPORT IN ACTION

Choose one of your GCSE sports and list the types of training you could do for it.

From your knowledge of the effects of training, write down the benefits they could bring.

MATCH IT

TERM	DEFINITION
Warm up	Making your body work harder than normal
FITT	Means of improving levels of fitness
Overload	Frequency, Intensity, Time, Type of activity
Cool down	Helps body get back to normal after exercise
Exercise	Helps prepare the body for physical exercise

QUICK QUIZ

1) Why do we need a warm up before exercise?

2) At what point in a training session would you do a cool down?

3) What are the three phases that all warm ups should contain?

4) What is the purpose of the first phase of the warm up?

✓ KEY WORDS

Tick each box when you understand the word

HEALTH ☐

FITNESS ☐

EXERCISE ☐

INTENSITY ☐

BALANCED DIET ☐

SHORT/LONG-TERM EXERCISE EFFECTS ☐

FITT ☐

WARM UP/COOL DOWN ☐

✓ REVISE IT!

For your exams you will need to know:

☐ What is meant by the FITT principles

☐ The role of diet in healthy living

☐ How under- or over-eating can affect health

☐ The importance of cleanliness and personal hygiene in promoting a healthy lifestyle

☐ How rest or fatigue can affect sporting performance

☐ The meaning of the key words for this chapter

Training Methods

The aim of this chapter is to help you to:

○ Understand the principles of training

○ Know the difference between the different forms of training

○ Explain and give examples of **endurance training**

○ Explain and give examples of **interval training**

○ Explain and give examples of **weight training**

○ Explain and give examples of **flexibility** of training

Everyone can benefit from training, not just top-class athletes, provided the training programme followed is at the right level.

In order for your training to be safe and effective, you must plan your programme carefully. We will discuss the basic principles of training below. By following these principles, you should be able to plan an effective training programme of your own.

◄◄ **REWIND**

FITNESS   see page 52

THE PRINCIPLES OF TRAINING

The five principles of training are designed to help you to get **fit** safely. They are:

● **Overload** Making the body work harder

● **Progression** Gradually increasing the workload as you train

● **Specificity** Choosing the right training for the sport

● **Reversibility** Understanding that fitness cannot be stored for future use and will disappear if you stop training

● **Variance** Varying the training in order to keep yourself motivated

Jogging and running are good examples of aerobic or endurance training

Endurance or aerobic training

Endurance training will help you to keep playing longer and at a higher intensity. This is also known as **aerobic training** since it improves the aerobic systems of the body. The aerobic systems include the heart, lungs and vascular system. Activities such as brisk walking, jogging, running, cycling, swimming and rowing are ideal examples of aerobic training.

Endurance training should involve the whole body. It is continuous, which means you do not stop to rest. It is also **sub-maximal**, meaning that you do not work flat out. In order to achieve adaptations this type of training should last at least 12 minutes.

> SUB-MAXIMAL
> Not working flat out, but hard enough to be breathless at the end of the session

'Fartlek' training, or 'speed play'

Fartlek is another type of training that can be used to develop endurance. This is a system of running where the performer runs fast and slow, both over hills and on the flat. A typical session will include steady-paced running, sprints, hill work and some slower 'recovery' running.

> FARTLEK
> Swedish for 'speed play'. System of running designed to develop endurance

> **INTERVAL TRAINING**
> Form of training in which periods of activity are interspersed with short periods of rest

Interval training

The purpose of **interval training** is to develop both the anaerobic and aerobic systems. This type of training is popular since a lot of sports require both types of system to produce energy.

In interval training, periods of exercise are followed by short periods of rest. The rest period is very important, since the quicker the body can replace oxygen and other fuels, the better it will work. There are four main components of an interval training session which can be combined in various ways:

- **Duration** – How long you work for
- **Intensity** – How hard you work
- **Duration** of the recovery period
- **Number** of work/recovery intervals

Examples of intervals used in training for track events are:

- 10 x 60 metres in 8 seconds with 90 seconds rest
- 10 x 200 metres in 30 seconds with 90 seconds rest
- 5 x 400 metres in 80 seconds with 160 seconds rest

> **REPETITION**
> The number of times that an athlete repeats a particular exercise – for example, ten arm curls

> **SET**
> A certain number of repetitions. For example, ten arm curls might equal one set

> **FREE WEIGHTS**
> Weights consisting of bars and discs, the discs being added to the bars to increase the weight

Weight training

In order to improve your strength, you need to work against some form of resistance. In **weight training** this resistance is provided either by the weights themselves or by the weight machine you lift or push against.

Weight training programmes are made up of **repetitions** and **sets**. The number of repetitions performed is one set. Usually three sets are completed in a session. Weight training has the advantage that a variety of activities can be performed and every part of the body can be exercised. Overload is developed by progressively increasing the weight you work against.

The amount of weight you lift can be varied. With **free weights** this is done by adding more weight discs to the bar. With a weights machine, this is usually achieved with a pin being moved down a stack of weights.

To improve strength you should train two or three times a week and your programme should continue for at least ten weeks.

Weight training can be used to develop strength throughout the body

WEIGHT TRAINING BENEFITS	
Exercise	**Body part worked**
Arm curl	Upper and lower arm
Bench press	Chest
Heel raise	Lower leg
Squat	Back and upper leg

Flexibility training

This type of training is very important, but is often overlooked by performers, even though it may be included in their warm up and cool down.

Flexibility is achieved by stretching and moving the joint to just beyond its point of resistance. The principle is to stretch the ligaments and tendons so that the joints are more mobile. This allows a greater range of movement and reduces the risk of joint injury. Swimmers, for example, will be able to produce more effective strokes if they are flexible.

For improvements in flexibility, a stretch should be held for at least ten seconds. This type of training needs to be done at least three times a week.

Examples of flexibility exercises

FLEXIBILITY
The range of movement around a joint, or how freely you can move limbs

QUICK TASK

Which stretching exercises would help develop flexibility in the following joints?

a) *Neck*
b) *Shoulder*
c) *Elbow*
d) *Hips*
e) *Knee*
f) *Ankle*

QUICK QUIZ

1) *In weight training, what provides the resistance to work against?*

2) *What type of weight training will produce explosive strength?*

3) *How would the principle of overload be applied to weight training?*

S P O R T   I N   A C T I O N

Three athletes at your school are: Dennis, a sprinter, Ian, a gymnast, and Kerry, a swimmer. They have asked you to help them develop a training programme that will enable them to improve their performance in their chosen sport.

Dennis

Ian

Kerry

1) What area do you think each of them needs to work on for their sport, e.g. strength, flexibility?

2) What type of training should they do, and how frequently? (Try and use the FITT principle discussed in the chapter.)

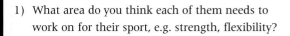

S P O R T   I N   A C T I O N

1) Describe some of the activities you might include in a Fartlek session.

2) Plan a 20-minute Fartlek session that would be appropriate for your level of fitness. You could you use your school fields or areas around your own home to run over different terrain.

M A T C H   I T

TRAINING	PURPOSE
Weight training	Increase range of mobility in the joints
Fartlek	Improve strength of the muscles
Flexibility training	Improving the body's aerobic capacity
Continuous running	Help to develop ability to change pace
Interval training	Improving the body's recovery systems

✓ K E Y   W O R D S

Tick each box when you understand the word

SUB-MAXIMAL ☐

FARTLEK ☐

INTERVAL TRAINING ☐

REPETITION ☐

SET ☐

FLEXIBILITY ☐

✓ R E V I S E   I T !

For your exams you will need to know:

☐ The five principles of training and how they are used in planning training programmes

☐ The following methods of training:

- Continuous
- Fartlek
- Interval
- Weight/resistance
- Flexibility

☐ What is meant by repetitions and sets

☐ The meaning of the key words for this chapter

Effects of Training
and Activity

The aim of this chapter is to help you:

- Understand the **short-term effects** of activity on the body

- Learn the effects of training on the **skeletal** system

- Learn the effect of training on the **muscular** system

- Learn the effect of training on the **cardiovascular** system

- Learn the effect of training on the **respiratory** system.

In Chapter 14 we identified the long-term and short-term effects of training. In this chapter we will discuss these in more detail and look specifically at how training affects the different body systems. As we saw earlier, regular training will result in adaptation of our bodies. This is one of the reasons we train. The type of training undertaken determines what adaptations take place.

SHORT-TERM EFFECTS OF TRAINING

When the body starts to do physical activity, a number of changes take place. When the body is working, it needs to transport more fuel and oxygen to the muscles and take away waste products more quickly. However, when the activity finishes, these effects will cease and the body will return to its normal state.

The exact amount of change will depend on the intensity (low or hard) and duration (how long) of the exercise.

The following changes will take place during exercise:

The heart

Exercise will cause the brain to increase the number of nerve signals it sends to the heart. This will cause an increase in **heart rate.**

◀◀ **REWIND**

LONG AND   see page 108
SHORT-TERM
EFFECTS OF TRAINING

SHORT-TERM EFFECT
Temporary changes to the body that occur during physical activity

◀◀ **REWIND**

HEART RATE   see page 26

SHORT TERM BENEFITS OF TRAINING

Body part	Effect
Heart	Increase in heart rate More blood pumped around body
Lungs	Increase in breathing rate and depth More oxygen taken into body
Blood	Pumped faster around body Becomes more acidic as lactic acid increases Blood pressure rises
Muscles	Produce heat Use up energy fuels Produce energy/movement

As these athletes start the race, their bodies will experience a number of changes

◀◀ REWIND

HORMONES   see page 44

◀◀ REWIND

LACTIC ACID   see page 36

Hormones

Just before exercise and during the initial exercising period, the body will also release a **hormone** called **adrenaline**, which increases both the heart rate and how hard the heart pumps out the blood. This happens so that the working parts of the body (the muscles) receive enough blood to work properly.

Lungs

Because the body is working hard, it requires more oxygen. To meet this demand, the lungs have to work harder and faster. They take in more air (inspiration) and blow more air out (expiration).

Blood

This is the major transport system of the body. It carries fuel and oxygen to the muscles and takes away the waste products of energy production. **Lactic acid** is the main waste product from the working muscle, and the blood takes this to the liver, where it can be disposed of.

The rate at which the blood passes around the body, and blood pressure, will also increase during exercise. The **arterieoles** (smaller arteries) dilate, or get bigger, so that more blood can pass through them. This is called **vasodilation**. In areas of the body that are not needed during exercise, such as the kidneys and stomach, the opposite may occur: the arteries get smaller, so restricting the amount of blood that can flow through them. This is called **vasoconstriction**.

The muscles

When the muscles work hard they use up more energy, so more energy has to be produced. In some cases the fuel store may become completely exhausted. This may happen if the body has to work for a very long time, as in a marathon.

Heat is produced by the working muscles and this will cause the body's temperature to rise. In order to get rid of this heat, the body sweats.

> VASODILATION
> *Where the diameter of a blood vessel increases as surrounding muscles relax*

> VASOCONSTRICTION
> *Where the diameter of a blood vessel decreases as surrounding muscles contract*

S P O R T   I N   A C T I O N

Draw a simple diagram of the human body and identify each main body part. Summarise the short-term effects of physical activity on each of the organs you have identified.

Make sure you put the effects in the right place!

LONG-TERM EFFECTS OF TRAINING AND ACTIVITY

Effects of training on the skeletal system

One of the long-term effects of training is the strengthening of the skeleton. The skeleton plays a key role in all physical activity. It provides the frame so that we can move around, and provides attachment to the muscles. A healthy skeleton is essential for a healthy life. As we get older, our bones and joints begin to wear out. Exercise can be used in order to slow down this process.

The main effects of regular training on the skeletal system are:

- Tendons become stronger

- **Ligaments** are stretched so they become looser and more flexible

- Calcium is added to bony tissue, strengthening the bones

- Cartilage at the ends of the bones gets thicker, cushioning more of the shock in the joints

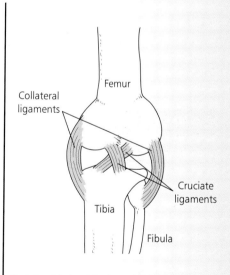

Front view of the knee joint showing how ligaments bind the joint together

> LIGAMENT
> *Strong non-elastic tissue that connects bone to bone, normally found at a joint*

HYPERTROPHY
Where a body part grows in size due to increased use

MUSCLE MYOGLOBIN
The substance that absorbs oxygen from the blood and takes it to mitochondria in the muscles

MITOCHONDRIA
'Powerhouse' sites where most of the energy for muscle movement is produced

QUICK QUIZ

1) *Which type of training effects occur during exercise – short or long-term?*

2) *During physical activity, what happens to the heart rate?*

3) *When vasoconstriction occurs, what happens to the blood vessels?*

4) *What effect does adrenaline have on the body?*

The muscular system

Several changes occur in the muscles as result of regular training. First, the muscle will increase in both size and strength. This is called **muscle hypertrophy**.

As oxygen is important in producing energy in the muscle, much of the adaptations to training are concerned with increasing the amount of oxygen the muscle can use.

The main effects are:

● An increase in **muscle myoglobin**

● An increase in **muscle mitochondria**

● The muscle energy stores are improved. This allows the muscle to work harder and longer

Regular weight training will lead to muscle hypertrophy

SPORT IN ACTION

Look at the table on page 118. Can you summarise the *long-term* effects of training in a similar table?

The cardiovascular system

The cardiovascular system is the system that takes the blood carrying the oxygen and energy stores around the body. **Aerobic exercise** leads to positive physiological adaptations to this system after a few weeks of regular training.

The cardio-vascular system is made up of two parts: the heart and the blood vessels. The main effects on this system are:

- The heart responds in the same way as other muscles, and regular training will cause hypertrophy of the heart. This means it will get bigger and stronger, so that it can pump more blood with each beat. When the body is at rest, the heart rate will actually be lower, as the heart can pump the same amount of blood in fewer beats

- Blood volume will increase. This will be of benefit, since the blood will then be able to carry more oxygen.

The respiratory system

As the oxygen transport system improves with exercise, the body will require more oxygen to use. This is provided by the lungs, which also improve with training. The main effects of exercise on the respiratory system are:

- The muscles around the ribs become more efficient, making breathing more efficient

- The amount of air the lungs can take in, i.e. the **lung volume**, will increase

- Because the surface area of the lungs is increased, more oxygen can be transferred from the air in the lungs to the blood capillaries

- Because more oxygen reaches the muscles, the **VO$_2$ max** will also increase

◄◄ **REWIND**

AEROBIC SYSTEM see page 36

QUICK QUIZ

1) What effect will hypertrophy have on the strength of the heart?

2) What does the cardiovascular system include?

3) What happens to the number of red blood cells as a result of regular training?

4) Will the heart rate at rest be lower or higher as a result of training?

◄◄ **REWIND**

LUNG VOLUME see page 33

◄◄ **REWIND**

VO$_2$ MAX see page 53

QUICK TASK

Look at the following exercises that might be included in a training session. Which joint or joints are being used for each exercise? (You may find it helpful to refer back to Chapter 2, page 8.)

M A T C H   I T

ADAPTATION	BODY SYSTEM
Muscle hypertrophy	Cardiovascular
Increased capillaries	Skeletal
More efficient respiratory muscles	Respiratory system
Increase in myoglobin	Muscular system
Better deposition of calcium	Muscular system

✓ K E Y   W O R D S

Tick each box when you understand the word

SHORT-TERM EFFECT ☐

VASODILATION ☐

VASOCONSTRICTION ☐

HYPERTROPHY ☐

✓ R E V I S E   I T !

For your exams you will need to know:

☐ Long-term and short-term effects of exercise on the body

☐ Specific effects on the body's systems, muscles (size) and joints

☐ Long-term effect of training on the heart (heart rate and output)

☐ Long-term effect of training on the respiratory system (rate, amount, VO_2 max)

☐ The meaning of the key words for this chapter

Safe Practice in PE and Sport

The aim of this chapter is to help you:

- Understand the importance of **health and safety** when planning or taking part in sports and games

- Recognise the importance of wearing the correct **clothing** and **footwear** for specific activities

- Recognise the importance of using the correct **equipment** and **playing surfaces**

- Be able to use the correct principles of health and safety when planning sports activities

Sport can be fast and thrilling. But it can often involve equipment and apparatus that could, if used wrongly, cause injury and harm. Sport often involves lots of people in confined spaces where the risk of collision is great. It is therefore important that all concerned in leading and participating in sports abide by the rules and guidelines. Some general principles relate to all sports. Others are more specific and are written down in rule books issued by sports governing bodies.

HEALTH AND SAFETY

The **Health and Safety at Work Act of 1974** applies to all activities in schools. It ensures that both teachers and pupils work in a safe and healthy environment. As PE and sport take place in a number of different environments and involve potentially dangerous activities, all PE departments have to have specific health and safety plans to ensure that activities are carried out in a safe and controlled way.

Similarly, each sports governing body produces health and safety guidelines for their sport. These enable all those playing these sports to do so in safety.

A PE lesson will often start with the teacher explaining the safety rules for an activity

> HEALTH AND SAFETY AT WORK ACT
> Legislation designed to ensure that pupils and teachers work in a safe and healthy environment

Safety guidelines

There are a number of key safety guidelines that apply to all sports:

- **Obey the rules** The rules of sport are written to ensure fair competition and safety for all

- **Wear the correct clothing or footwear** This is particularly important for outdoor sports such as skiing and canoeing

- **Only use the correct equipment** The equipment you use should not be faulty or broken

- **Always remember to warm up before and cool down at the end** This is discussed more fully in Chapter 14

- **Games should always be balanced in competition** This usually means that only people of the same age, size and sex should play against each other. Playing against people who are much older or bigger than you could cause you injury.

◄◄ REWIND

WARM UP/COOL DOWN
see page 109

SPORT IN ACTION

Can you think of any safety rules you have been taught in your practical PE lessons? Give some safety guidelines for the following PE activities:

1) Swimming   2) Throwing events in athletics   3) Gymnastics

---

QUICK TASK

Below is a list of sports. Write down the correct clothing and/or footwear and equipment for each activity:

a) Swimming
b) Hockey
c) Netball
d) Squash
e) Athletics
f) Cycling
g) Badminton
h) Trampoline
i) Judo
j) American football

SAFETY CLOTHING
Clothing or sports wear designed to prevent injury to the wearer and allow free movement. Can include lifesaving properties

CLOTHING AND FOOTWEAR

To ensure the safety of those taking part, different activities require different clothing. Correct clothing and footwear will also allow the person to perform to the best of their ability.

You should always change into a different set of clothing when you are doing PE or playing sport. Kit should prevent injury to the wearer and should allow free movement. Jewellery and other personal effects should be removed. These could cause injury to the wearer and to others.

In outdoor sports, correct clothing is even more important. Often **safety clothing** will include lifesaving qualities, such as the warmth and protection of a good coat when walking, or a lifejacket for sailing or canoeing.

Here are some key guidelines for wearing the correct kit:

- Clothing should allow unrestricted movement, but not be too loose

- Jewellery and watches, etc., should be taken off and long hair tied back

- In contact sports, players should always wear protective clothing such as shin pads and gum/mouth shields to help prevent injury

- On grass surfaces, studded boots should be worn, but these should be regularly checked for wear and tear and sharp edges. Many sports now insist that studs meet kitemark regulations

- For general games, wear good footwear that provides grip and support, especially for the ankle.

- Never chew gum or sweets while playing sports

Sports equipment

Sports equipment comes in a variety of shapes and sizes and may have many different functions. Some equipment may be thrown (javelin and discus), while in other sports, equipment may be part of the actual pitch you play on – for example, the posts in football and rugby. In sports such as cricket, the equipment is an essential part of the game. In all cases you should always check equipment before starting to play.

Faulty equipment can lead to injury to yourself or other players. Here is a quick checklist for anybody who uses equipment in a sport:

- **Look** Are there any signs of damage or wear?

- **Feel** Pick up the bat or stick. Does it feel stable? Are there any rough or sharp edges?

- If in doubt, ask your teacher or coach to take a look

- **Goalposts** should be firmly anchored in the ground. Posts for games such as rugby and American football should be padded to prevent injury in the event of collision

- In throwing events such as discus and javelin, equipment should be especially carefully checked. These are potentially very dangerous objects and should never be thrown when people are in the line of flight. Most athletics tracks have special cages which should always be used when throwing.

In some outdoor activities, correct clothing can mean the difference between life and death

QUICK QUIZ

1) Where would you find the rules for a specific sport?

2) The rules of sport ensure safety for all. What else do they help to enforce?

3) What should you do before any sporting activity?

Far left: Padding must be used on posts to prevent injuries

Left: Safety equipment such as the throwing cage has been specially developed to reduce the risk of injury

QUICK TASK

Below is a list of several sports you may have taken part in at school or college. Make a list of the equipment needed for each. What are the safety factors that must be checked for each one?

a)   *Football*
b)   *Hockey*
c)   *Gymnastics*
d)   *Cricket/rounders*
e)   *Basketball/netball*
f)   *Athletics*

GENERAL SAFETY PRINCIPLES
Commonsense procedures to avoid the risk of accidents or injuries when playing sport

SAFETY EQUIPMENT
Sports equipment specially developed to reduce the risk of accident or injury

FAST FORWARD ▷▷

FIRST AID   see page 132

Playing surface

The playing surface is an important element in the safety of a game. Hard or uneven surfaces can cause injury if players trip and fall, or if the ball – say, in hockey or cricket – is hit towards them and bounces unpredictably.

There may also be objects on the pitch or court that can cause injury. Litter such as glass and tin cans can often accumulate on playing fields that are open to the public. This should always be removed before play starts. In winter, outdoor pitches may be affected by frost, making them too hard to play on. Football and rugby matches often have to be cancelled for this reason during the winter months.

Fallen leaves can also pose a hazard on playing areas such as netball pitches, creating a slippery surface.

GENERAL SAFETY PRINCIPLES

If you are planning a sports activity, you need to think carefully about **general safety principles**. The success and enjoyment of the activity will be spoilt if players are injured. Although accidents do happen, it is important to make both the environment and the activities themselves as safe as possible.

Safety checklist

Some of the areas to consider are:

● **Group size** How many people will take part? Is there enough space and equipment? Will there be enough teachers or officials to supervise everyone?

● **Equipment** Has it been checked for damage or wear? Where necessary, have you provided **safety equipment** such as pads or helmets?

● **Playing surface** Is the ground or pitch fit to play on? Often it will be the job of the referee in a match to inspect the pitch. Are there any objects on it such as stones, glass or litter that could cause injury?

● **Rules of the game** Do all the players know the rules of the sport? The safest way to play is to obey the rules. It may be necessary to remind players of the rules, especially those that deal specifically with safety

● **First Aid** Is there provision for First Aid, including a First Aid kit with basic materials to treat injuries? Just as important, is there somebody who knows how to use it?

● **Emergency procedures** In the event of an accident or injury, is there a phone nearby or a medically trained person on standby?

MATCH IT

HAZARD	PREVENTION
Pulled muscles	Make sure posts are padded at bottom
Broken glass on pitch	Wear mouth guards/gum shields in contact sports
Damage to teeth/mouth	Always check equipment for damage before playing
Sharp edges to hockey stick	Always check playing surface before playing
Injury from collision with posts	Always check nobody is in the throwing area or line of flight
People being hit by thrown objects	Always warm up before starting to play

✓ REVISE IT!

For your exams you will need to know:

☐ Why it is important to try and prevent injury

☐ The safety precautions you should take when planning sports sessions

☐ The importance of:
- Warm up/cool down
- Safe playing surface
- Safe equipment
- Correct use of technique and obeying of rules

☐ What is meant by First Aid provision and emergency procedure

☐ The meaning of the key words for this chapter

✓ KEY WORDS

Tick each box when you understand the word

HEALTH AND SAFETY AT WORK ACT ☐

SAFETY EQUIPMENT ☐

SAFETY CLOTHING ☐

GENERAL SAFETY PRINCIPLES ☐

18

Sports Injuries and First Aid

The aim of this chapter is to help you:

◯ Understand the nature of **injury** in sport

◯ Look at the way injuries can occur in sport

◯ Look at the way injuries can be treated

◯ Understand and be able to use the principles of **First Aid**

QUICK TASK

Find out which organisations provide First Aid training in your area. Your local library may be a good place to start.

Sport is a dynamic activity. When we play, we push our bodies to the limit and this can lead to injury. There are several different types of sports injury and we will discuss these below, together with the basic principles of First Aid treatment.

Note: **If you want to be able to help someone who is injured, it is recommended that you complete a recognised First Aid course before practising any of the activities suggested here.**

THE NATURE OF SPORTS INJURY

Injuries in sport tend to fall into two categories:

● **Impact injuries** occur where there is a sudden stress on the body – for example, from a collision between players in rugby, or from being hit by the ball in hockey. Impact injuries tend to be associated with **contact sports**

● **Overuse injuries** develop over time – for example, tennis and golf elbow, or leg injuries to runners. They tend to be associated with sports that demand a lot of training, but they can occur in any sport and at any level of performance

Injuries in sport can also result from environmental factors – for example, playing on a surface which has been made slippery by rain.

The dynamic nature of sport means that there is always a risk of injury

CONTACT SPORTS
Team sports in which physical contact such as tackling is allowed

Joint and muscle injuries

These can result from either stress or overuse. They include:

- **Strains** The muscle is overstretched or twisted, causing pain and restricting movement

- **Pulled muscle** The muscle fibres are torn or over-stretched, as with a strain. Can be a very painful injury

- **Sprains** The ligaments are overstretched or torn at a joint, causing pain and limiting movement

- **Dislocation** The bone is jolted out of its normal position at the joint. Dislocations are serious injuries and require treatment by experts. They are often caused by collisions and are especially common at the shoulder and fingers

- **Tennis and golf elbow** Overuse injuries to the lower arm. In tennis elbow, the elbow becomes inflamed around the end of the ulna, making it painful and tender to the touch. In golf elbow there are similar symptoms, but the pain is on the inside of the elbow. In both cases, the only treatment is rest

Skin damage and injury

The skin is often the most vulnerable part of the body. Cuts, grazes and blisters are common injuries when playing sport.

- **Cuts** The skin is broken and bleeding occurs. Often caused by severe rubbing or by a sharp object coming into contact with the skin. Where bleeding occurs, there is an added risk of infection, so cuts should be treated immediately

- **Grazes** Caused by friction between the skin and another surface, often the playing surface. Best avoided by wearing knee and elbow pads when skateboarding or rollerblading

- **Blisters** Repeated friction on the skin causes the layers to separate and fill with fluid, creating a small swelling. Best avoided by wearing the correct size and type of footwear

- **Bruises** Swelling caused by sudden impact. Broken blood vessels leak blood which is trapped beneath the skin. Although painful, bruises are not generally serious

Concussion

In a severe collision or fall, you could suffer from concussion or even lose consciousness. **Concussion** is caused by the brain being violently shaken or jolted. It is a serious injury and should be treated by experts. Symptoms include dizziness and feeling sick. The victim should not continue playing, but should rest and receive appropriate medical treatment. After suffering concussion you should not play sport until you are completely recovered. This could take several weeks.

QUICK TASK

Of the following sports, which would you expect to be associated with stress and which with overuse injuries?

a)   Tennis
b)   Rugby
c)   American football
d)   Marathon running
e)   Rowing
f)   Hockey
g)   Javelin

Overuse of the arm can lead to a condition known as tennis elbow

AVOIDING INJURY IN SPORT

- *MAKE SURE YOU ARE FIT TO PLAY THE SPORT YOU CHOOSE*

- *USE THE CORRECT EQUIPMENT AND WEAR THE CORRECT CLOTHING AND FOOTWEAR*

- *ALWAYS OBEY THE RULES OF THE GAME*

- *ALWAYS START WITH A WARM UP AND FINISH WITH A COOL DOWN*

- *KNOW THE SAFETY PRECAUTIONS FOR YOUR SPORT*

- *KNOW YOUR LIMITATIONS AND DO NOT TRY TO EXCEED THEM*

Wearing the correct safety equipment will help prevent injury in the event of falls

Dehydration

This occurs when the body loses too much water, usually as a result of sweating. Dehydration can seriously affect performance, and all sports performers should take plenty to drink before, during and after sport. In endurance events such as marathon running and cycling, it is especially important to take regular drinks of water or special sports drinks.

Hypothermia

This is a potentially fatal condition in which the temperature of the body drops below its normal level of 37°C following prolonged exposure to cold or wet conditions. Although the risk is confined to outdoor sports – for example, canoeing or mountain walking – it is vital to recognise the signs of hypothermia and give treatment immediately.

TREATMENT OF INJURIES

If you suffer an injury while playing sport, stop playing, identify the problem and try to treat it. The immediate action is to get away from the pitch or playing area and seek appropriate help.

The RICE Principle

> RICE
> Rest, Ice, Compression, Elevation

For some injuries, using the RICE principle *(below)* will help reduce pain and swelling and prevent further damage.

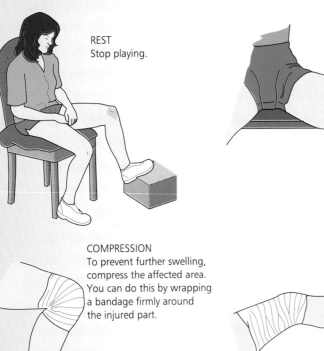

REST
Stop playing.

ICE
Try and put an ice pack or something cold on the injured part (a bag of frozen vegetables works well).

COMPRESSION
To prevent further swelling, compress the affected area. You can do this by wrapping a bandage firmly around the injured part.

ELEVATION
Swelling will also be reduced if you can raise (elevate) the injured part. This will reduce the blood flow.

Treatment of bleeding

If there is bleeding, the first priority is to try and stop the blood flow. For small cuts, it is quite easy to do this simply by applying pressure. If the cut is more severe, raising the injured part will help. If the blood is spurting out, this means an artery has been damaged. This is a serious injury and you should seek medical help immediately.

The next priority is to clean the wound using fresh water and, if possible, an antiseptic wipe. The wound should then be dressed using a pad of gauze or a sticking plaster. Where a cut is deep, **stitches** may be needed to pull the skin together. For these, you will need to go to the nearest hospital Accident and Emergency Department.

Broken bones and joints

Broken bones are called **fractures**. They are very painful and require specialist medical help. **Symptoms** include:

- Hearing or feeling a snap or crack

- Restricted movement of limb

- Injured part is very painful and there may be swelling

- Victim may feel sick and/or dizzy

- The arm or leg may look deformed compared with the opposite limb

When dealing with broken bones, the procedure is as follows:

- Call for medical help, e.g. ring 999

- Do not try and move the casualty. Try and keep them as comfortable and calm as possible

- Try and support the injured limb using cushions or a sling. Be very gentle when working around the injured part

Dislocations

Symptoms for **dislocations** are similar to those for fractures but the pain and swelling will be more centred on the actual joint. Follow similar procedure to fractures *(above)*.

Concussion

Seek medical help. Keep the injured person lying down and warm. If they do not regain consciousness, try and put them into the **recovery position** *(see below)*. This is the safest position for an **unconscious** person, until expert medical help arrives.

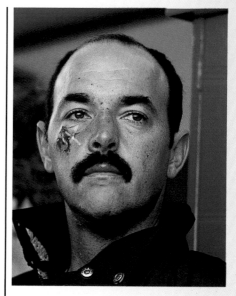

For severe cuts, it may be necessary for stitches to be used to repair the skin

SYMPTOMS
Physical signs that will give you a clue to the type of injury you are dealing with

QUICK QUIZ

1) What do we call injuries where a muscle is overstretched?

2) What do we call injuries where ligaments are overstretched?

3) In what types of sports are dislocations most common?

4) Is tennis elbow an overuse or stress injury?

UNCONSCIOUSNESS
Serious condition often caused by a collision or blow to the head. Medical help should be called for immediately

The recovery position

> **RECOVERY POSITION**
> *Position in which a casualty lies on their side to ensure the airway remains open*

> **ABC ROUTINE**
> *Airway, Breathing, Circulation – the key points to check when dealing with an injured person*

QUICK QUIZ

1) *Why might deep cuts require hospital treatment?*

2) *What part of the body is injured in a fracture?*

3) *For what type of injury do you need to put the casualty into the recovery position?*

The recovery position

The key priority is to make sure that the casualty's airway remains open. This is achieved by tilting the head back and pulling the chin forward.

Concussion is often associated with spinal injuries, so as soon as the casualty regains consciousness, ask them if they can move their toes or fingers, and if there is any pain in their neck or spine or any tingling sensation in their limbs.

Even if they regain consciousness straight away after a bump, the symptoms could still persist, so keep a close eye on any one who has a hard knock to the head.

FIRST AID PRINCIPLES

If you are confronted with an injured person, the first priority is to get an idea of how badly they are injured. The two most common methods are the **ABC routine** ('Airway, Breathing, Circulation') or the more thorough **DRABC check** outlined below:

- **D is for Dange**r Make sure that the casualty and yourself are in no further danger. If you cannot help them without putting yourself at risk, you should wait until help arrives

- **R is for Response** Can the casualty respond to you? Are they able to tell you where the pain is?

- **A is for Airway** Can they breathe freely? Is there any blockage of the airway? Remember how important it is to tilt the head back for the recovery position

- **B is for Breathing** Is the casualty breathing? Look at their chest. Is it moving? Listen for the sounds of breathing. If the casualty has stopped breathing you may have to begin mouth-to-mouth ventilation *(see opposite)*

- **C is for Circulation** Check if the blood is circulating by feeling for a **pulse** at either the wrist or at the carotid artery in the neck. If a pulse is present but the casualty is not breathing, you will have to administer mouth-to-mouth ventilation. If there is no breathing and no pulse, you will need to do mouth-to-mouth and also **cardiac massage** *(see page 134)*

Mouth-to-mouth ventilation

This is an emergency method of getting a casualty breathing again by inflating their lungs with your own breath. This will usually start them breathing on their own again, and may well save their life. The main stages of mouth-to-mouth ventilation are illustrated in the diagram opposite. If the casualty begins breathing again, put them into the recovery position and call for a medical expert as soon as possible. While you attempt artificial respiration, make sure somebody rings for an ambulance.

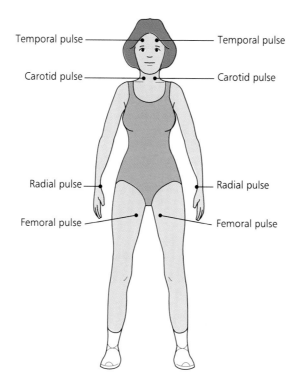

Temporal pulse — ... — Temporal pulse

Carotid pulse — ... — Carotid pulse

Radial pulse — ... — Radial pulse

Femoral pulse — ... — Femoral pulse

The main pulse points on the human body

• Tilt the head back to keep the airway open

• Pinch nose to stop air escaping through the nostrils

• Take a deep breath and breathe into the mouth of the casualty. Breathe out hard, and for as long as you can

• Lift your head up and take in a breath, looking to see if the casualty's chest is moving.

• Breathe into casualty's mouth once every six seconds. At the same time, keep checking for a pulse and watching the movement of the casualty's chest.

The main stages of mouth-to-mouth ventilation

Cardiac massage

If you cannot find a pulse on your casualty, their heart must have stopped beating. This is a serious condition, and you must act quickly. After trying mouth-to-mouth, the next stage is to try **cardiac massage** and then combine the two methods with a ratio of 5 compressions to 1 ventilation. The four stages are:

● Find the casualty's breastbone – the large, flat bone at the front of the ribs. The cardiac massage point is just above the top of this

● Place the palms of your hands one on top of the other, just above the breastbone. Keeping your arms straight, push down on the chest to a depth of about 4 cm. Stop pushing and allow the chest to expand again. Repeat this for a minute, at a rate of one compression a second

● Check again for any pulse

● If there is still no pulse, repeat and also combine with mouth-to-mouth ventilation.

> **CARDIAC MASSAGE**
> *Means of reviving a casualty whose heart has stopped beating*

QUICK QUIZ

1) What do you the initials DRABC stand for?

2) In mouth-to-mouth ventilation, why is the head tilted back?

3) Where in the body can you check for a pulse?

4) In cardiac massage, how many compressions should you do in a minute?

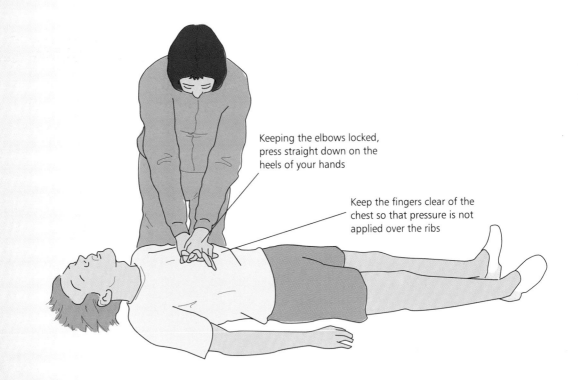

Keeping the elbows locked, press straight down on the heels of your hands

Keep the fingers clear of the chest so that pressure is not applied over the ribs

The four stages of cardiac massage

S P O R T   I N   A C T I O N

While you are walking by a river with a friend, a child comes running to you for help. His friend has fallen into the river and banged his head. Although he has managed to drag him back on to the bank, he is not breathing.

What would you do?

MATCH IT

INJURY	TREATMENT
Fracture of leg bone	Cardiac massage
Slight concussion after a bang on head	Support injured part using a sling
Casualty with no pulse or breathing	Mouth-to-mouth ventilation
Casualty not breathing	Get casualty to sit down, test for clarity of vision and do simple mental tasks, e.g. sums
Casualty with no pulse	Mouth-to-mouth and cardiac massage combined

✓ REVISE IT!

For your exams you will need to know:

☐ How to recognise and treat:

- – Muscle strains and sprains
- – Fractures
- – Joint injuries, such as dislocations
- – Cuts, grazes and blisters
- – Concussion
- – Dehydration and hypothermia

☐ The meaning and use of RICE

☐ The meaning and use of DRABC and ABC

☐ How to prevent injury occurring

☐ The meaning of the key words for this chapter

✓ KEY WORDS

Tick each box when you understand the word

CONTACT SPORTS	☐
STRAINS	☐
SPRAINS	☐
DISLOCATION	☐
CONCUSSION	☐
DEHYDRATION	☐
HYPOTHERMIA	☐
RICE	☐
SYMPTOMS	☐
RECOVERY POSITION	☐
ABC ROUTINE	☐
CARDIAC MASSAGE	☐

Exam questions: Health, safety and training

The questions below are typical of those that you might have to answer in your examination. Try answering each, remembering that the number of marks available for each question gives you a clue to the type of answer required.

Maximum possible marks

1   What are the four components that make up a healthy lifestyle?   [4]

2   How can fatigue or lack of sleep affect sporting performance?   [2]

3   Explain what is meant by the **FITT principles** in exercise planning.   [8]

4   An essential part of any training session should be the **warm up**. This avoids the risk of injuring your body and also enables you to concentrate better on the activity.

   What elements should be included in a warm up?   [3]

5   Using the principle of **overload,** explain how a weightlifter can train to increase the amount of weight they can lift.   [2]

6   Explain **interval training** methods and suggest a sport that would benefit from this type of training.   [3]

7   What are the differences between the **short-term** and **long-term** effects of training?   [2]

8   What is the long-term effect of exercise on the cardiovascular system?   [4]

9   Briefly outline some key safety guidelines you should follow before taking part in any sport. Try and use examples in your answer.   [5]

10   When choosing **footwear** for a specific sport, what should you be looking for?   [3]

11   Adhering to the rules is an important safety principle that all participants should follow. As an official or coach, how could you ensure that rules are adhered to?   [3]

12   You are organising a five-a-side football competition for young people at a local park. How will you plan your **First Aid** and **emergency provision?**   [8]

13   Why is injury more likely in **contact sports?**   [2]

14   **Tennis** and **golf elbow** are examples of which injury type?   [1]

15   What is **concussion** and how should it be treated?   [3]

Maximum possible marks

16 What does the **RICE principle** stand for in the treatment of injuries? [4]

17 Can you describe one of the First Aid methods that can be used to identify
what is wrong with a casualty? [4]

18 Can you describe the stages of mouth-to-mouth ventilation? [5]

19 There is an accident in a crowd at a sports event. You are in charge of First Aid.
Suggest four ways in which you could use some other spectators to help you. [4]

20 During a rugby match at your school, a player is cut and is bleeding severely.
Explain how would you deal with this major external bleeding. [6]

21 Can you list four basic safety guidelines that apply to all sports? [4]

22 When using an item of sports equipment, what should you look for before
playing to ensure that it will be safe to use? [3]

23 *a* Explain the difference between **impact** and **overuse** injuries. [2]

    b Can you give two examples of overuse injuries? [2]

24 Where in the body could you check a casualty's pulse? [2]

Revision guide: Health, safety and training

These pages summarise the most important areas covered in Chapters 14–18 on health, safety and training. By fully understanding everything below you will be better prepared to succeed in your examination.

Definitions
Make sure you know the meaning of the terms:
- **Health:** state of physical, mental and emotional well being
- **Fitness:** strength, speed, endurance, flexibility, body composition
- **Exercise:** activities that keep the body in good physical condition

A person's **diet** can affect their health. Problems such as overweight, obesity, under-eating all have an effect on sporting performance.

Healthy lifestyle also includes **cleanliness, personal hygiene** and **rest.**

FITT principles
Planning activity sessions using the **FITT principles**:
- **Frequency**
- **Intensity**
- **Time**
- **Type**

Training
When training, the following terms need to be used and understood:
- **Overload**: working the body harder to improve fitness
- **Progression**: increase the workload
- **Reversibility**: fitness cannot be stored
- **Specificity**: training needs to be specific to the sports you play
- **Variance**: keep training fun by varying the activities
- **Repetitions**: the number of times you repeat an exercise
- **Sets**: a certain number of repetitions

Different types of training produce differing results:
- **Continuous**: endurance
- **Fartlek**: endurance
- **Interval**: speed
- **Weight/resistance**: strength
- **Flexibility**: flexibility

Different types of exercise
- **Short-term effects** of exercise: changes to the body during physical activity
- **Long-term effects** of exercise: adaptations to the body that result from regular physical activity

Long-term effects on the muscles and skeleton include:
- Stronger tendons and joints
- Ligaments more flexible
- Additional calcium, making bones stronger
- Thickening of cartilage at bone ends
- Muscle hypertrophy

Long-term effects on the cardiovascular system include:
- Hypertrophy of heart muscle
- Increased blood volume
- Blood vessels more elastic
- Respiratory muscles more efficient
- Increase in surface area of lungs

Prevention of injury
Before playing sport, always:
- Warm up
- Check the condition of the playing surface
- Check the condition of the equipment
- Make sure you know correct techniques and obey rules

First Aid provision
This should include a filled First Aid kit. A qualified First Aider should be in attendance.

Using the RICE principle
RICE stands for:
- Rest
- Ice
- Compression
- Elevation

Other methods of injury treatment include the **DRABC** and **ABC** principles:

DRABC = Danger
Response
Airway
Breathing
Circulation

ABC =   Airway
Breathing
Circulation

Emergency procedure
In the event of an accident or emergency, the key is to call for assistance and summon the emergency services.

Further reading

- Davis, D., Kimmer, T., and Auty. M., *Physical Education: Theory And Practice*, Macmillan Australia, 1986

- Dick, F., *Sports Training Principles*, A & C Black, 1989

- Hazeldine, R., *Fitness For Sport*, Gowood Press 1985

- Honeybourne, J., Hill, M., and Moors, H., *Advanced Physical Education And Sport*, Stanley Thornes, 1996

- Parish, W., *Training For Peak Performance*, A & C Black, 1991

CHAPTER 19

Definitions and History of Sport

The aim of this chapter is to help you to:

○ Understand the terms used in the study of sport and PE

○ Be able to define terms such as **sport** and **leisure**

○ Understand the role sport and PE play in our **society**

○ Develop your knowledge of the **history** of sport

○ Suggest things that might affect **sport in the future**

In this section of the book we are going to investigate an area of study called **sports sociology**. We will identify how society can affect the sports performer and also the effect sport may have on **society.** We shall begin by looking at the different terms used to describe the sociological aspects of sport and physical education.

SOCIETY
The human community in which we live, and the people and things that surround us and affect how we live

Football in Costa Rica

SPORTS SCIENCE TERMS

Sports science terms often have different meanings according to where and how they are used, and we must define each so that we fully understand them. You will then be able to recognise them in other books you read.

Many of these terms are used without a true understanding of their meaning. Since we are approaching our study as sports scientists, we need to be precise in our use of these terms, so let us begin with the term **sport.**

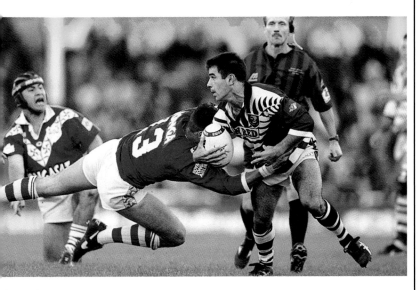
Sport involves competition

SPORT
Organised contests, involving physical activity between individuals or teams

QUICK TASK

Look at the sports listed below. What were the origins of these activities, and what might they have been used for in ancient times?

a) Steeple-chasing in athletics
b) Fencing
c) Ice hockey
d) Discus

What is sport?

We know that human beings have played sport for a very long time. Some sports, such as wrestling, date back thousands of years; others have arisen and been adapted from other activities.

Today there are hundreds of different sports. This makes our job of defining what a sport is very difficult. However, we can identify a number of characteristics that are shared by all sports. Try doing the quick task on the right then check your answers with the list below.

Sport – common features

Most of the world's sports contain the following features:

- **Competition** between individuals or teams

- **Physical activity**

- **Winners and losers** (in some sports you can have a **draw**)

- **Rules** to ensure fair competition

- A special **place to play** (e.g. a pitch, court or ring)

- Special **equipment**

- **Spontaneity**

QUICK TASK

1) *Look at the sports below and list the characteristics they have in common. We have already said that sports must involve **competition** – so there is the first word for your list.*

a) Football   b) Netball
c) Cricket   d) Rounders
e) Boxing

2) *Now compare your answer to Task1 above with the list given in the main text, under the heading 'Sport – common features'. How did you do?*

According to the list, which of the following activities qualify as 'sports'?

a) Darts
b) TV's Gladiators
c) Jogging
d) WWF American wrestling

QUICK TASK

1) List four labour-saving devices that have enabled people who do housework to have more leisure time.

2) Old age pensioners and retired people may have a lot of time for leisure, but what factors might limit what they can do during this time?

LEISURE
Free time in which you can choose what to do and when and where to do it

Outdoor recreation often offers the chance to escape and 'get away from it all'

RECREATION
An enjoyable activity that refreshes you and gives you more energy

Leisure

Another term we will come across frequently is **leisure**. If we listed all the different things we do in a typical day, we would end up with a very long list. However, most of our activities could be categorised under the following headings:

- **Work** What we do for a living, also school and housework
- **Bodily needs** E.g. sleeping and eating
- **Duties** Tasks we have to do for family, friends, etc.
- **Leisure** Free time after all the above have been completed

The average 'split' of a person's daily activities is shown below:

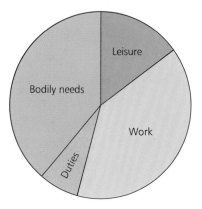

Pie chart showing average 'split' of daily activities

We often hear that leisure time is increasing and that we are living in a 'leisured society'. An increase in in the use of machines and computers means that people have more free time than they used to. The leisure industry has also grown in importance since the decline of the manufacturing industry in Britain. It now provides employment for many people and forms an important part of our economy.

Recreation

Another term we come across is **recreation**. This is an active form of leisure. Often, when people have leisure time, they are too tired or lazy to do anything and end up slumped in front of the TV. Recreation means using this time more constructively – either in order to produce something, as in cooking or DIY, or to get fit through sport.

S P O R T   I N   A C T I O N

Make a record of how you spend your time over the next few days. Sort your activities into categories and produce your own pie chart like the one shown above.

Physical education

Physical education takes place in schools, colleges and universities. It always involves a 'teacher' passing on knowledge to a group of students, and is almost always concerned with physical movement. We now have a **National Curriculum** for PE which sets out what kind of knowledge and experiences all children in the UK should be taught.

In recent years the interest in PE has grown greatly and it is now studied at many levels.

Most PE time is spent teaching traditional team games such as football, netball and hockey, but no two schools offer precisely the same programme of instruction. Swimming, gymnastics and athletics are the main individual activities, but new ideas such as health-related fitness, dance, aerobics and activities such as trampolining are also gaining in popularity.

PE helps you to learn to work with other people

S P O R T   I N   A C T I O N

Produce a table showing the different sports activities you have taken part in at school. Include columns for practical and social skills. For each activity, try and fill in skills that you developed through those activities. For example:

ACTIVITY	PRACTICAL SKILLS	SOCIAL SKILLS
Swimming	Swim strokes Diving skills Life- saving skills	Self confidence Appreciation of danger Communication skills

---

THE HISTORY OF SPORT

Throughout history, sport has played a variety of important functions in society: as a form of recreation; as a preparation for war or the hunt; or later, as a substitute for war. It has undergone many changes. Some sports such as wrestling have stayed much the same; others, such as football, have adapted with the times. New sports are always being invented and developed. Snowboarding and street hockey are two examples of recently invented sports. Often, changes in sport reflect changes in the history of the countries in which it is played. This can make it a fascinating area of study.

In the next few pages, we aim to give you a brief taste of the history of sport so that you have an idea of how it has developed into its present form.

The Coliseum, a sports stadium built by the Romans over 2,000 years ago

FAST FORWARD ▷▷

OLYMPIC GAMES   see page 178

MEDIEVAL
Belonging to the period in history called the Middle Ages: 786 AD to 1485 AD

Sport in ancient times

The oldest sport-like activities were probably gymnastic displays in religious festivals. One of the oldest recorded forms of sport was on the Greek island of Crete. Archaeological evidence shows pictures and descriptions of 'bull leaping' where slaves leapt over the horns of the bull. They regarded the bull as one of their gods, and by leaping over it they kept their god happy as well as providing an exciting spectacle.

It was also in Ancient Greece that the most famous of the ancient sports was developed: the **Olympic Games**. These date back to 776 BC, and were again linked to religious festivals. The Games included a wide range of activities and each athlete had to take part in all events. Many of the sports were linked to the training given to soldiers, and many such as discus and javelin are still used in the modern Olympics.

The Romans also held large sporting events, though these were much more violent and spectacular occasions. The main activities were chariot-racing and the popular gladiator fights. Here individuals or teams of men would fight animals or each other, usually to the death.

Medieval sports and games

After the fall of Rome, we enter a period of history called the **Dark Ages**. There are far fewer historical records and pieces of evidence to tell us about life during this time, and it is really only in medieval times that we can take up the study of sport again.

The most famous sport of medieval times was **jousting**, in which knights would practise their fighting skills in mock battles, the most popular being on horseback with lances.

During this time we begin to see the roots of many modern sports. These were played by the peasants in their villages. As most people worked on the land, leisure time was limited and these 'people's sports' were closely associated with the church calendar of holy days and festivals. Sports such as **mob football** were a chance for the entire village to get together and 'let off steam'.

Unlike today's sports, these games had very few, if any, rules and were more in the nature of a free-for-all. They were also not played often – perhaps only once a year. For example the annual Ashbourne Football Game in Derbyshire was played once a year on Shrove Tuesday.

The effects of the Industrial Revolution

At the start of the nineteenth century, a number of **public schools** started to develop sport as a means of educating young gentlemen. They took many of the people's games and began to make them more organised. This started the process that finally gave us the range of sports we play today.

PUBLIC SCHOOLS
Large boarding schools where parents who could afford to do so paid for their children to be educated. The most famous examples are Eton, Harrow and Rugby

Mob football in medieval times

The **Industrial Revolution** also played an important part in the development of modern sport. Machinery was developed that could be used in the production of goods, and this resulted in the movement of population from rural areas to towns and cities. This meant that the village games died out, and new town sports grew up to take their place.

The development of railways also meant that for the first time, teams could travel around the country to compete against each other, leading to the development of leagues and cup competitions.

Sport in the 20th century

Several factors have had an effect on sport since the start of the 20th century. There has been a steady move away from playing sports to watching sports. Initially, this was due to what is called **spectatorism**, but the most significant factor today is the growth of televised sport.

> SPECTATORISM
> People paying money to watch football, rugby and cricket teams play

The future of sport

Just as sport has changed since Roman times, so it will continue to change in the future. New sports, such as snowboarding and Quasar will be developed as technology progresses. Other sports will adapt to make use of new technology like the third umpire in cricket.

The media will play an ever-increasing role in the development of sport. Already we have 'sports-only' satellite channels in Britain, and more will certainly follow. Computers will play an increasing part in sports and may further decrease our actual physical involvement. No doubt most of us have already played golf or football on a computer game.

S P O R T   I N   A C T I O N

Pick one of your favourite sports and try and find out something about its history. How old is it? When were the rules first written down? Who played it in the past? Use the school or local library to help you.

You may have access to CD encyclopedias. Produce a chart showing how your sport has developed. Perhaps your class could research a number of different sports.

M A T C H   I T

SPORT	HISTORICAL PERIOD
Mob football	Ancient Rome
Jousting	20th century
Ancient Olympic Games	Medieval times
Snowboarding	Medieval times
Gladiatorial combat	Ancient Greece
Professional football	20th century

✓ K E Y   W O R D S

Tick each box when you understand the word

SOCIETY ☐

SPORT ☐

LEISURE ☐

RECREATION ☐

PHYSICAL EDUCATION ☐

PUBLIC SCHOOL ☐

✓ R E V I S E   I T !

For your exams you will need to know:

☐ Reasons and motives for participation in physical activity

☐ Reasons for increased leisure time for people in the UK

☐ Reasons for the growth of the leisure industry

☐ The role of the school in promoting participation in physical education

☐ The meaning of the key words for this chapter

Reasons for Participation

The aim of this chapter is to help you:

- Understand the **reasons** why people play sport

- Look at **where** people play sport

- Investigate **factors** that affect what sports we play

- Learn about **career opportunities** in sport and leisure

The Sports Council estimate that one in three people in the UK regularly take part in sport. In this part of the book we look at the reasons why people take part in sport and recreation.

Sport is all about participation

QUICK TASK

1) Write down four short sentences to describe a healthy person.

2) Write down four short sentences explaining the benefits of regular exercise.

3) How could sports be useful in places such as prisons?

STRESS
Tension in the body and mind. High stress levels are harmful since they put increased strain on organs such as the heart

'SPORT FOR ALL'
Campaign launched by the Sports Council in 1972 to encourage all people to take part in sporting activities

WHY PLAY SPORT?

Individuals take up sport for many different reasons. Throughout the UK, all young people have to do PE at school and this is often an important influence on the amount of sport they do, and which sports they take up. We can split the reasons for playing sport into two main categories:

1 Health benefits

Sport and physical activities help to keep us healthy. By working the body, we strengthen it and are less likely to become ill. However, keeping physically fit is hard work. This is because fitness cannot be stored and must be maintained by following a regular training programme. The key benefits of fitness are:

- The body functions better
- The risk of heart disease is reduced
- Problems with muscles and joints are reduced
- The body's ability to recover from illness is strengthened
- Levels of **stress** can be reduced
- Keeping fit is a good way to make and meet friends
- Being fit makes us feel good about ourselves

2 Social benefits

Sport is a positive use of spare time and an important way of releasing and harnessing energy. The more people play sport, the fitter they will be, and the less likely they are to be a burden on the health service. People will also work more efficiently and need less time off work due to illness or injury.

In order to encourage more people to play sport, bodies such as the Sports Council have set up campaigns such as **Sport For All**. This aims to promote the benefits of sport and also to provide funds to help build and develop more sports facilities.

Everyone should be able to take part in sport

SPORT IN ACTION

Tim and Claire both want to get fit, but for different reasons. Tim wants to build up his muscles, while Claire wants to lose weight. Try and find out which kind of exercise activities would help each of them achieve what they want.

OPPORTUNITIES TO TAKE PART IN SPORT

Local provision

Most people who take part in sport use local facilities and clubs. **Local authorities** such as city and town councils are the biggest providers of facilities. Councils provide a vast range of sports and recreational facilities, including parks, leisure centres, swimming pools, golf courses and community halls.

The idea of these facilities is to get as many people as possible to participate in sport, so prices are often **subsidised** to make them more affordable.

In order to take part in competitive sport, most people have to join a **club**. These are groups who join together to play a particular sport on a regular basis. These clubs rely for support on membership fees and fundraising.

Increasingly, private companies are also developing sports facilities. These private leisure companies tend to cater for specific types of activity, such as fitness or water sports.

The cost of participation

Sport can be an expensive hobby, and there are many costs involved. To join a sports club you usually have to pay a yearly membership fee of around £20–£40, plus weekly subs or match fees. More **exclusive** clubs for sports such as golf can charge much more – often hundreds of pounds a year. Other costs involved in taking part in sports are buying the correct kit – including clothing and equipment.

Access

By **accessibility** we mean how easy it is to play a sport. For example, how easy is it for you to get to your local sports centre and take part in sporting activity?

Some people are a lot less well off than others. Pensioners and the unemployed may be limited in the number of sports they can play, if they cannot afford the costs mentioned above.

For other people, time is a limiting factor. Doctors have very demanding jobs that leave them little time to get to the sports centre. To solve the problem, some centres such as swimming pools run 'early bird' sessions, opening very early in the morning so that people have the chance to take exercise before going to work.

QUICK TASK

Make a list of all the sports and leisure facilities provided by your local council. Against each one, note the activities available.

SUBSIDISED
Partly paid for by the local council

EXCLUSIVE
Only open to certain people. The more exclusive a club, the more expensive it is to join

Waterskiing – an ideal sport to try on holiday

Football remains one of the UK's most popular sports

1) Work out how much it costs you to play your sport, both per week and over a whole year. Remember to include things like match fees, equipment and travel costs.

2) Ask friends who play other sports to work out similar figures. Draw up a table showing the most expensive sports, and the cheapest.

3) To increase accessibility, many sports centres use a technique called **programming**. This involves organising special sessions or times for specific groups of people. Look at your local sports centre or swimming pool. What specific sessions are available?

Fashion in sport

The sports that people take up are often influenced by fashion.

Traditionally in the UK, team games like football and cricket have been the most popular. These were sports that are taught to everyone at school, and many thousands of people play and watch them.

But recently, other trends have begun to influence sporting activity. For example, the 1980s health boom in both America and Europe led many people to take up activities such as aerobics, jogging and working out in the gym.

Snowboarding and in-line skating are other examples of new sports that have become very fashionable and popular, with more and more people taking them up.

The biggest influence on sport now is undoubtedly television. Sports shown on TV tend to be the most popular, as they are in the public eye. TV also tends to give sports a glamorous image that can motivate people to get involved.

Snowboarding – a new sport

SPORT IN ACTION

Investigate the cost of sports facilities in your area. Find out the cost of activities such as the following:

- Hire of a Badminton court for one hour
- Hire of squash court for one hour
- Cost for an adult to swim
- Cost of a five-a-side football pitch for one hour

Try and contact or visit a number of different facilities and compare prices.

CAREERS IN SPORT AND LEISURE

As we saw in Chapter 19, leisure time is on the increase. There are a number of reasons for this:

- People are working fewer hours a week
- People are taking more holidays
- Part-time work has grown as a proportion of total employment
- People are staying at school and college longer
- People are retiring earlier and living longer
- Increasing automation and the development of labour-saving devices means more time is available for other things

With this growth in leisure time, there has also been a significant growth in the number of jobs and career opportunities available in the sport and leisure sector. Although the actual number of jobs in sport and leisure is still limited, the variety of jobs available is very wide.

Qualifications

The range of qualifications now available in sport and leisure is expanding rapidly. Many people take qualifications because they want to take up jobs in the leisure industry. Others do so because they enjoy sport and are good enough to gain reward for their sporting ability.

- At school, it is possible to study Physical Education at both **GCSE** and **Advanced Level**. For both courses, students have to study, and are assessed in, theoretical and practical aspects of sport and PE
- There are also **GNVQ** or **BTEC** First and National qualifications in leisure. These are more **vocational** in approach
- For those working in the leisure industry, the **Institute of Leisure and Amenities Management** and the **Institute of Sport and Recreation Management** also offer industrial qualifications
- **Sports governing bodies** and the **National Coaching Foundation (NCF)** offer specific courses for sports leaders, coaches and referees. These are usually short courses pitched at different levels. They are designed to help develop skills and knowledge and teach you how to coach teams and individuals

Coaches and sports development officers

As well as professional players, a number of sports also support coaches. These work either with individual performers or teams, helping to prepare them for competition and improving their fitness, skills and tactics.

QUICK TASK

1) Give four reasons why people might have more leisure time in the future.

2) How might TV coverage of a sport encourage people to get involved?

3) How might TV coverage of a sport discourage people from getting involved?

AUTOMATION
The use of machines and computers to do work that used to be done by hand

VOCATIONAL
Courses closely linked to skills and experience needed in leisure and recreation careers

The job of a coach is to improve fitness, skills and tactics

GCSE PE includes the teaching of both practical and theoretical elements

Both types of job require skills and experience in the particular sport, as well as personal skills such as communication and organisational ability. Often ex-performers go on to take up careers in coaching.

PE teachers

If you like helping other people develop their sporting skills, teaching PE or sport in a school or college may be for you. Full-time PE teachers need a degree, but if you teach fitness or sports at evening classes or community centres you can do so without a degree, although you will need to take sports governing body courses. Remember, if you want to become a PE teacher, you need to be able to teach *all* sports, not just your favourite!

Sports management

This is a wide-ranging and developing field. Increasingly, professional clubs are being run by commercially trained managers, while sports stars are turning to professional agents to handle their sponsorship deals and TV appearances.

The majority of jobs in sports management have less to do with practical sport and more to do with commerce and marketing. Most are in managing sports facilities such as local leisure centres and swimming pools.

Ground staff

These tend to be based at professional sports clubs such as football, cricket and golf clubs, though there are positions with local councils. The work varies, but usually involves looking after the pitches and surrounding areas. Most ground staff start as parks workers employed by local councils, then progress to craftsman/groundsman through courses or on-the-job training.

Sports medicine

Again, this is a growing career area. There are three main types of sports medical specialists:

- **Doctor** Although most doctors treat sports injuries, usually this is only a small part of their duties. In order to become a doctor, you need to study medicine at university – a very demanding course

- **Physiotherapist** The 'physio's' job is to aid recovery after injury and help the performer get fit to play sport again. There are a number of opportunities for physiotherapists in hospitals, sports clinics and at professional sports clubs. Many train and work on a voluntary basis for their local clubs and teams

- **Osteopath** Like physiotherapists, osteopaths aid recovery after injury by manipulating bones and joints. At present, job opportunities for osteopaths are relatively few, and most work as private practitioners. If you want to train to become an osteopath, you will need to attend a degree course with a registered institution like the British School of Osteopathy in London

Sports journalism

Sports journalists work for local and national newspapers, magazines and radio and television stations. Although there are many openings for people who want to write about or photograph sport, sports journalism is a highly competitive profession and very few make it to the top.

There are a number of ways to become a sports journalist. The traditional route is to start at a local newspaper or radio station and work your way up, but university courses in sports journalism are also available.

Professional sports performer

A small number of very talented performers can live purely from playing sports. The sports concerned are limited to those that attract large amounts of money from spectators, sponsors and TV. These include football, tennis, boxing and cricket.

Manchester United's Andy Cole is a full-time professional sportman

SPORT IN ACTION

Collect examples of job vacancies in sport and leisure.

Look for adverts in your local paper and explore the 'Appointments' section of a national paper or magazine.

Look at the different skills required – and how much they get paid!

MATCH IT

JOB	SKILLS
Sports journalist	Very good at sport
PE teacher	Knowledgeable about how the body works
Sports coach	Able to organise training sessions
Sports centre manager	Able to give clear instructions to others
Physiotherapist	Able to deal with customer complaints
Professional sports performer	Knowing how to drain a sports pitch
Grounds keeper	Able to record the details of a sports match

✓ KEY WORDS

Tick each box when you understand the word

OPPORTUNITY ☐

PARTICIPATION ☐

STRESS ☐

'SPORT FOR ALL' ☐

SUBSIDISED ☐

EXCLUSIVE ☐

AUTOMATION ☐

VOCATIONAL ☐

✓ REVISE IT!

For your exams you will need to know:

☐ The reasons for people taking part in sport

☐ The reasons for people not taking part in sport

☐ The reasons for increased leisure time

☐ The role of bodies such as the Sports Council in encouraging participation in sport

☐ The meaning of the key words for this chapter

Factors Affecting Participation

The aim of this chapter is to help you:

- Understand the terms **provision, opportunity** and **esteem** in the context of sport and leisure

- Identify groups in the population that may not have **equal access** to sport and leisure

- Understand how sports bodies can **motivate** people to take part in physical activity

In the last chapter we looked at reasons why people take part in sport and physical activity. But not all groups in society are equally able to participate in sport. In this chapter we look at the reasons for this and examine ways in which access and participation in sport can be improved.

PROVISION, OPPORTUNITY AND ESTEEM

Three key factors affecting people's participation in sport are **provision**, **opportunity** and **esteem**.

1 Provision

How easily you can get to a sports centre or playing field depends very much on where you live. City-dwellers tend to have better access to sports facilities. Cities also usually have good transport systems, such as buses. People who live in the countryside may have to travel much further to play sport.

Local councils provide most of the sport facilities in the UK. But the Sports Council argue that in many areas of Britain there are too few sporting facilities available.

The five sports councils (that is, the UKSC plus the sports councils of England, Scotalnd, Wales and Northern Ireland) and other bodies such as local authorities try to improve provision by giving grants to build new sports facilties.

> **PROVISION**
> Providing recreational facilities so that people can take part in sport

> **UK SPORTS COUNCIL**
> The body responsible for sport at the national level and for promoting UK sporting excellence on the world stage

sports council

QUICK TASK

1) How far would you have to travel in order to take part in the following sports? Use a map to help you.

   a) Swimming
   b) Tennis
   c) Golf
   d) Sailing
   e) Ice skating
   f) Hockey
   g) Skiing on a dry ski slope
   h) Weight training
   i) Cricket
   j) Horse riding

2) Look at your answers. Do you think your area is well catered for in terms of sport?

STEREOTYPING
Assuming that all members of a group of people share the same image or characteristics

2 Opportunity

Even if there are sports facilities available in your area, there may be other factors that prevent you from taking part.

When we looked at leisure in Chapter 20, we saw that free time is limited for some people. Women in particular are often faced with this problem. The demands of work and family mean that they have little time left to play sport. Surveys show that fewer women take part in sport than men.

Another factor is cost. In the UK, most people have to pay to take part in sport. There may be the cost of hiring a pitch or court, or the entrance fee to the local swimming pool. Other costs may be the cost of getting to the sports facility (the bus fare, for example). Sportswear and equipment also cost money.

3 Esteem

Another obstacle to participation is how we feel about ourselves. We tend to be attracted to sports that we feel suit us, and we are nervous about taking up sports that are new or different.

It is often said that certain sports are more suited to boys or girls – for example, that boys look stupid playing netball. Most of us don't like to be made fun of, particularly when playing sport. This has to do with what is known as **stereotyping**.

Stereotyping is often directed at different racial or gender groups. The result is that certain groups of people tend to be steered into certain sports and away from others.

SOCIAL AND CULTURAL FACTORS

The factors described above have a powerful effect on the amount of sport we play and the kind of sports we play. But there also a number of other issues that affect our opportunity to participate. We can put these under the following headings:

- Age
- Gender
- Social class
- Race and religion
- Ability

Age

In the UK, age is a very important factor in how much sport we play. Government surveys have found that those who participate most in sport are in the 16–24 age group. Sixty per cent of this age group take part in a wide range of sporting activity. In older age groups the rate drops, with only 16% of the over-60s taking part in sporting activities.

Some sports such as golf can be played by all ages

The reasons for this are the same as those mentioned above:

● Most sports facilities are aimed at the young. In the past young people have always been the biggest market for sports

● Older people have traditionally had less time and money to take part in sport. They may also be less able physically to take part in some activities

● In terms of esteem and image, sport tends to be seen as a young person's activity

Some sports centres and swimming pools try to encourage more older people to take part in sport by arranging special sessions exclusively for the 'over fifties'.

Gender

The Sports Council estimates that each year, 33% of all men participate in some form of sporting activity. Only 10% of women take part in sporting activity. As women make up over 50% of the UK population, this must mean that women have less opportunity than men to participate.

We have already highlighted some of the problems that many mothers have in making time for leisure activities. Another factor is provision. There tend to be fewer facilities for women's sport. For sports such as basketball, where there are limited facilities anyway, women's teams may have to wait for the men's team to finish before they can get time on court.

Again, sport centres try and get more women involved in sport by having special women-only sessions. Some also offer crèches where mothers can leave their children while they play. Also, the sports councils and the **Womens Sports Foundation** are working towards getting more women involved in sport.

QUICK QUIZ

1) In the UK, which age group plays the most sport?

2) What kind of sports do you think are most suitable for older people to take part in?

3) Why might old age pensioners have less money to spend on sport than younger people?

GENDER
The two sexes, male or female

womens SPORTS FOUNDATION

WOMENS SPORTS FOUNDATION
A body founded in 1984 to promote women's sport

S P O R T   I N   A C T I O N

Look at the picture below. It shows women playing football – a game traditionally played by men

Women's football – breaking the gender stereotype

1) How do you feel about the picture? Does it look 'wrong'?

2) What do the women in the picture get out of playing football?

3) Why in the past do you think women were discouraged from playing games like football?

S P O R T   I N   A C T I O N

Compare a variety of newspapers printed on the same day. Go through the sports pages and count how many of the articles cover men's sport and how many cover women's sport. Compare the number of articles for each.

Social class

In the UK, people tend to be divided up according to social class. Broadly speaking, this is based on the amount of money they earn, the kind of job they do, their housing and their general lifestyle. We have three main types of social class in the UK, though these are only vague sub-divisions in our society and are less clear now than – say – fifty years ago.

In the past, the upper classes had the most leisure time and money to spend on sport. They played an important role in developing many modern sports. We still tend to associate sports such as hunting and polo with the upper classes. Although their importance is declining, they still tend to have the most opportunity for participation.

The middle classes who prospered during the Industrial Revolution also had time to play sport. Many of our modern sports were developed during the nineteenth century at **public schools** attended by middle-class children. Middle-class businessmen nowadays often combine their work with sport. They see games such as golf and squash as a good way of meeting and socialising with other businessmen.

◀◀ **REWIND**

PUBLIC SCHOOLS   see page 144

Sports such as polo are traditionally associated with the upper classes

The working class have always had the least opportunity to participate in sport. As we have seen in Chapter 19, in **medieval** times, 'organised' sporting activity only took place a few times a year. The emphasis tended to be on spectator sports, with large numbers gathering to watch sports such as football and boxing. Today, however, most people are able to keep their weekends free for leisure activities.

◀◀ **REWIND**

MEDIEVAL SPORT   see page 144

Race and religion

Racial origin and religion can also affect people's choice of sport. Many people think that different racial groups are better suited to some sports than others. As a result, members of **ethnic minorities** tend to be steered towards sports in which they traditionally excel. For example, Asian people are encouraged to play cricket and Irish people to follow horse racing.

Religion can also affect people's opportunity to take part in sport. Although in the past people had to work long hours, they did have Sunday free from work. However, because Sunday was set aside as a holy day, most sports were banned. Recently our society has become less religious, and many sports are now allowed to take place on a Sunday. However, followers of some religions, such as Muslims and Hindus, have strict rules on what they can do in their spare time. Again, it is women who are affected most.

ETHNIC MINORITIES
Groups who are of different ethnic origin from the majority of the population. Examples in the UK would be Asian, Irish and Caribbean people

Ability and disability

In this section, we shall look at how access to sport is affected by ability – both in the sense of 'skill' and simply 'being **able-bodied'**.

In the past, people with disabilities had little opportunity to take part in sport. Nearly all sports facilities were built for the able-bodied.

Opportunities for disabled people are now increasing and all new sports facilities provide access for people of all abilities. Events such as the **Paralympics** and the **London Marathon** have helped raise awareness of sport for disabled people. Disabled athletes have shown that they can take part in a wide range of sports just like anyone else.

Improving access to sports centres for disabled people means ensuring that there are ramps as well as stairs. Doors also need to be wide enough to allow wheelchairs to pass through and changing facilities have to be adapted for use by disabled people.

Disabled people need to be able to participate fully in sport like able-bodied people

SPORT IN ACTION

If you were a wheelchair sports person, could you use all your local sports facilities? Visit the centres and check that they have ramps and lifts. Are disabled people encouraged to use the centre? If not, produce some suggestions on how they might make their facility more user-friendly for disabled people.

M A T C H   I T

SPORT	SOCIAL CLASS
Squash	Working class
Boxing	Middle class
Rugby league	Upper class
Pheasant shooting	Upper class
Tennis	Middle class
Polo	Working class

✓ K E Y   W O R D S

Tick each box when you understand the word

PROVISION ☐

UK SPORTS COUNCIL ☐

STEREOTYPING ☐

GENDER ☐

WOMEN'S SPORTS FOUNDATION ☐

ETHNIC MINORITY GROUP ☐

ABLE-BODIED ☐

✓ R E V I S E   I T !

For your exams you will need to know:

☐ The meaning of access and provision in sport, leisure and PE

☐ How to identify groups in the population who may not be able to participate in physical activity

☐ How sports bodies can motivate people to participate in sport

☐ The meaning of the key words for this chapter

The Local Organisation of Sport

CHAPTER 22

The aim of this chapter is to help you:

- Learn who provides **facilities** for sport and leisure

- Learn how sport is run at **local level**

- Look at how a local **sports club** is organised

- Look at how a **leisure centre** is run

This chapter looks at how sport is organised at local level. The five sports councils estimate that one in three people in the UK play sport, mostly in their local area. However, there are many national bodies that look after sport across the country. We will look at these in Chapter 23, but we must remember that these bodies also affect sport at local level as well.

OVERVIEW

The UK was the first modern country to develop sport, and each sport has followed its own separate course. Performers and clubs have always been free to play when and where they like, and government has never involved itself directly.

Today the **UK Sports Council (UKSC)** is responsible for sport at an elite level; it also deals with issues of UK significance, such as doping in sport. The **English, Scottish, Welsh** and **Northern Ireland Sports Councils** each look after sport in their area, promoting participation and allocating funds for sports facilities at regional level.

Each sport is controlled by its own **governing body**. There are well over 200 of these in the UK. They make the rules for the sport and look after the interests of clubs who participate.

Other important **sports agencies** are the **Central Council for Physical Recreation (CCPR)**, the **British Olympic Association (BOA)** and the **Sports Aid Foundation (SAF)**. We will look at them in more detail in Chapter 23.

FAST FORWARD ▷▷

UK SPORTS COUNCIL   see page 167

FAST FORWARD ▷▷

SPORTS AGENCIES   see page 171

ADMINISTRATION
How sports are organised, who is in control and how the sport is funded

QUICK TASK

Below are the initials of several sports governing bodies. Can you find out which sports they administer?

a) FA   b) LTA
c) ASA   d) RFU
e) HA   f) AENA

SPORT AT LOCAL LEVEL

Sport at local level takes place in what we call **facilities**. These include swimming pools, sports centres and local parks. Some facilities are provided free, but mostly a fee is charged to use them.

Sports facilities can be grouped under three headings:

- **Public sector** – owned by the public and usually run by a local council

- **Private sector** – owned or run by an individual or commercial company

- **Voluntary sector** – run by volunteers and supported through fundraising. For example, this could include bodies like churches or scouts which provide halls.

Who provides the facilities?

There are about 1,500 swimming pools and 2,000 local sports centres in the UK. According to the Sports Council, this is not enough and more sports centres need to be built. Other countries in Europe have far more facilities per head of population than the UK.

Most sports facilities in the UK are provided by:

- **Local authorities** (public sector)
- **Schools and colleges** (public sector)
- The **private sector**

Local authority provision

Local authorities are the biggest providers of sports and leisure facilities in the UK. Each local authority controls its own administrative area. This may be a city, borough, town or district. The local authority provides a vast range of facilities, including parks, leisure centres, swimming pools, golf courses and community halls.

Councils cater for the needs of the local community. The money to pay for these facilities comes from local taxes and central government grants. Although sports facilities are usually subsidised by the local authority, most sports centres also charge a small admission fee. The aim is to get as many people as possible to play sport, so prices are kept as low as possible.

Often sports centres offer **concessions** (reduced admission prices) for people who have to manage on low incomes, such as the unemployed, students or OAPs.

Although councils may own sports facilities, they do not necessarily run them. To increase efficiency, the government has recently introduced a scheme called **compulsory competitive tendering** in which commercial firms compete to run council-owned facilities and contracts are given to the firm who put in the most competitive bid or 'tender'.

QUICK TASK

1) *What is the name of your local council?*
2) *Is it a city, borough, town or district council?*
3) *Quickly write down what sport and leisure facilities your council provides.*

Schools provision

Most schools have a good range of sports halls, pitches, tennis and squash courts and, in a few cases, swimming pools. These are used for PE lessons and by sports teams and clubs. Increasingly, other groups and members of the community are being allowed to use these facilities as well.

This policy of opening up school facilities to the public is called **dual use**.

The government has also encouraged schools to open up their sports facilities by allowing them more say in how they run their own affairs – an initiative known as **Local Management of Schools (LMS)**. Many schools are now approaching the National Lottery to gain more funds for building better sports facilities that will be used by the local community.

Private sector provision

This is made up of two main groups:

- **Commercial** (i.e. profit-making) **companies** who provide sport and leisure facilities to the public in return for payment

- **Companies** who provide sports facilities for their employees

Leisure is an expanding industry, and there are many companies now building and running sport and leisure facilities. These companies tend to cater for specific areas such as fitness or water sports. Often the facilities are well equipped and offer a very good service.

Some companies also provide sports facilities for their employees and their families. Often these are either free or very low-priced, with most of the cost being borne by the company. Companies want their workers to be fitter, happier and have a place to socialise after work. They hope that this will make them work harder and more productively.

SCHOOLS PROVISION
Sports halls, pitches and other facilities in schools

DUAL USE
Making school sports facilities available to the general public outside school hours

QUICK TASK

Referring back to Chapter 21, try and identify groups of people in the community who may not be able to pay the high price of private sector facilities.

QUICK QUIZ

1) *What do the initials **SAF** stand for?*

2) *Which sector provides the most sport and leisure facilities?*

3) *Which body looks after all Olympic matters in the UK?*

4) *How many swimming pools are there in the UK?*

S P O R T   I N   A C T I O N

Using a map of your local area and perhaps a telephone directory, make a list of all the sport and leisure facilities in a three-mile radius of your home or school. Try and find out where the money comes from to fund each of the facilities and group them under the three headings of Public sector, Private sector and Voluntary. For example:

LOCAL SPORTS AND LEISURE FACILITIES

	Public sector	Private sector	Voluntary
Everglades Fitness Centre		✘	
Marleigh Leisure Centre	✘		
St Crispin's Community School	✘		

QUICK QUIZ

1) In what leisure sector would you place a council-run swimming pool?

2) In what leisure sector would you place a private health club?

3) In what sector would you place a scout group five-a-side football team?

SPORTS CLUBS

Most people who play sport regularly belong to a **sports club** where they can play with and against other people. The club will also be a member of a **league** or competition, so that players can compete against other clubs. Most clubs belong to the voluntary sector, i.e. they are run by volunteers who simply play for enjoyment.

Local sports clubs tend to be administered and organised by small voluntary committees. Everyone who joins a club becomes a member. This means they can play for the club and use the club facilities. It also means they have the right to elect members to serve on the organising committee.

Sports club management

There are several key officers that all sports clubs require. Their roles are generally as follows:

- **Chair** – oversees the running of the club, organises and runs meetings and signs cheques

- **Secretary** – organises the day-to-day running of the club, deals with correspondence and club rules, and makes sure the club and its players are registered to play in competitions and leagues

- **Treasurer** – deals with the financial side of the club, records money raised and pays the costs of equipment or rent

- **Coach** – responsible for improving the performance of the players or teams and supervising training or practice sessions. May also be involved in selection of team members

- **Captain** – acts as a figurehead for the club, representing members on and off the pitch. Also represents players and is closely involved in the selection of teams

LOCAL SPORTS CLUBS IN THE UK

Activity/sport	Number of clubs	Total membership
Athletics	19,000	110,000
Bowls (outdoor)	3,529	161,672
Football	42,000	1,250,000
Hockey	1,850	80,000
Golf	1,700	238,000
Netball	3,300	60,000
Swimming	1,784	300,000
Tennis	2,432	131,800

THE SPORTS CENTRE

Most towns in the UK have their own **sports centre**. Sports centres tend to be council-owned and offer a range of sports and leisure facilities. 'Dry' centres provide halls and courts for indoor and outdoor sports; 'wet' centres offer swimming and diving facilities. Newer centres often combine both types.

Most sports centres are easily accessible by local roads and bus services, and are open for a large part of the day. In the middle of the day they are often used by local schools who travel to and fro by coach, while in the evenings they are used by teams and individuals to train or play matches.

In order to attract different people to use the facilities, centres use a technique called **programming** at certain times of the day or week.

◄◄ REWIND

PROGRAMMING   see page 150

Sports centre staff

Key positions for running a sports centre are as follows:

● The **centre manager** has overall responsibility for the running of the centre. Looks after all members of staff and knows their jobs and duties. Will be involved in the recruitment and training of staff

● The **assistant manager** helps the manager in the running of the centre. At certain times in the week may become 'duty manager', i.e. deputise for the manager, if required

● **Reception** staff are responsible for welcoming customers and giving them their first impression of the centre. They also deal with admissions and give customers information about facilities and activities on offer

● **Recreation assistants** are responsible for the practical work in the centre. In the pool, lifeguards are responsible for ensuring everyone is safe and also for putting out equipment. In a dry sports centre, staff will set out the courts and may be involved in coaching or leading activities such as aerobics

● **Service staff** are responsible for making sure all areas of the centre are clean and tidy, maintaining plant – i.e. heating or air conditioning, water filtration system, etc. – and generally ensuring the centre runs smoothly behind the scenes. In busy centres, areas such as changing rooms will need constant cleaning

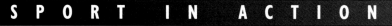

S P O R T   I N   A C T I O N

Tim and Claire are both interested in working in a sports centre but are not quite sure which job would suit them best. To help them, look at the jobs mentioned above and, for each one, list the characteristics and skills that are needed. You may want to read through Chapter 20 to help with this task.

M A T C H   I T

FACILITY	SECTOR
Club run by unpaid helpers	Voluntary
Keele Municipal Golf Course	Public
Centre run for profit	Private
Church hall badminton club	Public
Compulsory competitive tendering	Voluntary
Price concession for low income groups	Public
Esporta Health & Fitness Club	Private

✓ KEY WORDS

Tick each box when you understand the word

ADMINISTRATION ☐

DUAL USE ☐

SCHOOLS PROVISION ☐

✓ R E V I S E   I T !

For your exams you will need to know:

☐ About local provision of public sector sports facilities

☐ About local provision of private sector sports facilities

☐ The role of the local sports club

☐ The role of sports club committee members

☐ The meaning of the key words for this chapter

The National Organisation of Sport

The aim of this chapter is to help you:

◗ Understand the role of the **UK Sports Council** in the organisation of sport in the UK

◗ Look at the role of the **national governing bodies** of sport

◗ Identify and explore how the different **sports agencies** organise sport in the UK

◗ Learn how PE is organised in **UK schools**

As we saw in Chapter 22, UK sport does not follow a set pattern, and government has had little control over its development. A number of bodies try to bring some overall coordination to UK sport. Other agencies have specific roles.

THE UK SPORTS COUNCIL

As we saw earlier, the **UK Sports Council** is responsible for sport at an elite level in the UK and for dealing with sporting issues of national importance. It fulfils its role through three separate bodies:

● The **Performance Development Team** works to ensure that the UK's top athletes receive the highest standards of coaching and support

● The **International Relations and Major Events Directorate** supports British representatives on international sports federations and works with agencies such as the British Council, the Overseas Development Agency and VSO. It also works to attract major sporting events such as the Olympics and the football World Cup to the UK

● The **Ethics and Anti-doping Directorate** works with athletes and governing bodies to develop a fair and drug-free sporting environment for all

◀◀ REWIND

UK SPORTS COUNCIL   see page 161

QUICK TASK

1) Find out which sports council region your school or college is in.

2) Find out the names of all 10 regional sports councils in England.

FAST FORWARD ▷▷

UK SPORTS INSTITUTE
see page 189

TARGET GROUP
Section of the community identified as being under-represented in sport

◁◁ **REWIND**

DISABILITY   see page 159

Disabled athletes have been an important target group for past sports council campaigns

ROLE MODEL
Someone who is held up as a positive example to others

Each of the national sports councils is further split into regions, and each region has its own sports coordinating body. In England, there are ten sports council regions.

The sports councils are funded by means of an annual grant from the government. This pays for staff and buildings and enables them to provide information services to the public. Some of the money also goes directly to sports bodies and clubs.

Recently the sports councils have been able to draw on funding from the **Sports Lottery Fund**. The twice-weekly draw is a major source of funding for sport, and the sports councils are responsible for deciding how this money is spent.

With the help of National Lottery funding, the UKSC has also developed the **UK Sports Institute** (formerly the 'British Academy of Sport'). This will provide the very best facilities to put the UK's top athletes on a par with competitors from other countries. The four sports councils of England, Scotland, Wales and Northern Ireland have also spent money improving sporting facilities for use by the public and participants at club level.

Sports council campaigns

A major objective of the sports councils is to get more people involved in sport – especially so-called **target groups** who have been shown to be under-represented in sport. One major campaign, 'Sport For All', was launched in 1970s. Other targeted campaigns include:

● **Sport For All For The Disabled** Aimed at encouraging more disabled people to become interested in sport and raising awareness of the problems disabled men and women face in trying to take part in sport

● **50+ And All To Play For** Sport has tended to be regarded as a young person's activity. Aimed particularly at older people, this campaign tried to show that all ages can take part

● **Ever Thought Of Sport?** Set up to try and encourage school leavers to take up sport. Many people never play sport after leaving school. As part of the campaign, sports centres were encouraged to work with schools in giving 'taster sessions' so that young people could try a wide range of activities and get used to using local leisure centres

● **What's Your Sport?** In general, women are less likely to play sport than men. Aimed at getting more women to play sport, this campaign used sportswomen as **role models** to show that women can play sport as well as men

Since the launch of the Lottery Sports Fund in 1995, the **English Sports Council (ESC)** has distributed over £600 million to develop and improve sports facilities across the country. Its current priorities are to encourage more young people to take part in sport through its National Junior Sport Programme, and to raise standards and encourage individuals and teams to improve their placings in international competitions.

Target groups

As mentioned above, past sports council campaigns have sometimes been aimed at particular sections of society called **target groups**. **Women** remain the largest target group. Other target groups include:

- Old people
- The unemployed
- Ethnic minorities
- Inner-city communities

FAST FORWARD ▶▶

WOMEN IN SPORT   see page 219

Sally Gunnell – a positive role model for young female athletes

MATCH IT

CAMPAIGN	TARGET GROUP
50+ And All To Play For	Women
Ever Thought Of Sport?	Families
What's Your Sport?	Old people
Sport For All The Family	School leavers

QUICK QUIZ

1) How many national sports councils are there in the UK?
2) How are the sports councils funded?
3) Which body gives out Lottery money to sports clubs and teams?
4) What was the aim of the 'Sport For All' campaign?

GOVERNING BODY
An organising body that looks after all matters affecting a sport

FAST FORWARD ▷▷

RULES   see page 235

SPORTS GOVERNING BODIES

Most modern sports were developed in the late nineteenth century. As sports became more popular, it became necessary for players to decide on a common set of **rules**. Before this, sports and games tended to be played only in one area. Teams did not travel very far, and each area played by its own set of rules.

To provide common rules, sports began to develop their own **governing bodies**. Examples of sports governing bodies today include **The Football Association (FA)**, **The Lawn Tennis Association (LTA)** and **The Amateur Swimming Association (ASA)**.

Role and structure

At present there are over 300 sport governing bodies in the UK, responsible for enforcing the rules of their sport and running competitions and leagues. Sports clubs and teams pay to join the governing body. In return, they have the right to take part in competitions and to be consulted on issues affecting the sport as a whole.

Most governing bodies are still firmly based in the voluntary sector. However, the demands of running a modern sport mean that many now employ full-time officials and coaches to help develop and organise their sport. Their main roles are:

- To make the **rules** for the sport
- To organise **competitions**
- To develop **coaching and leadership schemes**
- To look after sport at **local and national level**
- To select teams and competitors for **national teams**
- To represent the sport at **international level**

Individual sports clubs are organised into **regional** or **county associations**. The county association represents its member clubs on the national body.

Most governing bodies are also members of **international** sports governing bodies – FIFA in football, for example. These international federations decide the rules and regulations for international matches and competitions. This structure is outlined in the diagram on the left.

Many sports governing bodies in the UK are also members of the **British Olympic Association**. This allows them to send teams and individual contestants to the Olympic Games.

International Sports Federations
↑   ↓
National Governing Bodies
↑   ↓
County Associations
↑   ↓
Local clubs

Local clubs have an input at national and international level

---

S P O R T   I N   A C T I O N

Look at the diagram above showing the relation between sport at local and international level. Redraw the diagram, basing it on your chosen sport and naming the sport's controlling bodies.

NATIONAL SPORTS AGENCIES

Although most of the administration of individual sports is done by the sports governing body, there are a number of **national agencies** that coordinate particular areas of sport. These tend to be independent voluntary bodies.

Central Council of Physical Recreation (CCPR)

The CCPR is one of the oldest coordinating sports bodies. Set up in 1935, it acts as the 'voice of the governing bodies', representing their views to the Sports Council and to government. It also provides a forum where sports bodies can discuss issues of common concern. Like the sports councils, the CCPR promotes participation in sport and runs a number of courses in sports leadership which encourage more people to become actively involved. Examples are the **Sports Leader Award** and the **Basic Expedition Leader Award**.

British Olympic Association (BOA)

This independent, non-government funded body is responsible for all Olympic matters in Great Britain and Northern Ireland and for entering competitors for the Summer and Winter Olympic Games, held every four years. Sending a team to the Games costs a lot of money and the BOA raises the millions of pounds required, mostly through commercial sponsorship. You may have seen the BOA logo on chocolate bars and drink cans.

SportsAid Foundation (SAF)

SportsAid raises funds to help talented young athletes in the UK with training and equipment costs in the run-up to national and international competitions. The money is raised through sponsorship, fundraising and donations, and grants are given to individuals who show real sporting potential but who are not yet eligible for support from the National Lottery Sports Fund. In many countries, sportsmen and women are funded by their government, or by scholarships from schools and colleges. Some of those who have benefited from SAF grants are Linford Christie, Sally Gunnell, Jonathan Edwards and Sharron Davies.

National Coaching Foundation (NCF)

Set up by the Sports Council in 1983, the NCF looks after the development of coaches and coaching in the UK. With headquarters in Leeds, it has ten regional training units across England based at sports universities or National Sports Centres, and works closely with coaching centres for Northern Ireland Scotland and Wales. As well as running courses, the NCF produces and sells a range of coaching aids, including books and videos, and publishes a monthly magazine, *Supercoach,* which has details of new ideas and reports on the latest training courses. The NCF has also developed a multi-stage fitness test (bleep test) and abdominal curl test.

QUICK QUIZ

1) **FA, LTA** and **ASA** are the initials of three governing bodies. What are their full names?

2) How many sport governing bodies are there in the UK?

3) What changes in sport and society at the end of the last century led to the development of sport governing bodies?

QUICK TASK

1) Find out which is your nearest National Coaching Foundation centre.

2) Does your team coach/PE teacher have coaching qualifications? If so, what are they, and how were they achieved?

QUICK QUIZ

1) What do the initials **CCPR** stand for?

2) How often are the Olympic Games held?

3) Which sports agency's motto is 'Giving Britons A Sporting Chance'?

4) How does the Sports Aid Foundation help sports men and women to compete in international competitions?

NATIONAL CURRICULUM
The key subjects that all children in state primary and secondary schools are required to study

Dance is just one of the activity types that is included in the National Curriculum for PE

◀◀ **REWIND**

PE   see page 143

EXTRACURRICULAR SPORT
Sport played outside lesson time, usually after school or on Saturdays

THE TEACHING AND ORGANISATION OF PE

In the UK, PE is taught in schools, colleges and universities. Schools in the UK now have to follow a **National Curriculum** for PE, which is one of the group of foundation (i.e. non-core) subjects. The National Curriculum for PE identifies six areas of sports activities that should be taught:

- Games
- Dance
- Swimming
- Gymnastic activities
- Athletic activities
- Outdoor and adventure activities

All children aged 5 to 16 have to study PE. They also have to reach certain levels of attainment at the four Key Stage levels at 7, 11, 14 and 16 years of age.

The money for state schools comes from both central government and local taxes. The **Department for Education and Employment (DfEE)** has responsibility for education in the UK. They appoint people to inspect schools and also draw up the National Curriculum.

Academic courses in PE and sport

In recent years there has been a huge growth in the number of academic courses in **PE** and sport. Courses such as GCSE and A Level PE have been developed which test both theoretical and practical aspects. Most schools now offer such courses.

The other aspect of sport in schools is what is known as **extracurricular sport**. This is carried on outside the classroom – for example, at lunchtimes or after school. Most schools run teams and clubs, where more able sports performers can play for the school team or practise their skills. These are voluntary activities, and neither teachers nor pupils are obliged to take part. However, as teachers are not paid for this extra activity, many have had to reduce the amount they do, as pressure in other areas of their job has increased.

In 1997, the incoming Labour government announced that they would like all children to do at least two hours of extra-curricular activity per week. This may well mean a change in the way after-school courses are organised in future.

MATCH IT

ORGANISATION	ROLE
CCPR	Coordinates coaching in UK
NCF	Has overall responsibility for sport in Scotland
BOA	Body that makes rules and runs competitions for a sport
Scottish Sports Council	Voice of governing bodies
National governing body	Coordinates all Olympic sports in Britain

✓ REVISE IT!

For your exams you will need to know:

☐ About the various agencies that fund sport in the UK

☐ How PE is organised in the UK and the role of the National Curriculum

☐ How the sports councils target participants in sports

☐ About sports councils campaigns and policies

☐ The meaning of the key words for this chapter

✓ KEY WORDS

Tick each box when you understand the word

TARGET GROUP ☐

ROLE MODEL ☐

GOVERNING BODY ☐

NATIONAL CURRICULUM ☐

EXTRACURRICULAR SPORT ☐

24 The International Organisation of Sport

The aim of this chapter is to help you:

- Look at how sport is played around the world

- Investigate how sport is used to promote the politics and ideals of different countries

- Learn about sports events that have a **worldwide importance**

- Learn about problems that have occurred in the **Olympic Games**

Sport is a universal activity, played all over the world. In this chapter we discuss how countries have used sport to further political ideals and show how good their country is, and how this attitude has often affected the most important world sporting events such as the Olympic Games. We will also investigate how different countries organise and fund their sport.

Australian rules football –
one of Australia's most popular sports

SPORT AROUND THE WORLD

Many of the sports that were developed in the UK at the end of the last century such as football, rugby and cricket are now played around the globe. In some cases, countries have adapted them to create their own distinctive games. Examples include Australian rules football (*see photograph opposite*) and American football. Although both are based on rugby, they are very distinctive and unique.

The sports and games played in a country can tell us a lot about that country and how its people live. Football is a good example of this. Although all countries play the same game to the same rules, it is amazing how different countries add their own unique style. This is most evident in the World Cup, when we can marvel at the skill and flair of the Brazilians, the tactical brilliance of the Germans and the sheer fun and enjoyment of the Cameroon team.

Sport in developing countries

Developing countries are sometimes called **Third World** countries. They include most African, Asian and South American nations. Many of these countries used to be ruled by developed countries such as the UK and were introduced to sport by their colonial rulers.

During the last forty years, most have been given independence and now rule themselves. They have used sport to help build up their countries. Sport can be used to encourage the population to get fit and healthy, as well as to win recognition for the country when its athletes and teams do well.

The success of countries such as Kenya in running, the West Indies in cricket and Brazil in football has shown that developing countries can beat the most powerful nations in the world at sport.

Sport in former Eastern Bloc countries

Though the Eastern Bloc no longer exists, former **Communist** countries played a very important role in world sport. Communism is the political system in which everything is owned and controlled by the state. The former Soviet Union and East Germany were the most successful of the Eastern Bloc countries, though all placed some importance on sport.

In the 1990s, with the collapse of Soviet Communism, Eastern Bloc countries became independent again. Although they still win medals, they do not place as much emphasis on sport as before.

However, their legacy is still evident and many other countries including the UK are now using Eastern Bloc methods such as **sports schools** to raise standards and develop sporting excellence.

QUICK TASK

Which sports would you associate with the following countries? You may put down more than one answer.

a) USA   b) Ireland
c) India   d) New Zealand
e) Japan   f) Canada

To help you, here are some sports you might think about:

Ice hockey, Gaelic football, rugby, Kabbadi, hockey, American football, Sumo wrestling, baseball

Sport in the New World countries

New World countries are former British colonies such as Australia, New Zealand and South Africa, i.e. countries that used to be under British rule. They share a lot of culture and tradition with Britain, including sport. All are now independent and have developed into advanced and thriving countries with sporting traditions of their own.

In a few sports such as cricket and rugby, New World countries now compete for world honours. Australia in particular is a world leader in both rugby union, rugby league and cricket. South Africa, until recently excluded from international sport because of **apartheid**, is rapidly re-developing its sporting talent and is once again emerging as a powerful force in rugby, cricket and athletics.

> *APARTHEID*
> *System of laws and practices in South Africa that discriminated against black people and led to South Africa being banned from international sport*

Sport in the USA

America is the most technically advanced country in the world, as well as the most powerful and the richest. This is reflected in American sports. The USA has the most complex games, the richest sports stars and the best facilities for spectators and TV viewers anywhere in the world.

Despite this, basketball is the only truly all-American sport. It was invented by Dr James Naismith at Springfield, Massachusetts in 1891. American football derives from rugby, baseball from rounders and ice hockey from hockey.

Interestingly, America's major sports are not played anywhere else in the world – America is so far ahead that it can hold world championships in baseball and basketball in which only American teams compete!

Sport and big business

American sports are high-scoring, action-packed and very entertaining. They reflect the American way of life, where being a winner is all-important.

The commercial side of American sport makes it very different from other countries. Every level of sport from school to national leagues is run as a business. Nearly all the funding for American sport comes from advertising, sponsorship or the media. Sport stars in America are millionaires. Many, like Michael Jordan, are not only paid large salaries to play sport, but make huge sums of money outside sport as well, through advertising and **endorsing** products.

This commercial side of sport is even found in schools and colleges. Sports such as American football and basketball draw large crowds and most schools have their own stadiums. The money generated from these crowds is used to fund scholarships for players. Good players at high school and college can receive large amounts of money this way.

> *ENDORSEMENT*
> *Recommendation of products such as football boots or trainers by established sports 'stars'*

QUICK QUIZ

1) Which English sport provided the original model for American football?

2) In American sport, what is meant by **product endorsement**?

3) How are sports scholarships funded in American schools and colleges?

SPORT IN ACTION

Below is a copy of the final medal table from the 1996 Atlanta Olympics. Look at the top 25 countries. How many of these would you describe as 'developing countries'?

1996 ATLANTA OLYMPICS – MEDAL TABLE

USA	101	Germany	65	Russia	63	China	50
Australia	40	France	37	Italy	35	South Korea	27
Cuba	25	Ukraine	23	Canada	22	Hungary	21
Romania	20	Netherlands	19	Poland	17	Spain	17
Bulgaria	15	Britain	15	Belarus	15	Brazil	15
Japan	14	Czech Republic	11	Kazakstan	11	Greece	8
Kenya	8	Sweden	8	Switzerland	7	Norway	7
Denmark	6	Turkey	6	New Zealand	6	Belgium	6
Nigeria	6	Jamaica	6				

1) Draw up a table of the top developing nations.

2) Using an atlas or encyclopedia, find out the population for each of these top 25 countries. You would expect that countries with bigger populations would do better since they have more people to choose from.

3) Using a calculator and your data for the top 25 countries, divide the total number of medals by the population in millions. For example, for the UK the figures would be $15 \div 65 = 0.27$.

4) Redraw the table for the top 25 countries, placing the country with the highest number of medals per head of population at the top. Is there a difference between the two tables?

POLITICS AND SPORT

As we saw earlier, an important element of international sport is that different countries and systems compete with one another. For this reason, sport has long been used as a means of proving that one political system is better than another.

The best example of this is the rivalry between the USA and the USSR during the 1960s, 1970s and 1980s – the period of the so-called **Cold War**. During this time, both countries spent huge amounts of money trying to outdo each other in sport. A win at the Olympics, it was said, proved that one political system (**capitalism** or **communism**) was better than the other.

At different times, both countries have boycotted the Olympic Games for political reasons and used their power and influence to persuade other countries not to take part.

Human rights

Human rights issues have brought politics and sport together. **Human rights** are basic entitlements and opportunities that all people should have. In some countries, certain groups of people are denied these rights, such as black people under the former apartheid regime in South Africa.

Sport is one area in which other countries can express their feelings about human rights abuses and bring pressure to bear. They may do this by **boycotting** sporting events or persuading international sports organisations to ban a country from competition.

Many sports people argue that politics and sports should not mix. But as we have seen, it is very difficult to separate the two when so many governments around the world actively support and fund the sports organisations in their country. The Olympic Games has been a major focus for these political problems, and we will look at this in more detail below.

BOYCOTTING
Refusal by a country to compete in an event, usually for political reasons

SPORT ON THE WORLD STAGE

Sport is very popular around the world and major events like the Olympic Games or World Cup are televised in every country. Because of the enormous worldwide audience for these events, any person or organisation wishing to use the occasion in order to make a political statement is guaranteed maximum exposure.

We have already described how countries and governments manipulate sport, and sporting success, for their own ends. Other smaller groups have also used the Olympics as a stage on which to make their point to the world. This has meant that the security and safety systems at the Games have to be very complex and are therefore very expensive.

Below we will identify some of the political issues linked to Olympic Games in the past.

The Modern Olympics

The modern Olympic Games are held every four years, each time in a different city. There are actually two Olympics, winter and summer, but the Summer Games are the more prestigious of the two.

The Games have their origins in Ancient Greece, where they were held every four years as part of a religious ceremony dedicated to the god Zeus. At the end of the last century, a Frenchman called Baron de Coubertin revived the Games and also set up an International Olympic Committee. De Coubertin's idea was that the Games could be used to bring the people of the world together in friendly competition. He hoped that this might help prevent war and develop more international friendship. The first modern Games was held in Greece in 1896.

In the past the Olympics were used to promote all that was best in sport. All competitors were amateurs competing purely for enjoyment and although the winner received a medal, it had no monetary value. Sportsmanship was the central point of the Games, an ideal embodied by the Olympic oath which all athletes took before the Games began.

Politics and the Olympics

Berlin, 1936

The first Olympic Games where politics was openly evident were the so-called Nazi Games of 1936. Berlin had been awarded the Games in 1931, but by 1936 Adolf Hitler and the Nazi party had taken over Germany and Hitler was determined to use the Games to show the world the might of the German nation

Unfortunately for Hitler, a young black American athlete, Jesse Owens, dominated the Games, winning four gold medals. Owens was the only athlete not to receive his gold medals from Hitler, who had left the stadium in disgust. Three years later, Hitler's invasion of neighbouring countries led to the start of the Second World War.

Mexico City, 1968

Two main problems affected the Mexico Olympics. At the time, Mexico was a very poor country, and many people both in and outside Mexico felt that the huge amount of money needed to put on the Games would have been better spent helping to meet basic human needs.

Mexican students actively opposed the Games, holding a number of demonstrations days before the Games were due to begin. Over 10,000 people marched to the Square of the Three Cultures in Mexico City. Aware of the impact such a demon-tration could have so close to the start of the Games, the Mexican authorities sent in troops to surround the demon-strators. A fierce battle followed and by the end 260 people had been killed and several thousands injured. Amazingly, the Games went ahead without further trouble.

The next political problem occurred within the Olympic stadium. In America in the late 1960s, black civil rights groups had been protesting about the lack of opportunity for black people and the racist attitudes of American society. In full view of the world's media, two young black American athletes used the medal ceremony to show their support for the Black Power movement. In the 200m Final, Tommie Smith of USA took gold and John Carlos of the USA took bronze.

As they stood on the medal podium listening to the USA national anthem, they bowed their heads and raised one gloved hand in the Black Power salute. Both were expelled by the US Olympic Association and immediately sent home.

OLYMPIC OATH
Before the Games, all Olympic athletes are required to recite the following:

"We swear that we will take part in these Olympic Games in the true spirit of sportsmanship and that we will abide by the rules that govern them, for the glory of sport and the honour of our country."

Tommie Smith and John Carlos giving the black power salute at the 1968 Mexico Olympics

Munich, 1972

During the Games, Palestinian terrorists, determined to draw attention to Israel's occupation of the West Bank, stormed part of the Olympic village, taking several Israeli athletes hostage.

The German police attempted a dramatic rescue but things went badly wrong, ending in the deaths of nine athletes, a policeman and five terrorists. Many felt the Games should have been abandoned in honour of the athletes killed. But the IOC decided the Games should carry on, in order not to be seen to give in to terrorism.

Montreal, 1976

Two problems overshadowed the Montreal Games. The Canadian government underestimated the costs involved and ran out of money before all the facilities were completed. To increase financial backing for the Games, the IOC later decided to let more commercial companies get involved. On the international front, the Games were boycotted by several African countries in protest against New Zealand, whose rugby team had continued to play against South Africa.

Moscow, 1980

Again, boycotts dominated the Games. In December of the previous year the Soviet Union had invaded Afghanistan. In protest, the USA, Canada, West Germany, Japan and Kenya all refused to take part.

Los Angeles, 1984

In retaliation for the USA-led boycott of the Soviet Olympics in 1980, the Soviet Union led a boycott of the Los Angeles Games in 1984. No Eastern Bloc countries competed.

Seoul, 1988

Korea is a divided country, the North being a communist state, the South capitalist. Seoul in South Korea was awarded the Games by the IOC, but North Korea applied to stage some of the events. The IOC refused and North Korea and three other communist countries boycotted the Games. The 1988 Games were also the first to allow professional tennis players to take part, so ending another Olympic tradition.

Barcelona, 1992

The Barcelona Olympics were generally considered to be a highly successful Games. No boycotts took place, and through the development of the commercial side, the Games made a profit. Following the dismantling of Apartheid, South Africa was allowed back into the Olympic movement. The Soviet Union was replaced by the Commonwealth of Independent States, and West and East Germany took part as one team.

Atlanta, 1996

Many people felt that the centenary of the Games should have been held in Greece, home of both the ancient Olympics and also the first modern Games. In the event, the IOC chose Atlanta above Athens and a number of other cities. One of Atlanta's major claim to fame is that it is the home of Coca Cola, the Olympic movement's biggest sponsor.

Problems with transport and the very hot weather brought many complaints. The lowest point was when a terrorist bomb exploded during a concert in Centenary park, killing several people and injuring many others.

MATCH IT

INCIDENT	PLACE AND DATE
Eastern Bloc boycott	Munich, 1972
Black power protest	Seoul, 1988
North Korea boycott	Mexico City, 1968
Palestinian terrorist attack	Seoul, 1988
Professional tennis players allowed to take part	Los Angeles, 1984

REVISE IT!

For your exams you will need to know:

- [ ] The political and financial issues relating to major international sporting events

- [ ] Details of the problems associated with the following summer Olympic Games: 1936, 1968, 1972, 1976, 1980, 1984, 1988, 1992, 1996

- [ ] How different countries organise sport and the values they place on sport, together with examples from the USA, former Eastern Bloc countries and developing countries

- [ ] How the Olympic Games has been affected by the move from amateur to professional status

- [ ] The meaning of the key words for this chapter

KEY WORDS

Tick each box when you understand the word

APARTHEID [ ]

ENDORSEMENT [ ]

BOYCOTT [ ]

OLYMPIC OATH [ ]

Exam questions: Participation in sport

The questions below are typical of those that you might have to answer in your examination. Try answering each, remembering that the number of marks available for each question gives you a clue to the type of answer required.

Maximum possible marks

1   It is often said people in the 20th century enjoy more **leisure time** than any people before them. Can you identify four reasons why people today have more leisure time? [4]

2   **Physical Education** in schools gives pupils a range of skills. Can you list some of these skills developed through PE under the following two headings? [6]

   a Practical skills
   b Social skills

3   **Participation** in sport brings benefits for individuals and the community. Can you identify some of the benefits that arise from participating and put them under the following headings? [4]

   a Health benefits
   b Social benefits

4   How can sports facilities help **disadvantaged groups** such as OAPs and the unemployed to participate in sport? [3]

5   Access is one of the problems facing disabled people who want to take part in sport and physical activity. Using appropriate examples, can you explain what the term **access** means for disabled participants? [6]

6   Can you list four groups of the population targeted by the **UK Sports Council** in order to increase their participation in sport and physical activity? [4]

7   Can you explain the difference between a **private sector** sports facility and a **public sector** one? [2]

8   How do **dual use** schemes for school sports facilities help both participation and access? [2]

9   How does the **National Lottery** help sport in the UK? [3]

10   What was the aim of the UK Sports Council **Sport For All** campaign? [2]

11   The Football Association, Lawn Tennis Association and Amateur Swimming Association are all examples of **national governing bodies**. What is the role of a national governing body in the running of sport? [4]

Maximum possible marks

12 Can you describe how **commercial factors** have overtaken the original aims of the Olympic movement? [8]

13 Using examples, describe how some groups of people have used the Olympic Games to stage **political protests**. [4]

14 Can you name **four** UK national sport centres? [4]

15 What support would help a young person who is gifted in sport to reach their highest potential? [5]

16 Give four examples of commercial companies that sponsor national sports leagues in the UK. [4]

17 How can **sports sponsorship** benefit a commercial company? [3]

18 Can you explain why sports in the 1990s rely more and more on sponsorship? [5]

19 Using rugby union as an example, explain how the move from **amateurism** to **professionalism** has affected sports. [4]

20 Name **four** sports that remain mainly amateur at the top level. [4]

21 What are the **advantages** of sponsorship for a sport? [4]

22 What are four **disadvantages** of sports sponsorship for a sponsor. [4]

23 **Tobacco sponsorship** in sport is a controversial issue. How might the rules on sponsorship by tobacco companies change in future years, and what are the advantages and disadvantages of these changes? [6]

24 How has the status of **Physical Education** as a subject developed over the last few decades? [4]

Revision guide: Participation in sport

These pages summarise the most important areas covered in Chapters 19–24 on participation in sport. By fully understanding everything below you will be better prepared to succeed in your examination.

Definitions

Make sure you know the meanings of the terms:

- **Sport**: organised contests, using physical exertion between human beings or teams of human beings
- **Leisure**: time when you can choose what to do and when you do it
- **Recreation**: an enjoyable activity that refreshes you and gives you more energy
- **Physical Education**: teaching of knowledge, ideas and values through physical activity

Reasons for increased leisure time include:

- the widespread use of labour-saving devices
- shorter working weeks
- more paid holidays
- earlier retirement
- staying longer in education

Sport in schools

Schools promote sport and physical education in two ways:

- **Physical Education** in school timetables and **National Curriculum** requirements
- Outside lessons, sport and recreation promoted through **extra-curricular sports** and courses

Reasons for participation

Remember the two fundamental reasons:

- **Intrinsic benefits**: health and fitness, reducing stress, self-fulfilment
- **Extrinsic benefits**: fitter people, less strain on health service, less crime

Opportunities for recreation

Facilities are provided by:

- **Local authorities**: the councils, the largest providers, use subsidies to keep costs down
- **Private sector**: companies that make profit from facilities

Factors affecting participation

Be able to define and use the following terms:

- **Provision**: providing recreational facilities so that people can take part in sport
- **Opportunity**: having the chance to part in sport
- **Esteem**: how we feel about ourselves; we play sports that we feel suit us

The five key groups who face discrimination when participating in physical activity are:

- **The elderly**: sport tends to be a young person's activity, less facilities and activities for old
- **The young**: sport and recreation expensive to take part in, less accessible to young
- **Women**: tend to have less time and money for sport, fewer facilities and activities
- **The disabled**: problems of access and availability of facilities and activities
- **Ethnic minorities**: racial groups are often channelled into particular sports

Mass participation

The **Sport For All** campaign was set up by the then Sports Council in 1972, to try and get as many people as possible in the UK taking part in sport. The key reasons were:

- That only one in three play sport
- To improve fitness of population
- To reduce strain on Health Service
- To help people work harder and more efficiently
- To generate jobs and income

Encouraging participation

There are four main methods that can be used to motivate people to take part in sport:

- Subsidised costs
- Programming
- Better transport
- Outreach schemes: taking sport to the people

The organisation of sport

The **public sector** is run by local authorities, funded by admission prices and local taxes. The aim is to provide a service to the community.

The **private sector** is owned by companies or individuals, funded by admission prices. Their aim is to make a profit.

The **UK Sports Council** is responsible for UK sport at the national level, and for promoting UK sporting talent on the world stage. Past campaigns aimed at increasing participation include:

- **50+ And All To Play For**, aimed at elderly
- **What's Your Sport?** aimed at women
- **Ever Thought Of Sport?** aimed at school leavers

The **National Sports Centres** have three key roles:

- Developing sporting excellence
- Training centre for national teams
- Base for training of coaches and administrators

There are six centres:
- Lilleshall
- Crystal Palace
- Bisham Abbey
- Holme Pierrepont
- Plas Y Brenin
- Manchester Velodrome

The national organisation of sport

The rules and organisation of each individual sport are overseen by a **national governing body**.

The **Central Council of Physical Recreation** is the independent voice of the governing bodies, reporting to the UK Sports Council and government.

Other UK sports organisations
- **British Olympic Association (BOA)**: Olympic matters
- **SportsAid Foundation (SAF)**: helps fund amateur athletes
- **National Coaching Foundation (NCF)**: co-ordinates and trains sports coaches

International sport and politics

Political and financial issues are increasingly important in international sport: the **Olympic Games** have become **open**, i.e. moving from amateur to professional status.

International sport is in the spotlight, seen on TV around the world, providing a key opportunity for political protest.

Problems at Olympics

1936: Nazi propaganda
1968: Black Power protest
1972: Arab terrorists
1980: Western boycott
1984: Eastern boycott
1996: Bombing

Sport can be important to a country for political reasons. Winning teams bring prestige. Many governments put money and effort into developing sport in their country. The **'shop window' effect** is where a country uses sport to show itself off to other nations.

Sports funding and sponsorship

Sport and sport facilities cost money. Funding can come from many sources:
- **Government**: limited amount in UK, give grants to sports councils
- **Local councils**: from taxes
- **Grants** from the **National Lottery** and **Foundation for Sports and Arts**
- **Fundraising** and membership
- **Television**
- **Sponsorship** from commercial companies

Sponsorship in sport
Items sponsored include:
- Football team shirts
- Motor racing cars
- Team equipment

The need for sponsorship is increasing because players demand more money and costs have risen. Sponsors can aid individuals, clubs and teams, events.

Advantages of sponsorship

For sport:
- Cover costs
- Pay for grassroots schemes
- Receive equipment and goods provided

For sponsor:
- Publicity
- Reduce tax liability
- Association with success enhances image

Disadvantages of sponsorship

For sport:
- Reliance on sponsorship
- Loss of control/influence
- Less popular sports find it harder to attract sponsorship

For sponsor:
- Can be expensive to sponsor best teams
- Image can suffer if sponsored player/team loses, cheats, etc.

Further reading

- CCPR, *The Organisation Of Sport And Recreation In Britain*, Central Council of Physical Recreation, 1991

- Davis, D., Kimmer, T., and Auty. M., *Physical Education: Theory And Practice*, Macmillan 1986

- Holt, R., *Sport And The British*, Oxford University Press, 1990

- Honeybourne, J., Hill, M., and Moors, H., *Advanced Physical Education And Sport*, Stanley Thornes, 1996

- Lumpkin, A., *PE and Sport – A Contemporary Introduction*, Times Mirror, 1990

- Mason, T., *Sport In Britain*, Oxford University Press, 1988

Politics and Sport

The aim of this chapter is to help you:

○ Understand how **governments** get involved in sport

○ Look at how the government in the UK **influences** sport

○ Understand the role of the **Sports Minister**

○ Discuss the effect of the **National Lottery** on sport

○ Look at the UK government's latest proposals for sport as outlined in *Sport – Raising The Game*

Because sport is popular, people are keen to be associated with it. Many also try to use it to help them gain power or increase their popularity. In Chapter 24 we looked at several occasions at the Olympic Games when sport was used as a way of putting forward a political message. Many governments have also used sport in this way.

◄◄ **REWIND**

OLYMPICS   see page 144

Winning teams enhance the reputation of their country

STATE CONTROL OF SPORT

In some countries the government, or state, has a high degree of control over people's lives. One of the areas it may seek to control is sport. For example, it may decide what kinds of sport can be played and provide money to develop teams and individuals. Governments like their sports teams and stars to be successful, because it reflects well on the country as a whole.

All governments support or influence sport in some way, but the extent of their influence depends on the country's political system. In communist countries like China or the former Soviet Union, everything is controlled centrally by the government. In countries like the UK, the government has less control, leaving bodies such as the Sports Council to run sport independently.

In the former Soviet Union and East Germany, every aspect of sport, from selection to training and diet, was controlled by the state. The government used sport as a **'shop window'** to show off their country to the rest of the world. If their sports stars won gold medals, the government believed it showed that the Soviet Union – and the communist system – was the best.

To make sure that their athletes came up to standard, communist governments spent a lot of money training and preparing them. They developed carefully structured programmes to fitness-test the whole population and pick out potential sports stars. These few were then trained at special sports schools. The government also provided medical support, including performance-enhancing drugs, many of which were illegal. The need to win gold medals became so important that they were prepared to break the rules.

The UK government and its role in sport

Despite the popularity of sport over the last century, the government in the UK has had very little interest in controlling or influencing it. At the beginning of the 20th century, it made PE compulsory in schools, but this was mainly in order to ensure that the population were fit in case of war.

QUICK TASK

1) How do governments benefit from taking control of sport? Write down some advantages and disadvantages of the system.

2) How might a government use its power to make sports stars do what it wants?

'SHOP WINDOW' EFFECT
Using sport to 'show off' a country to the rest of the world

PE was introduced in the UK in order to get the population fit in case of war

Although government involvement in sport has increased since the Second World War, it was not until the 1960s that the position of **Sports Minister** was created *(see below)*. Recently the government has announced plans to support sport and, in particular, to try and help UK teams be more successful in world events *(see opposite)*.

One area where the government has intervened is in improving safety at football matches. In 1990, the **Taylor Report** into the Hillsborough stadium disaster prompted the government to introduce new laws concerning football stadiums. As a result, clubs in all divisions were required to provide all-seater stadiums by August 1999.

Most of the government's coordination of sport is now undertaken by the **Department of Heritage**. However, sporting concerns still do filter into other departments, mainly the **Department for Education and Employment (DfEE)**.

The Minister for Sport

Although the UK has had a Minister for Sport since the early 1960s, the role has never really risen in status above that of junior minister. Many sports bodies would like the Sports Minister to be given cabinet status so that sport is given a higher priority.

In 1992 the **Department of Heritage** was set up, with responsibility for sport and recreation, along with other areas including the arts, media and national heritage. The department has two ministers, a secretary of state and a deputy who also has the title of **Minister with Responsibility for Sport**.

In June 1997 the new Labour government renamed this department the **Department of Culture, Sport and Media**.

The National Lottery

The Department of Heritage's main influence on sport has been the establishment and development of the **National Lottery**.

The National Lottery was established by an Act of Parliament in 1993 and the first draw was made on the 14th November 1994. The now twice-weekly draw raises money for five groups of 'good causes':

- Sport
- Art
- Heritage
- Charities
- The Millennium Fund

Various bodies submit bids for funds to the UK Sports Council, which is the body responsible for allocating lottery money to sport. The amount of money to be distributed each year is approximately £125 million.

THE TAYLOR REPORT, 1990
Official inquiry into the Hillsborough Stadium disaster which led to the introduction of all-seater football stadiums

QUICK QUIZ

1) Which government report led to the change to all-seater football stadiums?
2) How did the former Soviet Union use sport as a 'shop window'?
3) Which government department is headed by the Sports Minister?
4) In what year was the Department of Heritage set up?

SPORT IN ACTION

Try to find out if any of your local sports bodies have received lottery funding. If so, how much, and what was it used for? Information should be available from your local library, council or regional sports council.

'Sport – Raising The Game'

In the summer of 1995, the Department of Heritage and the Prime Minister, John Major, published a sports policy document entitled *Sport – Raising The Game*. This set out the government's proposals for rebuilding British sport. The main emphasis of the proposals was to recognise the role of schools in the development of sport. It outlined what the government felt the different sports bodies should be doing to raise standards.

The other main proposal was that a **British Academy of Sport** should be set up to serve as a centre of excellence for British sporting talent. In 1998 the government announced that Sheffield will be the site of the now renamed **UK Sports Institute**. This will provide facilities for the UK's top athletes to train and prepare for competition.

QUICK TASK

Ask to borrow a copy of **Sport – Raising The Game** from your school, college or local library. Take a look at the proposals and summarise the main points.

✓ REVISE IT!

For your exams you will need to know:

- ☐ How the National Lottery helps to fund sport

- ☐ How the Taylor Report affected football

- ☐ The meaning of the key words for this chapter

✓ KEY WORDS

Tick the box when you understand the word

THE TAYLOR REPORT ☐

'SHOP WINDOW' EFFECT ☐

Coaching, Facilities and Finance

The aim of this chapter is to help you:

○ Understand the role of **coaching** in developing sports performance

○ Understand what is meant by **facilities** in sport

○ Identify where people can take part in sport

○ Identify the people who provide sports facilities

○ Understand what is meant by **funding** in sport and who provides it

In order to take part in sport, people need sports facilities. Building and maintaining facilities costs money. In this chapter, we look at the type of sports facilities available and who pays for them. We also examine the role of the coach in improving performance and helping players develop their skills.

COACHING

The role of the coach is to improve players' performance. Coaches need to have a good knowledge of their chosen sport. They should be able to pick out faults and correct them so that the performer becomes a better player. They also need to get on well with people and have good communication skills.

Coaches can work with teams or individuals. Their role and responsibilities vary depending on the sport or club they work for. In professional football, the coach is the club manager who is in charge of the team. Coaches have to improve the performance of their team or performers. They also have a major role in selecting players and buying players from other clubs.

Professional coaches have to get their teams to win – or risk the sack! Most coaches in the UK do not get paid for coaching, but do it in their spare time as volunteers. Many have qualifica-

A coach in action

Far left: *The role of the coach is to improve the skills of athletes and players*

Left: *Terry Venables, the former England coach and manager*

tions, and a number of bodies now offer coaching courses. In Chapter 23, we mentioned the work of the **National Coaching Foundation (NCF)**. The aim of the NCF is to develop coaching in the UK and to offer information and advice on training. Most sports governing bodies also run coaching awards for their particular sports.

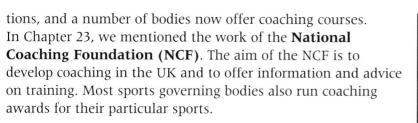

◀◀ **REWIND**

NATIONAL COACHING FOUNDATION see page 171

FACILITIES

The place where we play sport is called a **facility**. It may be a specially built indoor arena, or an outdoor pitch or playing field. Whichever the case, it will provide the basic requirements of the sport, i.e.:

- Space to play

- Pitch markings and goals

- Changing rooms

- Somewhere to socialise after the game

Sporting facilities can be found in a number of places and vary in shape, size and quality.

Where are the facilities?

Below is a list of the most common sports facilities. How many can you find in your area?

- Sports centres

- Playing fields

- Sports clubs

- Swimming pools

- National Sports Centres

Some sports use the natural environment as their 'sports facility'

FAST FORWARD ▷▷

NATIONAL SPORTS CENTRES see page 205

A commercial fitness centre

QUICK TASK

Referring to Chapter 28 or other sources of information, find out, and summarise in a table, which sports are catered for by each of the following national centres:

a) *The **National Indoor Arena, Birmingham***
b) *Wembley Stadium*
c) *Crystal Palace National Sports Centre*
d) *Don Valley Stadium, Sheffield*

◀◀ **REWIND**

FUNDING   see page 168

FOUNDATION FOR SPORT AND THE ARTS
Source of funding for sport, financed by a levy on the football pools

FAST FORWARD ▷▷

SPONSORSHIP   see page 196

User groups

The people who use sports facilities are called **user groups**. Some groups use sports facilities every week. Others visit less regularly. Different user groups will have different needs, but the facility must try and satisfy all of them. Many do this by scheduling special sessions for particular groups of users – a method known as **programming**.

Funding

The money to build and maintain sports facilities can come from a variety of sources. Due to the expense of new facilities, fundraising alone may not be enough, and most clubs and organisations have to look for financial help from outside sources.

The five sports councils are one such source. Money to help build new facilities is available through the sports councils' grant from government and also increasingly from the **National Lottery**.

Another is the **Foundation for Sport and the Arts** which is funded by a levy on the football pools. Again, clubs seeking grants have to make a formal application in writing.

Commercial sponsorship is another means of gaining funding. Many football clubs have been able to build major new stadiums with help from commercial companies. Recent examples include Bolton Wanderers' Reebok Stadium and Stoke City's Britannia Stadium.

S P O R T   I N   A C T I O N

1) Do you have a coach? Ask your coach or PE teacher what coaching qualifications they have, which body awarded them and how long it took.

2) As a class or group, compare different coaches and sports.

M A T C H   I T

SPORT	FACILITY
Ice skating	Lake or river
Canoeing	Municipal ice rink
Badminton	Indoor court
Skiing	Golf course
Golf	Mountain or dry ski slope

QUICK QUIZ

1) How many National Sports Centres are there in the UK?

2) In which city is the National Indoor Arena?

3) How can sports centres attract members of the population who may not be used to playing sport?

✓ R E V I S E   I T !

For your exams you will need to know:

☐ About local and national sports facilities

☐ About the role of the National Sports Centres

☐ What facilities are provided by:

- Local authorities
- Private sector
- Voluntary sector
- National authorities (e.g. the Sports Council)

☐ What finance is provided by:

- National government
- Local government
- Sports governing bodies
- The sports councils
- Business/private individuals
- Lottery and other gambling levies

☐ The meaning of the key words for this chapter

✓ K E Y   W O R D S

Tick each box when you understand the word

USER GROUP ☐

PROGRAMMING ☐

FOUNDATION FOR ☐
SPORT AND THE ARTS

27 *Sponsorship in Sport*

The aim of this chapter is to help you:

○ Understand the role **sponsorship** plays in sport

○ Identify who provides sponsorship for sport

○ Look at the **advantages** and **disadvantages** of sponsorship in sport

○ Explore other forms of **commercial funding** in sport

As we have seen in previous chapters, sport nowadays costs large sums of money. **Sponsorship** is an important way of providing that money. There are many advantages of sponsorship, both for individual sports and for the companies who provide it. However, sponsorship can also affect the way a sport is organised and presented. All these areas need to be explored in our study of sponsorship in sport.

QUICK TASK

How many commercial companies can you think of who sponsor sports events? Try and complete the table below

SPONSORSHIP AND SPORT

Item, event or activity	Sponsoring company
Football team shirt	
League or competition	
Motor racing car	
England cricket team equipment	
Drinking bottles at athletics events	

Left: *Footballers today are walking billboards for companies and commercial products*

Above: *Linford Christie – sponsored by Puma*

THE ROLE OF SPONSORSHIP

In the last twenty years, changes in sport have resulted in a dramatic increase in the amount of **sponsorship** by commercial companies. Many companies today are very willing to invest money in sport. Sport is very popular and reaches a wide audience via TV and the printed media.

The most common examples of sponsorship in sport are the company logos seen on football shirts during televised matches. As the UK's most popular sport, football attracts sponsorship from a large range of companies.

If you look at the sports pages of a newspaper, you will see that nearly all the sports leagues are sponsored. Many companies provide large sums of money to help cover league administration costs and provide prize money for the winners. Sports sponsorship helps both the sport and the sponsor. The performer receives money so they can buy the best equipment and clothing. They can also concentrate on their training, rather than having to spend time working to make ends meet.

In return, the sponsoring company benefits by being publicly associated with a successful performer or a winning team, and by being promoted to a very wide audience.

Although most companies take a strictly commercial view of sponsorship, some companies donate money to sport without asking for their name to be used in return. If the sports body is a registered charity, companies can use **Gift Aid Rules** which allow them to donate part of their profit without having to pay tax on it.

> *SPONSORSHIP*
> *Support by frms and companies for sports events and performers, usually in return for corporate publicity*

The Grand National – sponsored by Martell

Commercial sponsorship in sport

Commercial sponsorship of sport takes a variety of different forms. Sports performers in individual sports such as athletics and swimming often receive money to help with training and competition costs. Companies tend to favour existing stars, or at least performers who have the potential to be stars in the future.

For example:

- Linford Christie is sponsored by Puma, and even wears Puma Contact lenses!

- Martina Hingis, the young Swiss tennis player, is sponsored by Sergio Tacchini

Clubs and teams receive sponsorship from a variety of companies. The money can be used to help pay for kit and equipment or to develop facilities.

For example:

- Manchester United shirts are sponsored by the electronics firm Sharp

- The England cricket team kit is sponsored by Vodaphone

- The Scarborough Football Club ground is sponsored by the food manufacturers McCain

Major sporting events, competitions and leagues are extremely expensive to organise and administer, and sponsoring companies can be sure of a large amount of publicity and coverage in the media. Examples include:

- The London Flora Marathon

- The FA Carling Premiership

- The Martell Grand National

WHO SPONSORS WHAT?

Different companies tend to be attracted to different sports. This is because each sport attracts a certain audience which is also a potential **market** for the sponsor's products or services. Obviously, small local companies cannot afford to sponsor national sports events, and tend to spend their money on local events and teams.

Sports manufacturers have an obvious reason for sponsoring sports performers and events, and were the first to spot the potential of sports sponsorship. Nowadays nearly all sportswear carries the name or logo of the manufacturer.

Sports manufacturers want people to wear their kit and use their equipment. Big companies like Nike, Reebok and Adidas are prepared to spend millions sponsoring stars such as Michael Jordan in the hope that the public will associate the success of the performer with their particular product.

QUICK TASK

If you were organising a sports event such as a local marathon, what benefits could you offer local companies in return for sponsoring the event?

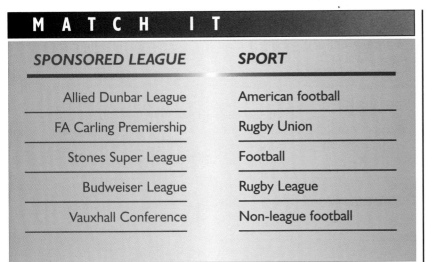

MATCH IT

SPONSORED LEAGUE	SPORT
Allied Dunbar League	American football
FA Carling Premiership	Rugby Union
Stones Super League	Football
Budweiser League	Rugby League
Vauxhall Conference	Non-league football

Insurance firms and banks have been involved in a wide range of sports sponsorship. Generally they have tended to favour sports such as cricket, rugby and hockey, but many banks also sponsor '**grassroots**' sports schemes and school sport awards. Examples are:

- TSB swimming awards for schools

- Midland Bank school tennis and hockey competitions

Breweries and tobacco companies spend a lot of money on sports sponsorship. Sports such as snooker and darts are obvious candidates since they are both 'pub sports'. Some sports have now rejected sponsorship from these companies as they do not wish to be associated with products that have been shown to be bad for health. Recent changes in advertising rules mean that sport is one of the very few areas where breweries and tobacco companies can still get their name on TV.

In the summer of 1997, the recently elected Labour government announced a proposal to ban all tobacco sponsorship in sport. Though later changed to allow existing sponsorship contracts to run their course, the decision represented a major shift in government policy.

> GRASSROOTS
> At beginner-level – i.e. for people, usually children, who are just starting out in sport

Advantages of sports sponsorship

For sports:

- In professional sport, sponsorship provides another source of income for players and clubs

- For amateurs, sponsorship helps cover the cost of training and competition and improve performance

- Sponsorship helps sports organisations fund grassroots schemes such as coaching and training courses

- Major events are very expensive to put on and require money from outside sources

For the sponsor

- Sponsors gain publicity for their company, image and products

- Companies can reduce the amount of tax they pay through sponsorship

- Sponsors can enhance their public image by being associated with sporting success

Disadvantages of sports sponsorship

For sports

- Sports can come to rely too heavily on sponsorship money. When this is withdrawn, teams or organisations which have no other source of income can face closure

- Sponsors can have too much influence over the sport, e.g. insisting that teams change their kit or influencing the timing of events

- Less popular sports attract less sponsorship, making it more difficult for them to survive

For the sponsor

- Sponsorship is a gamble. If the team/performer is successful, it is money well spent. If not, it can be a waste of money

- The company's image may suffer if the sponsored sportsperson or team behave disreputably – on or off the pitch

- Competition amongst companies means that sponsoring the top teams and performers is becoming more and more expensive

QUICK QUIZ

1) Give four examples of sporting items or events that can be sponsored, e.g. a tournament.

2) Give four example of companies that sponsor football teams

3) What are the disadvantages of sports sponsorship for the sports themselves?

SPORT IN ACTION

The pros and cons of tobacco sponsorship in sport makes a good topic for a debate. Divide into groups, and let each group take one of the following roles:

- A sports governing body
- A television company
- A tobacco company
- The Health Education Council

Each group needs to do some research into their role. After electing a chairperson, the group should make a short presentation and then open up to questions.

'Pyjama cricket' – coloured kit is considered to make the game more attractive to spectators and sponsors

EFFECTS OF SPORTS SPONSORSHIP

Because sports are costly to run, sponsors have a great deal of power. Some sports have had to change their rules in response to demands from sponsors. For example, sponsors' demand for maximum TV exposure has meant that the timing of football matches has changed from the traditional Saturday afternoon to **peaktime viewing** slots every night of the week. American football has even introduced more stoppages in play to allow more commercial breaks during the game.

Sportswear and equipment has also changed in response to commercial pressures. Cricket has abandoned its traditional white in favour of a range of colours for one-day matches. Shirts and equipment have been redesigned in order to allow more space to display the sponsor's logo. Formula One racing cars – even the drivers themselves – are covered in sponsors' logos.

Advertisement and endorsement

Many commercial companies nowadays are keen to use sports people to promote their products. These products may not necessarily be sports-related: Gary Lineker, for example, is well known for advertising Walkers Crisps. In return the sports people receive payment. Again, it is usually the better known performers that are used. Top sports stars often appear on TV and can become household names.

Endorsement is where top sports stars give their name or approval to a product. The company wants the public to believe that if they use that particular product they will be as good as the sports star. The best example is Nike Air Jordans, the training shoes worn by basketballer Michael Jordan.

Again, sport stars will receive large amounts of money for each endorsement – often millions of pounds. Michael Jordan also endorses breakfast cereals, cars, drinks and underwear.

> **PEAKTIME VIEWING**
> When most people are watching TV, usually in the early evening

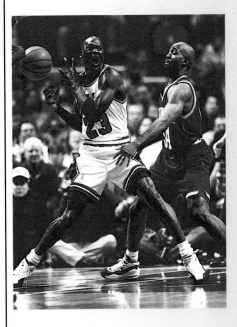

Basketballer Michael Jordan – sponsored by Nike

M A T C H   I T

SPONSORSHIP BENEFIT	WHO GAINS?
Source of income	Sponsor
Reduced tax liability	Sport
Gain public esteem through link with sporting success	Sport
Helps cover cost of training	Sponsor
Pays for administration of grassroots schemes	Sport

✓ KEY WORDS

Tick each box when you understand the word

SPONSORSHIP ☐

PEAKTIME VIEWING ☐

✓ R E V I S E   I T !

For your exams you will need to know:

☐ Examples of major events/competitions and their sponsors

☐ The advantages of sponsorship to the sports, the performers and sponsors

☐ The disadvantages of sponsorship to the sports, the performers and sponsors

☐ The effects of sponsorship on the organisation, equipment and timing of sports events

☐ The influence of sponsorship on amateurism and professionalism in sport

☐ The meaning of the key words for this chapter

Excellence in Sport

The aim of this chapter is to help you:

- Understand what is meant by **excellence** in sport

- Look at what makes a **sports champion**

- Understand the role **science** can play in developing sports champions

- Know about the role of the UK **National Sports Centres**

- Understand how the proposed **UK Sports Institute** will help develop sporting excellence in the future

Sebastian Coe in his book *More Than A Game* writes that 'Champions are made, not born'. In this section of the book we will discuss how champions are created in sport. Excellence in sport is an important issue in the UK. Many people feel that UK sporting performance is declining, and that, where we used to be one of the best sporting nations in the world, we are now slipping down the rankings.

WHAT IS EXCELLENCE?

First, let us try and define what we mean by the term **excellence**. In fact the word has two meanings which can be represented in the pyramid diagram on page 202:

- **Elitism** is about improving the performance of a selected few. Most of the time and money in modern sport goes into developing these top performers

- **Optimum performance** is about improving everybody. Here the aim is to get everyone in sport to perform to the very best of their ability

The best in the world – South Africa win the 1996 Rugby World Cup

> **ELITISM**
> Where facilities and opportunities in sport are provided for only a small number of the most highly talented people

> **OPTIMUM PERFORMANCE**
> The highest standard an individual can achieve

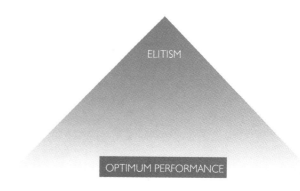

ELITISM

OPTIMUM PERFORMANCE

The pursuit of excellence: a visually handicapped athlete competing with the help of a sighted partner

---

SELECTION
Process of identifying sporting talent

SPORTS SCHOOLS
Facilities where young people can develop their sporting potential while carrying on with their academic studies

---

We can all aim to achieve a personal best in our own sport. This may mean swimming a length of the pool in the fastest time we can or managing to run a marathon. But to create national sporting champions, it is necessary for the nation to concentrate only on developing excellence in their very best performers. It would be far too expensive to train everyone in the country to achieve their best.

WHAT MAKES A CHAMPION?

There are three main stages in creating a sports champion:

I Selection

Identifying potential champions is the start of the process. The pyramid theory of sports development suggests that the wider the base, the greater the number of people at the top of the pyramid. The aim of the selection process is to make the base of the pyramid as wide as possible.

Usually, selection in sport begins at school. If you are good enough, you may be selected to play for your school team. Playing in matches and attending practices will develop your talent, and the next stage is to be selected for the district or county side. Often the better performers will go to trials and practice games, where selectors pick out the people who they think may have the potential to play at a higher level. The top players may then go on to represent their country in international events.

Sometimes individual sports will have a similar system, run through the clubs. Again, there will be a progression from local to district to country representation. Professional clubs may use **scouts**. These are people who watch games at school and local clubs and pick out performers to train at professional clubs.

There are also a number of **sports schools** in the UK. Here the best performers of school age are trained together. The most famous sports schools are the **FA School at Lilleshall** and the **LTA Tennis School** at Bisham Abbey *(see page 201)*.

2 Developing talent

Becoming a champion requires daily practice and a lot of dedication. You need to improve your skill in your sport and also your fitness. In order to do this, you need the best equipment, facilities and **coaching** available. Coaches may work for a club or sports organisation. Often good performers may have to travel a long way to get to the best facilities.

3 Winning

This is the most important part of all. If all your preparation is right, you should stand a good chance of winning. However, it is not just the physical side that needs to be trained. To be a winner, you need to develop the right **mental attitude** as well.

You need to be able to push yourself to the limit and have a determination to succeed. Many sports performers now use **sports psychologists** to help them prepare for competition. This involves strict concentration on performance and blocking out everything that might prevent them from winning.

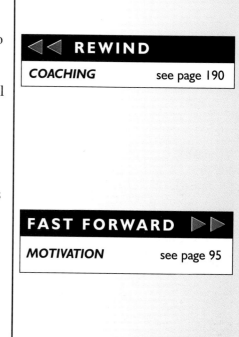

◀◀ **REWIND**

COACHING   see page 190

FAST FORWARD ▷▷

MOTIVATION   see page 95

QUICK QUIZ

1) Why do countries prefer to concentrate on developing a few top players rather than encouraging excellence for all?

2) What three stages go into making a sports champion?

3) What is the role of a selector in sport?

Linford Christie: success in sport depends on positive thinking

THE ROLE OF SPORTS SCIENCE

> **SPORTS SCIENCE**
> *Studies aimed at developing sporting excellence*

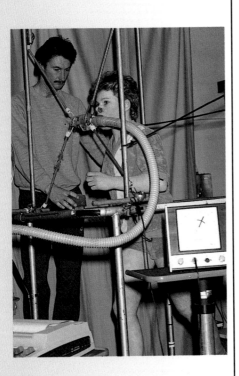

All top sports performers should be able to gain from the appliance of sports science

Sports science is a relatively new area of study. It covers a variety of subjects associated with sport and the development of sporting excellence.

- **Sports physiology** looks at the way the body functions and how its performance can be improved. Sports physiologists can help a performer by testing fitness and recommending ways to improve it

- **Biomechanics** is the study of the way the body moves. Studying performance on video can highlight problem areas that biomechanics can correct, and help performers with their techniques

- **Sports psychology** can help prepare performers mentally for competition. This may involve the use of relaxation techniques or methods of building up confidence and belief in the ability to win, both of which may improve performance

- **Sports nutrition** Performers are only as good as the food they eat. A nutritionist can help a performer by making sure their diet contains the right elements. Diets may need to be changed for training and competition

- **Physiotherapy** aims to help sports men and women recover from injury through a combination of exercise and physical manipulation. Physiotherapists identify problems and provide support and treatment to get performers playing again

QUICK TASK

What kind of factors affect your personal performance in sport? Make a list of things that a sports psychologist might tell you to ignore, such as the crowd and other competitors

M A T C H   I T

SUPPORT	SPORTS SCIENTIST
Treating injuries and promoting recovery	Psychologist
Helping performers relax before competition	Nutritionist
Testing fitness levels	Physiotherapist
Providing diet sheets	Physiologist
Analysing running action of a sprinter	Physiotherapist
Prescribing exercises for strained joints or muscles	Biomechanic

THE NATIONAL SPORT CENTRES

Many of the sports scientists described opposite work either in university sports departments or at the **National Sports Centres**. These six centres have been developed to help develop sporting excellence in the UK. They enable our international performers to train in top-quality facilities with all the equipment and expert help they need.

- **Bisham Abbey, Buckinghamshire** Home of the LTA National Tennis Centre. Also has facilities for football, hockey, squash, golf and weightlifting. England's football and rugby teams use Bisham Abbey as a base for training before matches

- **Crystal Palace, London** International-standard facilities for athletics, swimming, the martial arts and up to 40 other sports. Used as a training base for the national athletics and swimming squads

- **Holme Pierrepont, Nottingham** The national water sports centre, with international-standard facilities for canoeing, rowing, water-skiing and many other aquatic sports

- **Lilleshall, Shropshire** Home to the FA School of Soccer Excellence and the National Sports Injuries Clinic. The British Amateur Gymnastic Association also has a national training centre here

- **Plas Y Brenin, North Wales** The National Centre for Mountain Activities. Also caters for a wide range of outdoor sports

- **Manchester Velodrome** The National Centre for Cycling – the latest of the national sports centres

The UK Sports Institute

In the summer of 1995, the Heritage Department's policy document *Sport – Raising the Game* set out the Conservative government's proposals for rebuilding UK sport. One of the main proposals was the setting up of a **UK Sports Institute**, to be funded from the National Lottery.

In 1998 the government announced that Sheffield had been chosen as the site of the Institute. A similar initiative in Australia has been highly successful, and it is hoped that the UK Institute will prove equally so.

> NATIONAL SPORTS CENTRES
> The six centres of sporting excellence in the UK

> SPORT – RAISING THE GAME
> Published in 1995, the Conservative government's blueprint for rebuilding sport in the UK

> UK SPORTS INSTITUTE
> National sports training centre, to be located in Sheffield

S P O R T   I N   A C T I O N

How would you get to the top in your favourite sport?

Produce a chart to show how you might progress from school team to playing for your country.

MATCH IT

NATIONAL CENTRE	LOCATION
National base for swimming and athletics training	Lilleshall
LTA National Tennis Centre	Bisham Abbey
National Water Sports Centre	Holme Pierrepont
National Cycling Centre	Plas Y Brenin
National Centre for Mountain Activities	Sheffield
FA School of Soccer Excellence	Manchester Velodrome
UK Sports Institute	Crystal Palace

✓ KEY WORDS

Tick each box when you understand the word

ELITISM ☐

OPTIMUM PERFORMANCE ☐

SELECTION ☐

SPORTS SCIENCE ☐

NATIONAL SPORTS CENTRES ☐

UK SPORTS INSTITUTE ☐

✓ REVISE IT!

For your exams you will need to know:

☐ How sporting excellence is provided for

☐ How sporting excellence is developed

☐ The role of the National Sports Centres

☐ The meaning of the key words for this chapter

Amateurs and Professionals

The aim of this chapter is to help you:

Understand what we mean by **amateur** and **professional**

Understand some of the **history** of amateurism and professionalism in sport

Identify ways sports performers receive money

Understand how the **Olympics** have recently changed the rules on amateurism

When modern sports were developed towards the end of the last century, most performers still played sport in their spare time, simply for enjoyment. But as more and more people started watching sport, players began to receive payment in some sports. This chapter explores the rise of **professionalism** in sport.

COMMERCIALISM AND SPORT

Nowadays top performers in all sports are able to receive money from playing – and some stars can earn huge amounts. This was not always the case.

In the past **amateurs** played sport simply for the love of it. They receive little or no payment. Most people still play this way. There are hundreds of amateur football, rugby, hockey, netball, gymnastic, swimming and cricket clubs across the country.

A **professional** is someone who makes their living from sport. They receive money for playing, often earning more if they win. Professional performers will probably spend all their time preparing, training for, or playing their sports, whereas amateurs tend to have other jobs and commitments.

There are also sports which are **semi-professional** – for example, rugby league and non-league football. Here, players do receive money, but not enough to live on. They still need a regular job in order to support themselves.

Netball remains a popular amateur sport

QUICK TASK

1) Can you name four professional sports?
2) Can you name four sports that are still amateur?

3) List the reasons why amateurs play sport.

At the time of writing most Premiership footballers earn well over £70,000 a year

OPEN SPORT
One that allows amateurs and professionals to compete against one another

AMATEURISM AND THE CLASS SYSTEM

Historically, amateur sports such as athletics, rugby union and rowing have always been played and controlled by the upper classes, while the 'working classes' have played professional sports such as football and boxing.

When modern sports began to develop in the late 1800s, it was only the upper classes that had the time and money to take part in sport. They were not worried about making money from sport since they earned enough by other means.

It was not so easy for the working classes. In the 1870s, many worked six days a week, and playing sport would have meant missing an afternoon's work – and an afternoon's wages.

In sports such as football, it was recognised that lack of money was preventing many talented players from playing for their clubs and teams – and so clubs began to pay working-class players a small fee to make up for their lost wages. There had been limited professionalism in sports before this: boxing and foot races often had a money prize for the winner. But it was football that became the first truly professional sport.

Towards the end of the nineteenth century, laws were passed to give all workers a half-day off each week – generally Saturday afternoon. This meant that more people were free to play sport – and more importantly, to watch it. As the crowds grew at football matches, so did the wages players earned. Soon most of the top clubs employed professional footballers full-time.

However, in other sports, things developed differently. Many established sports such as rowing opposed the influx of working-class players into their clubs. They made strict rules allowing only amateurs to compete. This often ruled out working-class participants, who could not afford the costs.

Rugby union and rugby league
In rugby, the conflict between amateur and professional caused a major split. Many northern teams had large numbers of working-class players and wanted to pay them for the time they lost from work, as with football. However, the teams in the south of England, which were mainly middle class, were against this and persuaded the governing body of rugby, the RFU, to ban payment of any kind. This led in 1885 to the northern clubs leaving to form a new code of rugby, Northern Union, which later became **rugby league**. It was not until a century later that rugby union finally allowed players to receive payment.

The rise of 'open' sports

In the 1990s, pressure from commercial interests in sport has meant that most sports have now become **open**. This means they allow both amateurs and professionals to play. However, the demands on the modern sports performer mean that in reality only full-time players can compete at the highest level. In order to be full-time, players *have* to be professional.

The split between amateurs and professionals one hundred years ago led to the birth of a new sport – rugby league

Recently both rugby union and athletics have changed their rules to allow performers to receive payment. Athletics has for some time allowed performers to use trust funds to help cover the cost of their training, but rugby union had been a true amateur sport from the start. In both cases the influence of sponsors and the media has led to a change in the rules.

A **trust fund** is built up from sponsorship, appearance money and other income. However, the player does not receive the money directly. It is held in an account which can only be used for training and competition expenses. At the end of their career, players can draw all the money from their fund.

The funding of sports performers

Nowadays sports performers can receive money for playing sport in a number of ways. Usually, the more successful they are, the more they earn and the greater the variety of sources of income:

- **Wages** Some sports pay performers a wage for playing

- **Appearance money** In sports such as athletics and golf, players are paid for taking part, usually by the event's sponsors

- **Prize money** Here, the winner of an event will be given a sum of money and often other prizes such as cars as well. There may also be cash prizes for runners-up

- **Sponsorship** Financial backing from companies, who use the sport or performers to promote their products

- **Scholarships** Some schools and organisations pay talented performers scholarships to cover the cost of training and competition, as well as their education

- **TV appearance fees** Players can be paid for appearing on TV shows and commentating on matches

- **Publicity** Well-known performers can receive money for guest appearances, or for activities such as after-dinner speaking

> **TRUST FUNDS**
> *Schemes that allow amateur sports men and women to earn money from their sport*

QUICK QUIZ

1) Which social class is normally associated with amateurism?

2) In 1885, which sport split into a professional and an amateur code?

3) What change in working laws led to more people being free to watch sport?

◀◀ **REWIND**

OLYMPIC GAMES   see page 144

THE OLYMPIC IDEAL
The principle that performers should take part in sport for the pleasure of competing, not for money or reward

OPEN OLYMPICS
Since the late 1980s the Olympics have allowed both professionals and amateurs to compete

THE OPEN OLYMPICS

As we saw earlier, the modern **Olympics** were established in 1896. At the time, the International Olympic Committee who organised the Games stated that sports performers should not make a living or any sort of profit from sport. The Games were based around the **Olympic ideal**. According to this, the important thing was to take part and not to win.

Professionalism rules

However, the dramatic rise in the standards of performance and the increasing influence of the media and sponsors has led to the need for athletes to train all the year round. To do this, they require payment to enable them to concentrate on sport.

In the 1980s the Olympics became more open and the rules were altered so that both amateurs and professional could compete. It is likely that professionals will soon dominate the Olympic Games.

One of the first Olympic sports to admit professionals was basketball. At the 1988 and 1992 Olympic Games, the USA team was made up of professional basketball players from the American leagues. Not surprisingly, this 'dream team' took the gold medal on both occasions.

Commercialism in sport

As we have mentioned in earlier chapters, top-level sport is attracting more and more attention from commercial companies and the media. Although this affects some sports more than others, sport at all levels is becoming more and more dependent on sponsorship.

Television is a particularly important source of money. Companies such as Sky Sports have invested millions of pounds in sports such as football and rugby league. This has resulted in massive increases in the wages paid to top players.

Sports stars in America are millionaires. Most professional teams have a number of players on multi-million-pound annual contracts. Many stars like Michael Jordan and Shaquille O'Neil will make even more money through sponsorship deals and endorsements.

The USA 'dream team' – professional sportsmen playing in the Olympics

S P O R T   I N   A C T I O N

Try and list the various costs an athlete might have to pay in order to train for the Olympic games.

You could use the following headings to help you:

- Training costs
- Competition costs
- Medical and living costs

MATCH IT

SPORT	STATUS
Netball	Professional
Boxing	Amateur
Hockey	Professional
Rugby league	Amateur
Tennis	Amateur
Football	Professional
Swimming	Professional
Formula One motor racing	Professional

QUICK QUIZ

1) Explain the meaning of the term **professional** in sport.

2) Explain what the term **amateur** means in sport.

3) Why are sponsors so keen to use sports stars to advertise their products?

REVISE IT!

For your exams you will need to know:

☐ The traditional differences between between amateur and professional sport

☐ The origins of amateur and professional sport

☐ The development of amateur and professional sports

☐ Current isues relating to amateur and professional sport

☐ Specific examples of changes in athletics and rugby

☐ Amateurism and professionalism in the Olympics

☐ The influence of sponsorship and the media on amateur and professional sport

☐ The meaning of the key words for this Chapter

KEY WORDS

Tick each box when you understand the word

OPEN SPORT ☐

TRUST FUND ☐

THE OLYMPIC IDEAL ☐

OPEN OLYMPICS ☐

30

The Role of the Media in Sport

The aim of this chapter is to help you:

- Identify the different forms of media

- Investigate the way sport is covered by the media

- Explore the concept of the **sports star**

- Understand the positive and negative influence of the media on sport

Sport has been affected by many factors during the twentieth century. There has been a steady move away from participation and towards watching sport instead. To begin with, people watched sport live, but today most of us watch sport on television. Television is one of the **media** we shall be looking at in this chapter, and the one which has the biggest effect on sport today.

American football – a sport regularly seen on Channel 4 in the UK

FORMS OF MEDIA

Newspapers, television (**terrestrial**, cable and satellite), radio, magazines and films are all forms of **media**. All of them devote a great deal of time and space to reporting, discussing and analysing sport.

We can tell how important sport is to our culture by the amount of time and space the media devote to it. The BBC alone devotes at least 20 hours per week to sport, while most national newspapers devote 20–30 per cent of their pages to sport.

The media began to have an impact on sport in the late nineteenth century when newspapers first started reporting on games and events. Later, at the beginning of the twentieth century, radio began to broadcast live. This was to have an important effect on the development of modern sport.

The audience for sport

Suddenly the audience for sports events became much bigger. Whereas thousands of people might attend a football match, the same match broadcast on radio could reach an audience of millions. Radio helped turn occasions such as the FA Cup and the Derby into events the whole country could follow.

In the 1950s television turned many sports into entertainment packages, giving them a more glamorous image to attract viewers. In the 1990s satellite and cable television have transformed sport into a global phenomenon. We can now watch sports events from anywhere in the world, live in our own front room.

HOW IS SPORT COVERED?

The presence of the media has turned sport into a **commodity** – something that can be bought and sold. Television companies pay huge sums of money to cover sporting events. Advertisers and sponsors back sport because of the exposure they get in the media.

Individuals train and prepare for sport in the knowledge that the media will give them a stage on which to present their talents – and a valuable source of income.

As we saw above, television and radio allow us to experience live coverage of matches, but they also present many other types of sports programmes. Often programmes make use of **edited highlights** to give certain sports a better image and make them seem more lively. TV companies only want to show entertaining action and naturally tend to concentrate on the best moments of any sporting event.

TV and radio also increasingly feature **sports discussion programmes**, where people talk about events and performers. There are also a number of **sports quizzes** broadcast both on radio and TV.

TERRESTRIAL TV
The traditional, i.e. non-satellite, non-cable, channels in Britain – BBC1 and BBC2, ITV and Channels 4 and 5

THE MEDIA
Channels of mass-communication including the press, television and radio

QUICK TASK

1) Identify four sports shown regularly on TV.
2) Name two satellite TV channels that are devoted totally to sport.
3) Give examples of sports from other countries shown on Channel 4.

QUICK QUIZ

1) Which of the media first broadcast 'live' sport?
2) Can you name the UK's five terrestrial TV channels?
3) In what way does TV make sponsors more willing to give money to sport?

QUICK TASK

1) Can you name three sports quizzes on either radio or television?

2) List the main differences between each.

PAY-PER-VIEW
System whereby, in addition to their usual subscription or fee, the television viewer must pay to watch a particular programme

SENSATIONALISM
Use of attention-grabbing headlines or 'exclusives' to attract readers

The impact of technology

Televised sport today makes use of every conceivable technological trick to give the viewer the best possible vantage point on the action – from instant action replays to miniature cameras mounted in cricket stumps, snooker-table pockets or on the bonnet of racing cars.

Technology is also used to stop cheating in sport. Many sports now use video evidence to spot fouls which the referee or umpire may have missed during the game.

Because of the popularity of sport we now have radio and television channels devoted entirely to sport – a growing trend for the future. Discussions are already underway to bring in **pay-per-view** channels for football. Soon leading football clubs will have their own TV channels where all matches will be shown.

Press coverage of sport

The back pages of most newspapers in the UK are entirely devoted to sport. Papers in the UK are known collectively as the **press**, and tend to fall into two groups;

● Tabloids (e.g. the *Sun* and *Mirror*)

● Broadsheet or 'quality' papers (e.g. *The Times* and *The Telegraph*)

Although both types of newspaper carry sports reports, their style of coverage is very different.

Both types of newspaper include reports of matches and events, comments and sports news. Sometimes, especially on Monday and Sunday, they may carry a separate sports section.

The tabloid papers tend to report on a smaller number of sports – usually the more popular ones. They also tend to be more **sensationalist** in their coverage, reporting on the private lives of sports personalities or using outrageous headlines to attract readers' attention. Broadsheet papers tend to be more factual and cover a wider range of sports. However, male sport tends to dominate in both types of newspaper.

QUICK TASK

1) Can you name four specialist sports magazines? As a class, bring in some examples and compare them. Do you think they offer good value for money?

2) Find three sports magazines covering the same area (e.g. golf or football). Think about the differences between them, then complete the following table:

Title	Sports covered	No. of pages	Target audience

Magazines

Sports magazines are a growing area of the sports media. There are now hundreds of titles available. They tend to concentrate on specific sports and come out only once a month or fortnightly.

In order to attract readers, they are often very glossy and colourful, although this tends to make them expensive to buy.

QUICK QUIZ

1) Can you name four tabloid daily papers?

2) On which days do papers tend to have a separate sports section?

3) How do tabloid papers try to attract people to read their sports pages?

SPORT IN ACTION

Collect a tabloid and a broadsheet newspaper for the same day. Study the sports pages of both papers, then fill in the following table:

UK PRESS SPORTS COVERAGE

		Tabloid	Broadsheet
Title			
Number of sports covered			
Number of 'male-oriented' pieces			
Number of 'female-oriented' pieces			
Percentage of sports pages devoted to:	Photographs		
	Headlines		
	Text		
	Adverts		

As a class, look at a range of different papers, and compare the results. You could limit your study to the Sunday papers, which tend to have a separate sports section.

THE DEVELOPMENT OF THE 'SPORTS STAR'

The media – and the press in particular – have turned sports men and women into celebrities. Top performers become household names. As a result, they attract attention from sponsors and advertisers. Many also become stars in non-sporting areas such as TV chat shows and panel games.

This is good news up to a point, since it enables them to make a lot of money. But it also means they are public figures, whose every move off and on the pitch attracts massive media attention. Often, the spotlight focuses more on their private life than on their sporting talent. The result is that performers have to be very careful not to let the intense media pressure interfere with their sporting performance.

Sports such as gymnastics often find it hard to get coverage in the media

MINOR SPORT
A sport that is only played or watched by a small number of people

EXCLUSIVE RIGHT
An agreement whereby only one television company is allowed to broadcast a game or event

POSITIVE AND NEGATIVE EFFECTS OF THE MEDIA

The media have had a number of effects on sport, some of which have been very positive. For example, the media have:

● Brought more sponsors into sport

● Awakened public interest in sport, so that people either play or watch sport more often

● Made some sports performers rich and famous

● Given sports the technology to help referees and officials control the game more easily

● Allowed coaches and performers to study technique on video and improve their performance

But the media have also had a number of negative effects:

● Sports like football and racing get wide coverage, while others find it hard to get coverage in the media, and **minor sports** find it hard to attract sponsorship

● Live television coverage often means smaller crowds

● People may prefer to watch the game from the comfort of their home, and a club or event may lose money as a result

● As sports performers become media personalities, they may find their private life as well as their sporting talent in the spotlight

The power of the media

The media have now become so powerful that TV companies can dictate when, where and even how games are played:

● Tennis introduced the tie break so that games would fit in with TV schedules

● Squash now uses glass courts so that cameras can get a better view of the action

● Rugby league uses a 'video ref' to check decisions

The media and the Olympics

The influence of the media – especially television – is epitomised by coverage of the Olympic Games. This great event is now controlled by American television companies who pay well over $400 million for the **exclusive rights** to screen the Games.

This financial influence gives the American TV companies enormous power over the way the Games are conducted. For example, British TV audiences now have to stay up late at night to see key moments such as the 100 metres Final, so that the race can be screened at peak viewing time in America.

The Olympics – a great sporting event now dominated by powerful TV sponsors

QUICK QUIZ

1) How might television affect the size of the crowd at a live event?

2) Name two quality/broadsheet newspapers sold in the UK.

3) Identify two disadvantages of a sport being associated with TV.

M A T C H   I T

NEWSPAPER	TABLOID OR BROADSHEET?
The Sun	Tabloid
The Daily Express	Broadsheet
The Times	Tabloid
The Star	Tabloid
The Guardian	Broadsheet
The Mirror	Tabloid
The Independent	Broadsheet
The Daily Mail	Tabloid
The News of the World	Broadsheet
The Sunday Times	Tabloid

S P O R T   I N   A C T I O N

Collect one of the weekly TV listings guides from one of the national papers. For each channel, record how many programmes are devoted to sport each week.

1) Which channel shows the most sport?
2) Which sports are on television the most?

✓ K E Y   W O R D S

Tick each box when you understand the word

MEDIA ☐

TERRESTRIAL TV ☐

PAY-PER-VIEW ☐

SENSATIONALISM ☐

MINOR SPORT ☐

EXCLUSIVE RIGHT ☐

✓ R E V I S E   I T !

For your exams you will need to know:

☐ The different forms of the media

☐ How different media cover sport

☐ How the media has developed sports stars

☐ Positive effects of the media on sport

☐ Negative effects of the media on sport

☐ How the media and sponsorship work together in sport

☐ The meaning of the key words for this chapter

Women in Sport

CHAPTER 31

The aim of this chapter is to help you to:

- ⦰ Investigate the role of **women** in sport
- ⦰ Look at the **history** of women's sport
- ⦰ Understand the movement towards **equality** in sport
- ⦰ Understand the role of the **Womens Sport Foundation**

Gender is the term we use to differentiate between the sexes. There are two forms of gender, male and female. Each year in the UK, 33 per cent of men participate in some form of sporting activity, while the figure for women is only 10 per cent. As women make up just over half the population, this suggests some form of discrimination. In this chapter we look at women in sport and try to identify some of the reasons why fewer women play sport than men.

◀◀ REWIND	
GENDER	see page 157

Which of these sports do you think portrays a 'feminine' image?

QUICK QUIZ

1) What percentage of women regularly take part in sport?

2) In which sports do scientists suggest women might one day out-perform men?

3) What is the name of the image traditionally associated with women?

◄◄ REWIND

STEREOTYPING   see page 156

MYTH
A stereotype that has become so widely used that people accept it as fact

SPORT AND FEMININITY

Despite changes in society, many people still fundamentally believe that women ought to conform to a set image of 'femininity'. This stereotyped view of how women are expected to think, dress and behave also extends to the area of sport.

There have been many **myths** about what sports are 'suitable' for women. Although many of these are now seen to be untrue, many people still believe that women's sporting capabilities are inherently more limited than men's.

Before 1980, women were not allowed to compete in marathons in the Olympic Games. The athletic authorities took the view that 26 miles was too far for women to run, and that they did not have the physique for endurance sports.

However, in the last few years there have been many very good female runners, and performances are improving all the time. Sports scientists now even claim that women may be better suited to the longer, endurance-type events than men.

Hockey – a 'suitable' sport for women?

Practical difficulties

Apart from the issue of prejudice, women who want to participate in sport face a number of practical difficulties which are not encountered by men.

One of these is time. Because of the combined pressures of work and family, women tend to have less leisure time than men. When they do find time for sport, they are often exhausted from all their other activities.

Breaking the stereotype

However, more and more women are taking up sport – and slowly the media and public are becoming more interested.

So-called 'feminine' sports such as gymnastics, ice skating, netball and hockey have always attracted women participants and spectators, but recently women have begun to break the stereotype by taking up sports such as boxing, football and rugby as well. The success of the England women's rugby team, who are currently world champions, may encourage more women to take up a wider range of sports. Indeed, the fastest-growing sports in the UK are women's rugby and women's football.

However, some sports and events are still closed to women. In athletics, women are not allowed to compete in the Olympic pole vault, hammer or triple jump. Until recently it was illegal for women to box in the UK.

Could women one day out-perform men in the Marathon?

Although recently made legal in the UK, women's boxing still causes controversy

WOMEN'S SPORTS – A BRIEF HISTORY

Throughout history, women have taken part in sports. In ancien Greece, female athletes had their own version of the Olympic Games. Egyptian drawings called **hieroglyphics** show men and women competing in various sporting activities.

However, in nearly every society, women's sports have taken second place to men's. For men, sport was a substitute for war and a chance to show off their fighting skills, bravery and strength. But women were always constrained by society's narrow view of their role. This image was evident in many different cultures and countries. Women could play sports, but only if they were not too demanding or violent.

From 1800 to the present day

In the 1800s, some sports such as cricket and golf were very popular for women, and in a few sports such as tennis and badminton, women could play alongside men.

In the 1960s there was a 'battle of the sexes' when the top women's tennis player played against the top male tennis player – and won. Although there are now many high-profile female tennis players such as Steffi Graf, at most tournaments, women receive less prize money than the men. This is also true in athletics.

Women and the Oympics

At the first modern Olympics in 1896, women did not take part. At the next Games in 1902, they were only permitted to participate in a very small number of sports.

Although now there are many events for women to compete in at the Olympics, there are still not as many as for men. As we saw earlier, some sports such as boxing are still barred to women.

◀◀ **REWIND**

OLYMPICS   see page 144

QUICK QUIZ

1) Which are the UK's fastest-growing sports in terms of participation?

2) How can role models be used to increase participation in sport?

3) Why was it considered acceptable for women to play tennis in Victorian times?

In Victorian England, tennis was regarded as an acceptable sport for women

'Question of Sport' presenter,
Sue Barker. More women are now
seen on TV sports shows

QUICK TASK

What sports do girls at your school or
college play? Look at activities that are
offered:

a)   In PE lessons
b)   For extra-curricular sport
c)   In your local area

Present this information in the form of a
table. Do girls or boys have more
opportunity to play sport?

WOMEN, SPORT AND THE MEDIA

In the past, the media have shown little interest in women's
sport, and male sports still tend to dominate both TV and the
press. Because of this lack of attention, sponsors also tend to be
less enthusiastic about backing women's sport. When women
sports stars are used to advertise goods, they tend to be
associated with 'feminine' products such as shampoos.

However, in recent years there have been a number of
important developments. Channel 4 has had a policy of showing
a number of minority sports, including women's football. There
are also now a number of female broadcasters and reporters.
Role models such as Sue Barker, Helen Rollason and Sue Mott
are now regularly seen on television fronting sports
programmes.

QUICK TASK

1)   Look at the sports programmes
     shown on TV for the next week.
     How many women's sports are
     mentioned?
2)   How much airtime is given to
     women's sport compared to men's?

Towards equal opportunity in sport

The term **equal opportunity** means giving everybody equal
access to sport. This involves trying to remove obstacles that
prevent certain groups from taking part.

As we saw earlier, women have been identified by the Sports
Councils as one of the 'target groups' of people who are under-
represented in sport. The Sports Council's campaign 'What's
Your Sport?' was deliberately set up to try and encourage more
women to take part.

Many sports centres and swimming pools use **programming**
to provide special sessions for women – for example, mothers
and toddlers. This **positive discrimination** is an active attempt
to get more women to take part. Often women feel more
comfortable taking part in sport if only other women are
present.

EQUAL OPPORTUNITY
Giving everyone equal access to sport,
regardless of gender, race or background

QUICK TASK

We have discussed this idea of equal
opportunity earlier in the book. What
factors might prevent somebody from
taking part in sport? List the various
factors.

POSITIVE DISCRIMINATION
Deliberately trying to redress the balance
in favour of a disadvantaged group

ADMINISTRATORS
People who help organise and run sport bodies and clubs

Women in sports administration and management

Women are also under-represented in management and coaching, and most sports **administrators** are still men. The main reason for this is that in the past there have always been fewer women participants. Often when people retire from sport they move into sports administration.

As in the case of the media, however, this is slowly changing and there are now a small number of women referees in football and rugby. Hopefully, as more women take part in sport, more will also move into management and administration.

The Womens Sports Foundation

This organisation was founded in 1984 with the aim of improving and promoting opportunities for women in sport and increasing the participation rate among women. The Foundation runs campaigns and adverts, lobbies other bodies, including the media, and provides information and materials for schools and colleges. It also works closely with other bodies such as the UK Sports Council.

WOMENS SPORTS FOUNDATION

✔ KEY WORDS

Tick each box when you understand the word

GENDER ☐

STEREOTYPE ☐

MYTH ☐

EQUAL OPPORTUNITY ☐

POSITIVE DISCRIMI-NATION ☐

ADMINISTRATORS ☐

✔ REVISE IT!

For your exams you will need to know:

☐ How gender affects participation in sport

☐ The traditional role of women in sport

☐ How the media represent women's sport

☐ How gender can affect sponsorship

☐ How the development of equality in sport has affected women

☐ The role of the Womens Sports foundation in promoting women's sport

☐ How women have been identified as one of the UK Sports Council target groups

☐ The meaning of the key words for this chapter

Behaviour in Sport

CHAPTER 32

The aim of this chapter is to help you to:

- Understand what is meant by **sportsmanship**

- Look at how sports people can break sporting **rules**

- Understand how **violence** can sometimes occur in sport

- Look at how sports **spectators** behave

- Understand some of the problems associated with football **hooliganism**

Sport needs rules to ensure fair play and to protect participants from getting hurt. Sometimes people break these rules or cheat. There are many ways of cheating and we shall look at some of them in this chapter. People attending sports events can also behave badly. Some may use sports events in order to stage protests, knowing the media will be present. Others use sports events as an excuse to fight.

Hooliganism on the terraces

SPORTSMANSHIP AND 'FAIR PLAY'

Sport relies on sportsmanship, i.e. playing to the written and **unwritten rules** of the game.

- **Fair play** means treating your opponent as an equal. If you win, you do it by sticking to the rules

- **Sportsmanship** includes shaking hands and cheering the other team at the end of the game. Often this mutual respect between opponents is vital for players' own safety

Many sports involve high-speed contact with potentially lethal weapons such as hockey sticks. In such cases, disregarding the rules could cause serious injury.

> **UNWRITTEN RULES**
> The values, ethics or 'spirit of the game' which all sports men and women are expected to follow

FIFA
The International Federation of Association Football, the body responsible for administering international football

◀◀ **REWIND**

INTRINSIC   see page 95
REWARDS

GAMESMANSHIP
Where winning becomes the most important objective for a team or sportsperson

John McEnroe – sportsman or 'gamesman'?

◀◀ **REWIND**

DRUG ABUSE   see page 77

QUICK TASK

Write down five ways in which people cheat in sport. Why do you think they do this?

'Gamesmanship'

Fair play and sportsmanship are still an important part of sport in the UK, and sports governing bodies such as **FIFA** have tried to foster sportsmanship by giving **Fair Play awards**. But for many, the pressures to win – and the rewards of winning – are too great. If people cheat and win, this is often referred to as a 'hollow victory'. Although it may bring **extrinsic** gains, it will not produce the more satisfying **intrinsic** rewards.

Instead of sportsmanship, many sports performers have turned to **gamesmanship**, using whatever means they can to beat their opponent. The only aim here is to win – not so much by breaking the rules as bending them to their advantage.

Many sport stars of the last few years could be described as masters of gamesmanship. For example, John McEnroe used to distract his opponents by arguing with the umpire and the crowd. Boris Becker has also been disqualified from a tennis tournament for similar gamesmanship.

Gamesmanship has now become an acceptable part of modern sport. Unfortunately, the mood is changing from 'We shall play fairly' to 'If you can't beat them, join them.'

Cheating

There are an increasing number of ways in which people can **cheat** in sport. Some of these are listed below:

- Intentionally fouling or injuring a player

- Taking illegal drugs to enhance performance

- Hoodwinking the referee or officials to try and gain an advantage – 'diving' in football, for example

- Using illegal or banned equipment

When the pressure is on, players can be tempted to break the rules

Sports governing bodies now spend a lot of time and money trying to stamp out cheating. The increase in television coverage has helped cut down a little, since cameras can sometimes record evidence of fouls that the referee may have missed. But as the rewards of winning continue to grow, the incentive to cheat still proves to be too great for some.

Violence

Violence is also a growing phenomenon in modern sport. However, it is debatable whether sport is actually becoming more violent, or whether the presence of the media – and especially the use of TV action replays – simply makes it more obvious.

Once again, it is often the need to win that leads to violence in sport. If the opposition's best player is injured, they can no longer take a full role in the game. Although a professional foul may result in a penalty, there is a good chance that the goalkeeper will save it. Violence can also be caused by pent-up frustration: when the match is not going their way, players may get angry and vent their aggression on opponents or officials.

Violence in sport is another example of cheating

QUICK TASK

Frustration in sport can lead to violence. Can you list five things that might make a player frustrated during a game?

CROWD BEHAVIOUR

These same pressures and frustrations can affect spectators as well. Crowds at football matches are very passionate, and fans often experience extremes of emotion when supporting their team – especially at key matches. For many people, supporting a football team is almost like belonging to a tribe or religious cult.

We earlier defined **spectatorism** as 'people paying to watch sports'. Football attracts the biggest crowds in the UK, but other sports such as rugby, athletics and tennis also attract large numbers. It is only a minority of sports – notably football and boxing – that seem to give rise to problems of crowd behaviour.

As with the sport itself, spectating has certain rules – although they are less strictly observed now than they used to be. Crowds too can show sportsmanship by applauding good play by both teams, keeping quiet when players take penalties and accepting referees' decisions.

Racial abuse

Another aspect of crowd behaviour in recent years is verbal – and especially racial – abuse directed at officials or players. Again, this is a problem that tends to be associated with football, where abuse directed at players from ethnic minorities used to be common.

The campaign, 'Let's Kick Racism Out Of Football', which is supported by a range of footballing bodies, has had some success in trying to tackle the problem. It is now a criminal offence to use racist abuse at a football ground.

QUICK QUIZ

1) Can you name four sports that attract paying spectators in the UK?

2) What is the name of the campaign set up by the FA to combat racism?

3) What is a **professional foul** in football?

HEYSEL STADIUM DISASTER
Collapse of a wall causing the death of 39 people at the 1985 European Cup Final in Belgium, following rioting on the terraces by Liverpool fans

HILLSBOROUGH FOOTBALL DISASTER
Tragic death of 95 Liverpool fans following a sudden surge of spectators into the Sheffield Stadium at an FA Cup semi-final

Sport can stir up powerful emotions

QUICK TASK

1) List four examples of hooligan behaviour that may occur at football matches.

2) One method clubs have used to prevent hooligan behaviour is to try and get more families involved. Can you think of any schemes or activities that could be used to attract families to football matches?

◀◀ **REWIND**

ALCOHOL   see page 81

Hooliganism

The problem of football hooliganism has received a lot of attention in the media and has been widely studied. There are many theories to explain why some supporters become violent.

Although certain sports have always attracted a hooligan element, football hooliganism did not become a major problem until the 1960s. It continued to develop in the 1970s, until dramatic events at the **Heysel** stadium in Belgium and **Hillsborough** in the 1980s led to a much stricter approach to the problem by both the football and government authorities.

The Taylor Report

Following the fire at **Bradford City** football ground of 1985 and the **Hillsborough Stadium disaster** of 1989, the government commissioned a major investigation into spectator behaviour and the safety aspects of football grounds. The main conclusion of the **Taylor Report (1990)** was that all stadiums should become all-seater. This has now been fully implemented.

The media has played an important part in developing the image of the football hooligan. It has been argued that, by sensationalising a relatively minor form of rowdyism, the media have created a fashionable image for young men to follow.

The other major contributory factor to most outbreaks of hooliganism is **alcohol**. Drinking can cause people to be more aggressive than normal, and most grounds have now banned the sale of alcohol during matches.

Solutions to hooliganism

In recent years, football authorities and police have worked hard at tackling the problem of hooliganism. Schemes have included:

- **Segregation** The oldest form of crowd control, where fans from different teams are kept apart to prevent trouble

- **All-ticket games** Spectators can be controlled, and only those with tickets allowed near to the stadium

- **No away fans** A number of clubs have tried this policy for short periods, notably Manchester United and Luton. Though effective, it tends to result in a lack of atmosphere at matches

- **Early kick-off** Aimed at preventing fans from drinking too much before the game

- **Closed-circuit TV** Perhaps the most successful approach of all. Nearly all football grounds are now covered by closed-circuit cameras which can be used to pick out troublemakers in the crowd

- **Families** A family atmosphere was found to deter hooliganism. Many clubs have set up schemes to get more families into their grounds

M A T C H   I T

BEHAVIOUR	DESCRIPTION
Shaking hands at the end of the match	Gamesmanship
Diving in the penalty area in football	Sportsmanship
'Walking' in cricket	Sportsmanship
Helping an opponent up after a tackle	Gamesmanship
Arguing with the umpire's decision in tennis	Gamesmanship
Talking performance-enhancing drugs	Sportsmanship

QUICK QUIZ

1) How is alcohol linked to hooliganism?

2) What was the main conclusion of the Taylor Report?

3) How might an early kick off at a football match deter bad behaviour?

✔ R E V I S E   I T !

For your exams you will need to know:

☐ How the behaviour of performers varies from sport to sport

☐ What is meant by sporting etiquette or sportsmanship

☐ How participants and officials should behave during sport

☐ Why violence occurs on the sports pitch

☐ About anti-social behaviour by sports spectators

☐ Strategies for combatting football hooliganism, including segregation

☐ About the Taylor Report recommendations and all-seater stadiums

☐ The meaning of the key words for this chapter

✔ K E Y   W O R D S

Tick each box when you understand the word

UNWRITTEN RULES ☐

FIFA ☐

GAMESMANSHIP ☐

HEYSEL STADIUM DISASTER ☐

HILLSBOROUGH DISASTER ☐

Exam questions: Issues in PE and sport

The questions below are typical of those that you might have to answer in your examination. Try answering each, remembering that the number of marks available for each question gives you a clue to the type of answer required.

Maximum possible marks

1 Identify **four** sports shown regularly on TV. [4]

2 'The presence of the media has turned sport into a commodity.' Explain the meaning of this statement, using examples of sports sponsorship. [5]

3 How might **'pay per view'** TV affect sports coverage in the future? [3]

4 The **media** have had a number of effects on sport, some good, some bad. Describe some of these positive and negative effects of the media on sport. [6]

5 Give examples of how **stereotypes** affect the sports people choose to play. [2]

6 Name four **women's sports** regularly seen on television. [4]

7 Discuss the view that sponsors tend to be less enthusiastic about backing women's sport. [4]

8 How do some sports facilities use **positive discrimination** to increase the participation of certain groups of the population? [3]

9 Sport relies on sportsmanship – people playing to the written and unwritten rules of the game. Can you explain what we mean by the terms **written** and **unwritten rules**? [2]

10 'People cheat in sport, and the rewards are becoming so great that in future more may be tempted.' Can you give examples of how people can attempt to cheat in sport? [4]

11 Can you name four sports that attract paying spectators in the UK? [4]

12 In the 1970s and 1980s **football hooliganism** was a severe social problem. Can you describe some of the methods authorities used to tackle the problem? [5]

13 How do governments benefit from taking control of sport? [3]

14 What are the advantages and disadvantages of government control in sport? [6]

15 What does the term **shop window effect** refer to in international sport? [2]

Maximum possible marks

6 How does the **UK Sports Council** help fund sport in the UK? [3]

7 How could a sports centre attract members of the population who may not be used to playing sport? [4]

8 What does the term **endorsement** mean? Give two current examples. [4]

9 How has the increasing level of commercialism led to the change to 'open' status of most sports? [4]

0 What are the advantages of attending a sports school? [3]

1 What are the disadvantages of attending a sports school? [3]

2 How could a **sports psychologist** help prepare an athlete before an important competition? [4]

3 How does the history of rugby football reflect the problems over **amateurism** and **professionalism** in sport? [6]

4 How can professional performers earn money from sport? [5]

Revision guide: Issues in PE and sport

These pages summarise the most important areas covered in Chapters 25–32 on issues in PE and sport. By fully understanding everything below you will be better prepared to succeed in your examination.

The role of the media

Terms and definitions
Media: channels of mass communication including the press, radio and television.
  – **Newspapers**: tabloid (*The Sun*) and broadsheet (*The Times*)
  – **Magazines**: general sport (*Total Sport*) and sport-specific (*90 Minutes*)
  – **Television**: terrestrial (BBC, ITV, CH4) and satellite (Sky Sports, Eurosport)
  – **Films**: *Cool Running, White Men Can't Jump, Chariots Of Fire*

Sports coverage
Make sure you understand and use terms such as :
  – **Factual**: reporting what actually happens
  – **Sensational**: focusing on the personal life of stars/ use of headline-grabbing 'exclusives'
  – **Highlights**: where the best parts of a match are shown or reported on
  – **Educational**: information film or documentary that looks in detail at sports/performers

The 'sports star'
The sports star is a relatively new phenomenon.
  – Exposure of individuals/teams
  – Attraction to sponsors
  – Sports stars used to endorse and promote products

Effects of the media on sport

Positive:
  – Better-informed supporters
  – Greater number of spectators
  – Increase in participation: more people playing
  – Increase in sponsorship
  – Creation of sports personalities: the sports star or 'household name'

Negative:
  – Over-exposure of major sports such as football
  – Problems of exposure/sponsorship for minor sports
  – Decrease in attendances
  – Sensationalism and effect on personalities
  – Power of media in changing timings, rules, image of sport
  – Limiting access to view sport, e.g. introduction of **pay per view**

The media and sponsorship
Both need each other: the media to attract viewers, sponsors to attract buyers. Media exposure attracts sponsors and can help increase their market.

Women in sport

Gender and participation
Social attitudes, lack of time and cost affect women's participation in sport.
  Equal opportunity programmes try to even out the participation in sport between the sexes.
  Media coverage: women's sport receives less exposure, and is labelled as less exciting – feminine image only used.
  Women's participation also influenced by traditional role of women in society and in sport, i.e. subordinate status.
  Sports stereotypically regarded as 'suitable' for women are:
  – Tennis
  – Netball
  – Gymnastics

Encouraging participation
Various organisations and activities encourage womens' participation in sport:
  – Role of the **Womens Sport Foundation**
  – **UK Sport Council** tries to improve women's participation through the use of targeted campaigns
  – **Programming** at sports centres

Behaviour in sport

Behaviour of performers may differ from sport to sport. Sporting etiquette is linked to **sportsmanship**, defined as playing to the letter *and* spirit of the game.

Cheating in sport
Examples include:
  – Drug abuse
  – Bribing officials
  – Tampering with equipment
  – Violence
The reasons for cheating include:
  – Money or reward
  – Chance of getting away with it
  – Feeling that everyone else is doing it

Conduct of players and officials
Be able to compare the behaviour of players in different sports.

Spectator behaviour
Be aware of the effects of spectator behaviour, especially the problem of football hooliganism.

Strategies used to reduce this problem include:
- All-seater stadiums *(Taylor Report)*
- CCTV
- Segregation of fans
- Harsher penalties

Further reading

- Allison, L., *The Politics of Sport*, Manchester University Press, 1986

- Blue, A., *Grace Under Pressure*, Sidgwick & Jackson, 1987

- Cashmore, E., *Making Sense Of Sport*, Routledge, 1990

- Coe, S., Treasdale, D., and Wickham, D., *More Than A Game*, BBC Books, 1992

- Davis, R., Bull, R., Roscoe, J., Roscoe, D., *PE And The Study Of Sport*, 3rd Edition, Mosby, 1997

- Davis, D., Kimmer, T., and Auty. M., *Physical Education: Theory and Practice*, Macmillan Australia, 1986

- Honeybourne, J., Hill, M., and Moors, H., *Advanced Physical Education And Sport*, Stanley Thornes, 1996

Rules, Tactics and Techniques

All the current GCSE PE syllabuses offer students the opportunity to be assessed in practical activities. This section of the book is designed to help students prepare for some of these activities.

The following sports are covered:

Athletics	Badminton	Basketball
Cricket	Football	Hockey
Netball	Rugby league	Rugby union
Swimming	Tennis	

The tasks and questions are designed to help both students and their teachers to combine the practical and theoretical elements of the course in a straightforward way. The overview on page 235 could also be used to introduce the theoretical aspects of the practical activities.

Sport questions

The questions on pages 237–241 can be used in three ways:

● As part of a practical activity, with students using them as a checklist

● For assessment

● As preparation for final assessment or moderation

Shortage of space has meant it has not been possible to cover all the activities offered by all exam boards, and the number of exemplar questions is limited. However, it is hoped that students and teachers will use the examples given as a model to develop further questions of their own.

Students and teachers are advised to refer to other specific sources for the detail and information for each activity covered. In particular, the **Sports Action Packs** produced by the Royal Navy are a very useful resource.

OVERVIEW

Rules

All sports activities require **rules**. Their purpose is to ensure fair competition and protect participants from injury and accident during the game. All performers should have a good grasp of the rules before beginning an activity.

Usually an official such as a **referee** or **umpire** will administer the rules. Referees have a difficult job and should always be respected and listened to. Just because there is a referee present it does not mean you do not need to know the rules yourself!

Each sports governing body issues a **handbook** setting down the rules of the sport. These can change from year to year so it is important to keep up to date with the latest edition. It is a good idea to check if there are any new rules at the beginning of each new season and ask coaches or referees to explain them to you.

Ignoring rules can result in injury and foul play. Referees and umpires have the power to warn or send players off for breaking rules. In extreme circumstances governing bodies have the power to ban individuals from the sport altogether.

Skills

All practical activities need a level of **skill**. If you want to perform better you must improve your skills. Some skills such as hand-to-eye coordination and balance are needed in all sports, but most are specific to the particular sport and need to be practised.

Most sports require a number of different skills and you need to be able to identify what they are. You also need to identify which skills you are good at, and which skills need more work. Often your coach or teacher will be able to help you with this, identifying your strengths and weakness and giving you practice exercises to help.

Skills development takes **practice**. This means repeating a technique many times until you become proficient. Practices or **drills** can be used to develop skills, and you should know some examples of these.

When looking at particular skills you need to have an idea of what good technique is like. You can gain this from watching a good demonstration by someone, or by referring to videos, books or pictures. To make it easier to apply a skill, you need **coaching points**.

You should know the main coaching points for the major skill used in your practical activity.

◀◀ **REWIND**

SKILLS DEVELOPMENT see page 88

Tactics

In order to try and win your game, you need to **plan**. How you beat your opponent will depend on a number of different factors, such as the environment, how good he or she is and how you feel on the day. When you play in teams, the tactics become even more complex. It is usually the role of the coach to help decide on these tactics. However, if you are the **captain**, you also have some responsibility for deciding how you and the team will play.

As a team you can practise tactics for situations such as corners or free kicks/hits. Again, you should know some examples of drills and practices that can be used in each situation.

For most activities, the main tactics involve either **attack** or **defence.** You need to know the basic principles behind these for your activity.

Observation and correction

You also need to be able to pick out **faults** in both your own performance and that of others. What is going wrong? Why are you not being successful?

Having identified the problem, the next step is deciding what to do about it. Before you can do this, you need to have a sound knowledge of the skills and tactics required for each activity. Coaching qualifications and courses will help, but your PE lessons should also have given you enough information and experience to do some basic observation and correction.

What is the best way of observing someone performing?

Video has the advantage of allowing you to stop, repeat and slow down a player's performance. This makes it a lot easier to identify faults.

However, it is not always practical to use video, so you also need to be able to carry out **live observation**.

The first part of observation and correction is to have in your mind a clear picture of what you *should* be seeing – i.e. a perfect or near perfect attempt. Again, demonstrations or books can give you this.

Against this mental ideal you then need to judge the performance you are watching. You can make it a little easier by analysing the skill, or the performer's body, into smaller parts, and concentrating on these one at a time.

For example if you were looking at a long-jumper, you could divide up the activity as follows:

Skill	Body
Run-up	Legs
Take-off	Arms
Flight	Head
Landing	Torso

Splitting the skill up should make it easier to observe, identify faults and correct. However, this may mean your performer repeating the skill many times. Again, it helps to have a thorough knowledge of the relevant coaching points.

◀◀ **REWIND**

PART PRACTICE   see page 91

SPORT QUESTIONS

Athletics

Rules

1) On the track, which races require competitors to stay in their own lane?
2) Give two reasons why a throw may be a foul in the discus. (*Hint:* Think about the actual throw and where the discus lands.)
3) How many attempts does a high-jumper have at each height?

Skills

1) How might a hammer or discus thrower develop power in their upper body? (*Hint:* Think of different training methods.)
2) For each of the three phases of the sprint start, give two coaching points.
3) Describe two different types of long jump technique and give the advantages of each.

Tactics

1) Explain the use of check marks in long jumping and triple jumping.
2) Why do javelin throwers often use the crowd to help them prepare for their throw by clapping a rhythm? (*Hint:* Think about the mental side of the throw.)

3) Study the diagram of the hurdle above. Describe good practice for the next phase of the hurdle.

Observation and correction

1) Describe the techniques involved in the correct execution of the Fosbury high jump. Use the following headings:
   a) Approach
   b) Take-off
   c) Flight
   d) Landing
2) A right-handed discus thrower consistently throws to the right of the throwing sector. What might be causing this?
3) Give three points that a long-jumper should concentrate on when approaching the take-off board.

Badminton

Rules

1) After the service is won in doubles, from which side do you start to serve? (*Hint:* 50% chance!)
2) Using diagrams, describe the differences between the singles and the doubles court. (*Hint:* Think about the tram-lines)
3) At what scores in badminton do you have the opportunity to set? (*Hint:* Must be equal)

Skills

1) Identify and describe two types of forehand serve. (*Hint:* To front or to back)
2) Describe how the forehand overhead clear should be played. (*Hint:* Body and arm positions)
3) Describe the forehand smash under the following headings:
   Preparation   Racket movement
   Impact with shuttle   Follow-through
   (*Hint:* Body position, racket position)

Tactics

1) Explain the tactics that would be used in mixed doubles. (*Hint:* Front and back)
2) Suggest how the tactic of disguise could be used in a game of badminton. (*Hint:* Keep them guessing!)
3) Explain, with examples, how the movement of an opponent on court can influence the tactics you use. (*Hint:* If the opponent is at the net, on one side or at the back, what would you do?)

Observation and correction

1) Describe two shots that you could play from close to the net. (*Hint:* Soft or hard)
2) A player keeps hitting the shuttle into the net. Give three possible reasons for this. (*Hint:* Eyes, racket, feet)
3) Your opponent keeps smashing the shuttle and winning many points. What could you do to stop this happening? (*Hint:* Describe the shots that you would try to make)

Basketball

Rules

1) Describe the signal used by the referee to indicate travelling.
2) After how many fouls must a player leave the court and take no further part in the game?
3) Can you give two examples of time infringements that can occur in a game?

Skills

1) What coaching points should be emphasised when teaching the chest pass to young players? (*Hint:* Think about: Legs, Elbows, Head, Hands and wrists, Follow through)
2) How can a player protect the ball from the opposition while dribbling? (*Hint:* Think about the position of the body and the ball.)
3) The basic stance in basketball should try to match the 'triple threat position'. Explain what is meant by this, and draw a simple diagram to illustrate it.

Tactics

1) Can you give two occasions when your team would use a zone defence? (*Hint:* What kind of attacks and shots/drives does a zone defence prevent?)
2) What factors might make your team switch from zone to man-to-man defence?
3) How can you beat the defender when you are attacking in a one-to-one situation?

Observation and correction

1) Can you identify the phases or sub-routines that might be used when teaching a lay-up shot?
2) In a match situation, what suggestions could you give to help a player prepare mentally for taking set shots? (*Hint:* Think about the flight of the ball. Is there a focus word or phrase that might help?)

Cricket

Rules

1) If the ball hits the stumps without dislodging the bales, what is the umpire's decision?
2) What is the relationship between the bowler's front foot and the popping crease? (*Hint:* Why would the umpire call a no ball?
3) What is the maximum width of a cricket bat in centimetres?

Skills

1) Footwork is an important component of good batting. What are the key points concerning the feet and the following elements when batting?
   a) Balance
   b) Speed
   c) Power
2) Bowlers need to bowl a 'good line and length'. Can you give a more technical explanation of what this would mean for a medium-paced bowler?
3) When preparing to take a catch, what should a fielder be focussing on? (*Hint:* Think about hands, body, feet.)

Tactics

1) If an opposing batsman favours coming forward to meet the ball, as a bowler, how could you modify your line and length to put them under more pressure?
2) Draw a diagram to show how a side may set an attacking field against a left-handed batsman.
3) On a wet, humid morning, what factors would influence your choice after winning the toss?

Observation and correction

1) For a batsman, what would be a good body position for:
   a) the on drive
   b) the off drive
2) Bowlers should bowl with a smooth, economical run-up. What should you look for in their running style?
3) What factors should a wicket keeper think about when deciding how far back to stand from the stumps?

Football

Rules

1) State two laws that must be obeyed when a penalty kick is taken. (*Hint:* What rules apply to the kicker and to the goalkeeper?)
2) What two types of free kick can a referee award, and what is the main difference between them?
3) What is the height of the cross-bar in football?

Skills

1) Give three basic coaching points for heading the ball. What are the main differences in heading for attackers and defenders? (*Hint:* For the second question, think about the main aim of the defensive header and the attacking header.)
2) Ball control is a skill all players and positions should practise. Can you suggest some practices/drills that can be used to develop it?
3) Creating space and moving free are both essential skills in attack. How can they be achieved? Can you suggest some drills/practices that can be used to develop these skills?

Tactics

1) Your team has been awarded a corner. Can you suggest two tactics that would result in an attempt at goal?
2) In defence, how can a team play to the offside rule? Does this system have any disadvantages?
3) Your team is due to play against a team that plays a slow-build-up passing game, especially in midfield. What tactics might you use to counteract this and how might this affect your selection of players?

servation and correction

Tackling is an important skill. What are the key coaching points to emphasise to young players?

Your goal-keeper is having difficulty catching high crosses. What should he concentrate on? Can you give him some practices to help him develop confidence in this skill?

What skills does a player need to dribble the ball effectively? (*Hint:* Use these focus words to help you cover all the key points: Balance, Foot-to-ball contact, Vision, Body position)

ockey

les

When does an umpire award a penalty stroke? (*Hint:* 'deliberate')

How does a game of hockey start? (*Hint:* A push or hit)

The shooting area is an area where a goal can be scored. Give two other rules that apply in this area. (*Hint:* What you can and cannot do)

ills

Describe the position of the hands on the stick for:

a) striking the ball

b) stopping the ball

(*Hint:* One hand remains the same)

Describe in detail how you would perform a penalty flick. (*Hint:* Hands, feet, movement)

Describe how you would tackle a player who is coming towards you with the ball. (*Hint:* Positioning of feet and stick)

ctics

Describe two ways in which an attacking team could take a penalty corner to try to score. You may use diagrams to help you. (*Hint:* Different players could strike the ball.)

Using a free hit effectively is very important. Discuss how you would take a free hit so that it is effective. (*Hint:* Think about where the opposition is and where your fellow players are.)

Identify and explain two different marking systems. (*Hint:* Position of defenders in relation to attackers)

servation and correction

) A player keeps missing the ball. Identify two reasons why this should happen and suggest some coaching points that could be made. (*Hint:* Eyes, hands, feet)

2) Give reasons why a player may dribble the ball. (*Hint:* mostly in attack)

3) A team's defence is obviously not working because the opposition keep getting into scoring situations. Explain why might this happen and give two suggestions that might help the defensive players. (*Hint:* Defensive marking tactics)

Netball

Rules

1) How long does a game of netball take to play?

2) Which players (both attack and defence) are allowed only in zones B and C of the pitch (*see diagram*)?

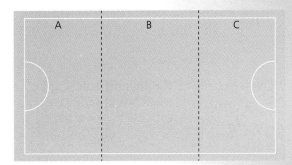

3) How is the game restarted after a team has scored?

Skills

1) What are the basic coaching points for passing the ball? (*Hint:* Think about hands, body position and weight of pass.)

2) What are the main fitness elements a good netballer should work on developing?

3) Getting free to receive a pass is an important skill. Can you suggest some ways of achieving this in a game?

Tactics

1) In a full court system of defence, explain what is meant by 'horizontal banding'.

2) Being able to execute a number of different passes correctly is an essential part of the netballer's game. Can you give some examples in a game when different passes may need to be used? (*Hint:* Think of the different kind of passes and give an example of each.)

3) Before passing a ball to another player what should the passer consider?

Observation and correction

1) What suggestions could you give to a player shooting that will help them prepare mentally for this stressful situation in a game? (*Hint:* Think about the flight of the ball)

2) What points would you coach to young people practising catching the ball on the run?
3) How could you help a player improve their marking skills? (*Hint:* Think of the main points and any drills/practices that you could use.)

Rugby league

Rules
1) After winning the toss at the start of the game, what choices does a captain have?
2) If the referee affords a team 'head and feed' at a scrum, what does this mean?
3) On the last tackle, an attacking player kicks the ball which hits a defending player and rebounds back to him. What could the referee award and what may affect it? (*Hint:* Who would get the decision – the attacking team or the defending team?)

Skills
1) A player taking up the 'dummy half position' needs to pick up the ball quickly and give an accurate pass. What should he concentrate on for the following when executing this role?
   a) Feet
   b) Hands
   c) Body position
2) Kicking is an essential skill. What are the key coaching points for punting from the hands?
3) Creating space in attack is an important skill. Explain what this means and suggest ways it can be achieved. (*Hint:* Think about how the ball can be moved quickly to space, or how the pass can be used in the tackle.)

Tactics
1) Kicking on the last tackle can put the defending team under pressure. What options does the kicker have? (*Hint:* Think about attacking or defensive kicks.)
2) Explain what is meant by a sliding defence.
3) How does the alignment of the backs change in attack and defence?

Observation and correction
1) A player consistently loses the ball in the tackle. What could be the possible causes of this error? (*Hint:* Think about the position of the ball, and body position in contact.)
2) Can you think of specific practices/drills that could help develop close support skills in young players? (*Hint:* They will need to be able to give and take short passes.)
3) Place kicking is an important skill that can win matches. Can you identify the key points for the following phases:

a) Approach
b) Leg swing
c) Point of impact
d) Follow through
(*Hint:* Think about the different parts of the body and the role they play in balance, power and accuracy.)

Rugby union

Rules
1) What would the referee award if a player kicked the ball directly into touch from inside his own 22? (*Hint:* Who would get the advantage?)
2) A side successfully get the ball over the try line, but the referee is not certain whether they have touched the ball down. What should he do?
3) A major area of concern for referees is the line-out. What potential offences should he be looking for? (*Hint:* Go through the players involved in the line-out – hooker, jumpers, backs.)

Skills
1) Explain the skills a scrum half needs to practise in order to be successful. (*Hint:* Scrum halves have to serve both forwards and backs.)
2) Kicking can be an important skill for the backs. What are the key coaching points for punting the ball from the hands?
3) Creating space is an important skill in attack. Explain what this means and suggest ways it can be achieved.

Tactics
1) Kicking can be an important part of a team's attack. After receiving the ball just inside the other team's half, what kicking options will a fly half have? (*Hint:* Think about angles and depth.)
2) A long throw at the line is often used by teams in attacking situations. How could a team defend against it? (*Hint:* Remember that forwards who are not needed in the line-out could be used in defence.)
3) If your opponents are known to have very strong forwards who are very good at mauling, what tactics might you practise and apply in the match? (*Hint:* Strong mauling forwards may be less mobile.)

Observation and correction
1) A hooker is having problems throwing straight at the line-out. Can you suggest some practices? (*Hint:* You may want to isolate this skill.)
2) What are the main points you should emphasise when teaching a young player to receive a pass?

3) Place kicking is an important skill that can win matches. Can you identify the key points for the following phases?
a) Approach
b) Leg swing
c) Point of impact
d) Follow through
(*Hint:* Think about the different parts of the body and the role they play in balance, power and accuracy.)

Swimming

Rules
1) Name two strokes that may be used during a medley relay race.
2) Give reasons why a breaststroke swimmer may be disqualified in a race.
3) What are the laws on turns for freestyle events?

Skills
1) What are the key coaching points for the leg kick in front crawl?
2) In a race, what are the key points for the forward start? (*Hint:* Use the following sub-routines to list the points:
a) Stance
b) Take off)
3) Throwing is an important part of life-saving skills. Before throwing a rescue aid, what should the rescuer consider?

Tactics
1) If a lifesaver is faced with more than one casualty in the water, what must he/she consider before attempting a rescue? (*Hint:* Who needs the most urgent help? Is either casualty capable of helping himself?)
2) If you were teaching young people about diving, what safety considerations would you explain at the outset?
3) For longer-distance swimming events, economy and efficiency of stroke is required rather than power. How can these qualities be developed?

Observation and correction
1) What are the major faults that can be identified in breast stroke leg kick?
2) Suggest drill practices that may be used to try and eliminate faults in the breast stroke leg kick.
3) Breathing is often a problem in front crawl. What are the key points to emphasise to young swimmers?

Tennis

Rules
1) Name three officials needed for a tennis competition. What is the role of each one in administering the tournament?
2) Can you explain the foot-fault rule, giving examples of when it is broken.
3) What rules does the server have to obey each time they serve?

Skills
1) Describe how you would perform an angled volley at the net during a game.
2) Give the main coaching points for the forehand drive. (*Hint:* Concentrate on where the racket is and what happens to it during the stroke.)
3) Using the sub-routines given, give the main coaching points for a forehand volley.
a) Grip
b) Feet
c) Movement of racket head
d) Point of impact

Tactics
1) What tactics would you use in a singles match against an unknown player? (*Hint:* How would you quickly assess the strengths and weaknesses of your opponent?)
2) Using a diagram, identify the basic positions for both players when receiving service in doubles. What are the reasons for this positioning?
3) The most attacking position in tennis is at the net. How would you build up to this position in a rally? (*Hint:* What shots would give you enough time to get to the net?)

Observation and correction
1) List the two possible grips for backhand strokes. Does either have any advantage?
3) How could you help a young player develop the correct timing for hitting the ball? (*Hint:* Think about where in terms of the ball bounce it should be hit, body position, and giving them a focus for the timing.)

Glossary

ABC routine   Airway, Breathing, Circulation: the key points to check when dealing with an injured person

Abduction   Movement of a limb away from an imaginary vertical line down the middle of the body

Able-bodied   Having full use of the whole body and its functions

Actin and myosin   Basic protein threads or filaments contained within myofibrils

Adduction   Movement of a limb towards an imaginary vertical line down the middle of the body

Adenosine triphosphate (ATP)   Substance which provides energy for muscle activity

Administration   How sports are organised, who is in control and how the sport is funded

Adrenal glands   Responsible for producing adrenaline which causes the 'fight or flight' reaction

Aerobic   System providing long-term energy for low-intensity physical activity

Agility   Ability to move quickly and change direction at speed

Altitude   High up, where there is less oxygen to breathe

Alveoli   Tiny hollow sacs at the end of the bronchioles which fill with air when we breathe in

Anabolic steroid   Drug illegally used by sports performers to increase strength, power and aggression

Anaerobic   Energy-producing systems which do not rely on oxygen

Antagonistic muscles   Muscles which work in pairs to control movement

Anxiety   State of apprehension or worry before a sporting event

Apartheid   System of laws and practices in South Africa that discriminated against black people

Appendicular skeleton   Bones not forming part of the axial skeleton

Arousal   State of mental and physical excitement before taking part in sport

Arteries   Vessels which carry blood away from the heart

Automation   Using machines and computers to do work formerly done by hand

Axial skeleton   Central part of the skeleton, made up of the skull, spine, ribs and breastbone

Balance   Ability to distribute the weight of the body evenly and maintain equilibrium

Balanced diet   Combination of nutrients the body needs in order to be healthy

Ball and socket joint   Joint in which the rounded head of one bone fits into a cup-like socket on another

Basic metabolic rate   The minimal level of energy needed by the body when resting

Blood   Classified as a connective tissue. Average total blood volume is about five litres

Blood doping   Artificially increasing the number of red blood cells in the body

Blood pressure (BP)   Pressure needed to pump blood around the human body

Body composition   The relative percentage of muscle, fat, bone, and other tissues

Body mass index   Calculated by dividing weight in kilograms by the square of height in metres

Boycott   Refusal by a country to compete in an event, usually for political reasons

Brain   The control centre for most of our actions

Bronchi   Two small branch-like passages at the end of the trachea

Bronchioles   Small branch-like passages formed by the division of the bronchi inside the lungs

Calorie   Amount of energy needed to increase $1cm^3$ of water by 1^oC

Capillaries Network of small vessels through which blood passes

Carbohydate loading Building up stocks of glycogen in the body

Carbohydrates Nutrients which provide energy for our muscles

Carbon dioxide Gas forming .04% of inhaled air and 4% of exhaled air

Cardiac massage Means of reviving a casualty whose heart has stopped beating

Cardiac output (Q̇) Volume of blood ejected from left ventricle in one minute

Cardiovascular endurance Ability of the heart, blood vessels, blood, and respiratory system to supply fuel and oxygen to the muscles

Cardiovascular system System governing the circulation of blood and the transport of oxygen and nutrients to the cells of the body and waste products away from these cells

Cartilage Connective tissue found in a variety of forms in the human body

Central nervous system System comprising the brain and spinal cord responsible for all conscious and unconscious actions

Cerebellum The 'little brain' under the cerebrum, responsible for balance and coordination

Cerebrum Largest part of the brain which controls thought, speech and movement

Cervical, thoracic, lumbar, sacral and coccyx The five components of the human vertebrae

Cholesterol Fat substance that can lead to disease by blocking arteries, particularly those around the heart

Circumduction Combination of flexion, extension, abduction, adduction and rotation

Compact and spongy bone Two types of tissue found in long bones

Concentric contraction Where a muscle shortens in length

Concussion Injury caused by the brain being violently shaken or jolted

Condyloid joint Joint allowing movement in two directions, e.g. the wrist

Contact sport Team sport in which physical contact is allowed

Coordination Ability to perform movements smoothly and with no waste of effort

Creatine phosphate (CP) Naturally occurring substance in muscle tissue used to generate energy

Dehydration Dangerous condition when the body loses too much water, usually as a result of sweating

Diaphragm Dome-shaped muscle in the thorax which regulates the flow of air to the lungs

Diastolic BP Blood pressure measured when the heart relaxes

Diffusion Process whereby gases pass through a membrane from an area of high concentration to an area of lower concentration

Digestive system System which breaks down food into usable nutrients

Dislocation Injury in which the bone is jolted out of its normal position at the joint

Diuretic Drug illegally used by sports performers to reduce body weight

Drug Medical substance or chemical used for relieving illness, pain or discomfort

Dual use Making school sports facilities available to the general public

Eccentric contraction Where a muscle is lengthened

Ectomorph Body type that is linear or long and thin

Effector organs Organs that receive information and instructions from the brain

Elitism Where facilities and opportunities in sport are provided only for a talented few

Endocrine system Body system governing the production of hormones which help the body to function correctly

Endomorph Body type that is mainly pear-shaped

Endorsement Recommendation of products by established sports 'stars'

Energy equation Energy Intake = Energy Expenditure

Enzyme Substance that helps to speed up chemical reactions, e.g saliva

Epimysium Fibrous layer of connective tissue which protects muscle

Equal opportunity Giving everyone equal access to sport, regardless of gender, race or background

Ethnic minority People of different ethnic origin from the majority of the population.

Exclusive Only open to certain people

Exclusive right Where only one television company can broadcast a sporting event

Exercise   Physical activity that improves health and fitness

Extension   Increase in the angle between two bones

External and internal intercostal muscles   Extra muscles located between the ribs which help us to inhale and exhale

Exteroceptors   Organs which receive information from outside the body, e.g. the eyes and ears

Extra-curricular sport   Sport played outside lesson times in school

Fartlek   System of running used to develop endurance

Fast and slow twitch fibre   The two major types of skeletal muscle fibre in the human body

Fat-free weight   The weight of the body excluding fat but including the organs, blood and other connective tissues

Fats   Used by the body as an energy source, especially when we are asleep or at rest

Fibre   Adds bulk to food, allowing it to pass more easily through the digestive system

FIFA   The International Federation of Association Football

Fight or flight syndrome   The body's instinctive response to a potentially threatening situation

Fitness testing   Measuring performance to assess a person's overall fitness

Fitness   The ability of the body to meet the demands placed on it

FITT   Frequency, Intensity, Time and Type – the four basic elements of a training programme

Fixators   Muscles situated near the point of origin of a prime mover muscle, which stabilise the body part

Flexibility   Having a wide range of motion in a joint

Flexibility   The range of movement around a joint

Flexion   Decrease in the angle between two bones

Fluid replacement   Drinking at regular intervals in order to replace lost fluid

Foundation for Sport and the Arts   Grant-making body funded by levy on football pools

Function/physiology   How the parts of the body work

Gamesmanship   Where winning becomes the most important objective in sport

Gender   The two sexes, male and female

General safety principles   Commonsense procedures to prevent accident or injury

Gliding joint   Joint in which one bone glides over another, e.g. between the tarsals of the feet

Goal-setting   Establishing aims or objectives to work towards

Governing body   An organising body that looks after all matters affecting a sport

Haemoglobin   Substance contained within red blood cells, giving them their colour. Its main function is to carry oxygen

Hand grip dynamometer   Device for measuring grip strength

Harvard Step Test   Involves stepping on and off a bench for five minutes, after which heart rate is recorded

Health and Safety At Work Act, 1974   Legislation to ensure that teachers and pupils work in a safe and healthy environment

Health   State of physical, mental and emotional well-being

Health-related fitness   Combination of cardio-vascular, endurance, muscular strength and endurance, flexibility, body composition and ability to cope with stress

Heart rate (HR)   Number of heart beats or pulses per minute. Average resting HR is 75 bpm

Heysel Stadium Disaster   Death of 39 people at the 1985 European Cup Final in Belgium

Hillsborough Disaster   Death of 95 Liverpool fans at an FA Cup semi-final in Sheffield

Hinge joint   Joint allowing movement in one direction only

Hormones   Chemical 'messengers' normally released into the bloodstream by the glands of the endocrine system

Hypertrophy   Where a body part grows in size due to increased use

Hypothermia   When body temperature drops below 37°C following prolonged exposure to cold or wet

Immovable, slightly movable, and movable/synovial joints   The three main types of joint found in the human body

Inhalation and exhalation   Process of breathing in and out

Intensity   How hard we exercise or exert ourselves

Interoceptors   Organs that receive information from inside the body, e.g. changes in the blood or lungs

Interval training   Form of exercise in which periods of activity are interspersed with short periods of rest

Involuntary muscle   Muscles that work automatically

Isometric contraction   When a muscle tenses but does not change in length

Kilocalorie   Measure of the energy value of food

Lactic acid (LA)   Substance which can build up in the muscles, causing pain and heaviness

Large intestine (colon)   Where undigested food is stored before being passed out of the body

Left/right atrium   Smaller chambers of the heart where blood is oxygenated and deoxygenated

Left and right ventricle   The two larger chambers of the heart which pump blood around the pulmonary circulation system

Leisure   Free time which we can spend as we like

Levers   System comprising pivot, load and effort, formed where muscle is attached to bone

Ligament   Strong non-elastic tissue that connects bone to bone, normally found at a joint

Limited channel capacity   The inability of the brain to process more than a certain amount of information at a time

Liver   The largest organ in the human body, responsible for producing bile

Location   Position of parts within the body

Long, short, flat, and irregular bones   The four main types of bone in the human body

Maximal oxygen uptake (VO$_2$ max)   The maximun amount of oxygen we can transport and use in one minute

Maximum HR   The maximum number of heart beats per minute of which a person is capable

Media   Channels of mass-communication

Memory   The brain's ability to store information

Mesomorph   Body type that is wedge-shaped and more muscular

Minerals   Substances found in a wide range of foods which are essential for healthy functioning of the body

Minor sport   A sport that is only played or watched by a small number of people

Minute ventilation   The amount of air we breathe in one minute

Modern Pentathlon   Olympic sport made up of five events including shooting and fencing, as well as horse riding, running and swimming

Motivation   The drive to do well in sport

Motor neurones   Transmit impulses from the brain to the effector organs, where the instructions are carried out

Muscular endurance   The ability of the muscles to repeatedly exert themselves

Muscular strength   The ability to exert an external force or to lift a heavy weight

Muscular system   Network of muscles mainly composed of skeletal muscle which is connected to bones by tendons

Myofibrils   Microscopic fibres which form skeletal muscle

Myth   A stereotype that has become so widely used that it is accepted as fact

Narcotic analgesic   Drug illegally used by sports performers to combat pain and aid relaxation

National Curriculum   The key subjects that all children in state schools are required to study

National Sports Centres   The six centres of sporting excellence in the UK

NCF Multi-stage Fitness Test   Designed to test cardiovascular endurance

Nervous system   Control system for voluntary and involuntary movements

Nucleus   Element usually located near the centre of a cell which controls how it functions

Olympic Ideal   Principle that performers should take part in sport for the pleasure of competing, not for money

Olympic Oath   Pledge of sportsmanship that all Olympic athletes are required to swear

Open Olympics   Allowing professionals and amateurs to compete in the Olympic Games

Open sport   Where amateurs and professionals compete together in the same sport

Open/closed skills   Skills which are affected by surrounding factors are **open**, while those which are less affected are **closed**

Opportunity   Having the chance to take part in sport or recreation

Optimum performance   The highest standard a sportsperson can achieve

Organ   Two or more types of tissue that work together to perform a common function

Ovaries/testes   Glands which control the development of secondary sexual characteristics in women (ovaries) and men (testes)

Overweight   Having over 20% body fat (males), and over 30% body fat (females)

Oxygen debt   Where the demand for oxygen is greater than the supply

Oxygen deficit   Where the supply of oxygen is greater than the demand

Oxygen   Gas which, together with carbon dioxide, makes up the air we breathe

Oxygenated/deoxygenated blood   Blood that contains/does not contain oxygen

Pancreas   Organ which produces insulin and other enzymes which aid digestion of food

Participation   The amount of sport people do, and the type of sports they choose

Passive smoking   Harmful effects of smoking on non-smokers who are present

Pay-per-view   Where viewers must pay extra to watch a particular TV programme

Peaktime viewing   When most people are watching TV, usually in the early evening

Percentage body fat   The proportion of total body weight that is made up of fat

Perception   Interpreting information received via the senses

Performance-enhancing drug   Drug misused by athletes in order to boost performance

Peripheral nervous system   The nerve fibres that branch out from the spinal cord, and the organs to which they are connected

Personal hygiene   Keeping your body clean and healthy

Physical Education   Teaching of sport and associated skills in schools and colleges

Physique   The size and shape of our body

Pituitary gland   Control centre of the endocrine system

Pivot joint   Joint resembling a peg and ring allowing rotation only

Point of origin/insertion   Points at which tendons connect muscle to bone

Positive discrimination   Trying to redress the balance in favour of a disadvantaged group

Power   Combination of speed and strength

Pre-match meal   Normally eaten 3–4 hours before a sporting fixture or endurance event

Prime mover   Muscle which contracts in order to perform a movement

Programming   Targeted sessions for special groups at local sports centres

Proprioceptors   Organs that receive information from within muscles, tendons and joints

Proteins   Vital nutrients for building and repairing cells and tissues in the body

Provision   Providing recreational facilities so that people can take part in sport

Puberty   Growth spurt that occurs between the ages of 10 and 20

Public schools   Large boarding schools where parents paid for their children to be educated

Pulmonary circulation   Passage of blood from the heart to the lungs

Random testing   Spot-checks on drug abuse carried out by sports bodies

Reaction time   Speed of response to external events

Receptor organs   Organs that transmit information to the brain

Recovery position   Position in which a casualty lies on their side to ensure the airway remains open

Recreation   An enjoyable spare-time activity

Repetition   The number of times that an athlete repeats a particular exercise

Respiration   Process of transporting oxygen to the cells and removing waste products

Respiratory rate   The rate at which we inhale and exhale when breathing normally

Respiratory system   System which regulates the breathing process, enabling us to take oxygen into our body and expel carbon dioxide

RICE   Rest, Ice, Compression, Elevation: procedure for reducing pain and swelling after an injury

Role model   Someone who is held up as a positive example to others

Rotation   Circular movement

Saddle joint   Joint allowing movement in two planes at right angles to each other

Safety clothing   Sportswear designed to prevent injury to the wearer and allow free movement

Safety equipment   Sports equipment specially developed to reduce the risk of accident

Schools provision   Sports facilities in schools

Selection   Identifying sporting talent

Selective attention   The ability to concentrate on what is important when performing a skill

Semi-lunar valves   Valves located at the 'exits' of the ventricles. The valve of the right ventricle is also known as the **pulmonary** valve, whilst the valve of the left ventricle is also known as the **aortic** valve

Sensationalism Using attention-grabbing techniques to attract readers/viewers

Sensory neurones Organs that receive information from receptor organs and transmit impulses to the brain

Set A certain number of repetitions of an exercise

'Shop window' effect Using sport to 'show off' a country to the rest of the world

Short\long-term exercise effects Temporary changes which take place in the body during physical activity, and lasting changes which result from regular exercise

Sit and reach test Test for measuring the flexibility of the lower back and hamstrings

Skeletal system The 206 bones of the human skeleton

Skill An action or set of actions in a sport

Skill-related fitness Combination of agility, balance, coordination, power, reaction-time and speed

Skills transfer The influence of learning or performing one skill on the learning and performance of another

Skinfold callipers Used to measure percentage body fat

Society The human community in which we live

Somatotypes System of classifying the human body according to certain basic types

Speed Ability to move quickly

Spinal cord Conducts nerve impulses to and from the brain

Spirometer Machine for measuring volume of air inhaled and exhaled

Sponsorship Support by firms and companies for sports events and performers, usually in return for corporate publicity

'Sport For All' Sports Council campaign to encourage people to take part in sport

Sport Organised contests, involving physical activity between individuals or teams

Sports science Studies aimed at developing sporting excellence

Sprain Injury in which the ligaments are overstretched or torn at a joint

Stereotyping Assuming that all members of a group of people share the same image or characteristics

Stomach Sac-like structure at the end of the oesophagus where food is mixed with gastric juices

Strains Injury in which the muscle is overstretched or twisted

Stress Tension in body and mind

Stroke volume (SV) Volume of blood ejected from the heart in one beat, measured in ml/beat

Structure/anatomy How the body is constructed

Sub-maximal Not working flat out, but enough to be breathless at the end of a session

Subsidised Partly paid for by the local council

Sympathetic nervous system Responsible for preparing the body for action, e.g. by stimulating the adrenal gland

Symptoms Physical signs of an injury or illness

Synergists Muscles which work actively to help a prime mover muscle

Systemic circulation Circulatory system that transports oxygenated blood from the left ventricle to the cells of the body

Systolic BP Blood pressure measured when the heart forcefully ejects blood

Target group Group identified by the Sports Council as being under-represented in sport

Tendon Strong tissue attaching muscle to bone

Terrestrial TV Non-satellite, non-cable, channels, e.g. BBC1 and BBC2

The Taylor Report, 1990 Official inquiry into the Hillsborough Stadium disaster

Tidal volume The amount of air moved each time we breathe, usually about 500ml

Tissues Cells that have a similar structure and function and work closely together

Trust fund Scheme enabling amateur sportsmen and women to earn money from their sport

Twelve-minute Cooper Test Running, walking or jogging as far as possible within 12 minutes

UK Sports Council The UK body responsible for sport at the national and for promoting UK sporting excellence on the world stage

UK Sports Institute National sports training centre, to be located in Sheffield

Unwritten rules The values, ethics or 'spirit of the game' which all sportsmen and women are expected to follow

User group The people who use sports facilities

Vasoconstriction Where the diameter of a blood vessel decreases as the surrounding muscles contracts

Vasodilation   Where the diameter of a blood vessel increases as the surrounding muscles relax

Veins   Blood vessels which carry blood back to the heart

Vitamins   Essential nutrients for the body's growth and healthy functioning

Vocational   Term used to describe college courses which are closely linked to careers

Voluntary muscle   Muscles that are under our conscious control

Warm-up/cool-down   Necessary routine before and after physical exercise

Water   Vital fluid that must be replaced to prevent dehydration

Withdrawal and stretch reflex actions   Impulse to remove ourselves from a source of pain (withdrawal) or to extend the leg when we receive a bang or tap on the knee (stretch)

Womens Sports Foundation   Body founded in 1984 to promote women's sport

Index

Abduction 12
Access 149
Actin 16
Adduction 12
Adenosine diphosphate (ADP) 36
Adenosine triphosphate (ATP) 36
Adrenal gland 5, 41
Adrenaline 5, 28
Aerobic system 36, 53
Age and sport 156, 157
Aggression 93
Agility 53, 84
Alcohol 81
Altitude 80
Alveoli 32
Amateur sport 207, 208, 209
Anaerobic system 36
Anxiety 97, 98
Appendicular skeleton 9
Arousal 96, 97
Arteries 5, 25
Articular cartilage 12
Athletics 237
Axial skeleton 9

Badminton 237
Balance 53
Basic metabolic rate 73
Basketball 237
Behaviour in sport 225, 226, 227, 228
Bleeding 131
Blood 23, 118
Blood plasma 24
Blood pressure 27
Blood vessels 25, 29
Body composition 53
Body types 62, 63, 64
Brain 40
Breathing 31, 32, 33, 34, 35
British Olympic Association 170, 171
Bronchi 32

Calories 72, 107
Capillaries 5, 7, 25
Carbohydrate loading 74
Carbohydrates 46, 68, 69, 74
Cardiac muscles 5, 15, 25
Cardiac output 26

Cardiovascular 3, 45, 23, 53, 121
Careers in sport 151, 152, 153
Cartilage 9, 11
Cells 2
Central Council for Physical Recreation 171
Cerebellum 39, 40
Cerebrum 39, 40
Cheating 226, 227
Cholesterol 69
Circumduction 12
Circuit training 109
Circulatory system 23, 28
Closed skills 87, 88
Clothing 124, 125
Coaching 190, 191
Collagen 7
Commercialism 207, 210
Compact bone 9
Concussion 129, 131
Connective tissue 2, 5
Contraction 20
Cool down, 109, 110
Cooper, 12-Minute Test 57
Coordination 53, 85
Cricket 238
Crowd behaviour 227

Dehydration 45, 71, 75, 130
Diaphragm 1, 33
Diet 46, 68, 71, 107
Diffusion 25, 34
Digestive system 5, 45, 46, 47, 48
Dilation 29
Disability 159
Drugs 77, 167
Dynamometer 58, 59, 85

Eastern Bloc countries 175
Effector organs 39
Electrolyte 75
Endocrine system 5, 44, 45
Endurance training 113
Energy 72
Energy systems 36
Enzymes 46
Equal opportunity 223
Equipment 125, 126

Esteem 146
Excellence in sport 161, 201, 202, 203
Excretion 46
Exercise 107, 108
Extension 12
Facilities 155, 162, 191, 192
Fair play 225

Fartlek 113
Fashion and sport 150
Fast twitch muscle fibres 18
Fats 46, 68, 69, 71, 74
Feedback 90
Femininity 220
Fibre 71
First Aid 132, 133, 134
Fitness testing 55, 56, 57, 58, 59
FITT principles 109
Flat bones 9
Flexibility 53, 55
Flexibility training 115
Flexion 12, 13
Football 238
Funding 168, 192, 209

Gamesmanship 226
Gaseous exchange 34
Gender and sport 157
Glycogen 36, 37, 74
Goal setting 98, 99, 100
Governing bodies 161, 170
Guidance 91, 92

Haemoglobin 24
Harvard Step Test 53, 57
Health 52, 106, 148
Health and safety 123, 124, 125, 126
Heart 3, 25, 117
Heart rate 26
History of sport 143, 144, 145, 222
Hockey 239
Hooliganism 228
Hormones 5, 44, 45, 118
Human rights 178
Hygiene 107
Hypertrophy 120
Hypothermia 130

Information processing 88, 89
Injuries 128, 129, 130
Insertion 19
Interval training 114
Inverted U Theory 96, 97
Irregular bones 9, 10, 14
Isotonic drinks 75

Joint capsule 11, 12
Joints 5, 11, 12, 13

Knee joint 12, 13

Lactic acid 118
Lactic acid system 36
Leisure 142
Levers 19, 20
Ligaments 11, 12
Limited channel capacity 90
Local authorities 162
Local provision for sport 149
Long bones 9
Losing weight 73
Lung volume 33, 34, 121
Lungs 31, 32, 33, 34, 35, 118

Marrow cavity 9
Media and sport 212, 214, 215, 216,
   217, 223
Medulla oblongata 41
Memory 88, 89
Minerals 7, 68, 70
Minister for Sport 188
Mitochondria 120
Motivation 92, 95, 96
Movement analysis 21
Multi-stage Fitness Test 56
Muscles 16, 17, 18, 19, 119
Muscular endurance 55
Muscular system 5, 15, 53, 120
Myoglobin 120
Myosin 16

National Coaching Foundation 171
National Curriculum 172
National Lottery 155, 188
National Sports Centres 205
Nerve cells 40
Nervous system 5, 39, 40, 41, 42
Netball 239
Neurones 40, 41
Nucleus 2
Nutrients 5, 45, 46, 47, 48
Nutrition 74

Obesity 64, 73
Observation and correction 236–41
Olympics 144, 170, 178, 179, 180,
   181, 216, 222
Open skills 87, 88
Opportunity 156

Origin 19
Ossification 11, 66
Overload 109
Oxygen debt 37
Oxygen uptake 35

Patella 9
Personality 92
Physical Education 143
Physique 61
Politics and sport 177, 186, 187, 188,
   189
Posture 8
Power 53, 84
Practice types 90, 91
Press coverage of sport 214, 215
Principles of training 112, 113, 114,
   115, 116
Private sector provision 163
Professional sport 207, 208, 209, 210
Proprioception 90
Proteins 46, 68, 69, 74
Provision for sport 155
Puberty 65
Pulmonary circulation 24

Race and religion 159
Racism 227
Reaction time 53, 84, 85, 86
Recovery position 132
Recovery process 37
Recovery rate 57
Recreation 142
Red blood cells 23, 24
Reflex actions 41, 42
Respiratory system 5, 31, 35, 121
RICE principle 130
Rotation 12
Rugby league 240
Rugby union 240
Rules 235–41

School sport 163
Selection 202, 203
Selective attention 89
Sesamoid bone 9
Sex differences 65
Short bones 9
Sit and Reach Test 59
Sit-up test 58, 59
Skeletal muscle 2, 16
Skeletal system 5, 7, 119
Skeleton 7, 8, 9, 12
Skill 83, 87, 108, 235–41
Skin 2
Skinfold callipers 64
Slow twitch muscle fibres 18
Smoking 81
Smooth muscle 5, 15
Social class 158
Social factors 156, 157, 158, 159

Sociology 140
Somatotypes 62, 63, 64
Spectatorism 145
Speed 53, 86
Sphygmomanometer 27
Spine 10, 40
Spirometer 34
Spongy bone 9
Sponsorship 194, 195, 196, 197, 198,
   199
Sport 141, 142
Sports agencies 171
SportsAid Foundation 171
Sports centres 165, 166
Sports clubs 164
Sports councils 147, 155, 161, 167,
   168, 169
Sports psychology 203, 204
Sports science 204
Stereotyping 156, 221
Strength 54, 85
Stress 53, 148
Stroke volume 26
Sugars 69, 71
Swimming 241
Synapse 41
Systemic circulation 26

Tactics 235–41
Target groups 168
Taylor Report 228
Teaching PE 172
Television and sport 210, 213, 214,
   216
Tendons 16, 18
Tennis 241

UK Sports Institute 205
USA sport 176

Valves of the heart 25
Vasoconstriction 119
Vasodilation 119
Veins 5, 25
Vertebrae 10
Violence 93, 227
Vital capacity 34
Vitamins 68, 70
VO$_2$ max 35, 53, 121
Voluntary muscle 16

Warm up 109, 110
Water 71, 75
Weight training 114
White blood cells 24
Women and sport 219, 220, 221, 222,
   223, 224
Womens Sports Foundation 224